Making Knowledge Makable

Joseph Hilger • Zachary Wahl

Making Knowledge Management Clickable

Knowledge Management Systems
Strategy, Design, and Implementation

 Springer

Joseph Hilger
Enterprise Knowledge, LLC
Arlington, VA, USA

Zachary Wahl
Enterprise Knowledge, LLC
Arlington, VA, USA

ISBN 978-3-030-92384-6   ISBN 978-3-030-92385-3   (eBook)
https://doi.org/10.1007/978-3-030-92385-3

© The Editor(s) (if applicable) and The Author(s), under exclusive license to Springer Nature Switzerland AG 2022

This work is subject to copyright. All rights are solely and exclusively licensed by the Publisher, whether the whole or part of the material is concerned, specifically the rights of translation, reprinting, reuse of illustrations, recitation, broadcasting, reproduction on microfilms or in any other physical way, and transmission or information storage and retrieval, electronic adaptation, computer software, or by similar or dissimilar methodology now known or hereafter developed.

The use of general descriptive names, registered names, trademarks, service marks, etc. in this publication does not imply, even in the absence of a specific statement, that such names are exempt from the relevant protective laws and regulations and therefore free for general use.

The publisher, the authors and the editors are safe to assume that the advice and information in this book are believed to be true and accurate at the date of publication. Neither the publisher nor the authors or the editors give a warranty, expressed or implied, with respect to the material contained herein or for any errors or omissions that may have been made. The publisher remains neutral with regard to jurisdictional claims in published maps and institutional affiliations.

This Springer imprint is published by the registered company Springer Nature Switzerland AG
The registered company address is: Gewerbestrasse 11, 6330 Cham, Switzerland

To our loving families, who will likely never read this, and to our wonderful colleagues, whom we certainly hope do!

Preface

Now more than ever, organizations are realizing the critical role that knowledge management (KM) plays within their enterprise. Organizations today face great challenges in the form of remote work, global diffusion of resources, tightening budgets, and greater competition. These all mean that organizations must focus on maximizing their productivity and ensuring their knowledge is treated as it should be: as one of their most valuable assets.

Big and small, local and global, as organizations are confronting these increasing and evolving operational challenges, they must face the reality that they are unprepared. Although many of these organizations have knowledge, content, and data programs, few have successfully woven them together and connected the complete spectrum of information, from tacit to explicit and from unstructured to structured.

Far fewer have made the critical leap to designing, implementing, and maintaining KM systems that make it easy for their end users to create, capture, manage, enhance, and find the knowledge they need, enabling them to learn from it and act on it. Fewer still have created an enterprise knowledge management ecosystem that connects not only knowledge, but also systems, processes, people, and all types of information and data. This type of ecosystem allows organizations to excel and set their employees up for success. Individuals in the organization feel supported in their growth and find themselves learning and being more productive.

Though few have succeeded fully, many organizations have attempted to achieve an enterprise knowledge management ecosystem. One of the major reasons that enterprise KM transformations fail is that the end users do not feel the impact fast enough, or even at all. This is due to a failure on the part of the organization to adequately understand the role of technology in making KM real for end users. This is a huge, missed opportunity to yield appropriate business value for the organization. A more thorough analysis of this phenomenon is provided in Chap. 17: Common KMS Project Challenges and Mistakes.

This is not to say that organizations do not invest in technology. Indeed, many do to a fault, front-loading purchases of the latest and greatest technology without consideration for the foundational KM designs, processes, and structures required to make it work. Too many organizations treat KM and information technology (IT) as two distinct areas, perhaps with touchpoints and overlaps, but divided nonetheless.

As a result, it is difficult to realize the potential value of KM transformations. This is frustrating at both ends of an organization. Employees are asked to adopt KM without sufficient explanation or proof that their changes will be beneficial to themselves and their colleagues. Meanwhile, executives have been asked to fund a KM transformation and disrupt business practices but are left searching in vain for return on investment and frustrated that their employees are left reluctant to adopt new systems and reverting to old behaviors.

There are already many books about knowledge management. They range from academic to practical and from highly technical to disappointingly simplistic. However, the existing books and manuals fail to do one very important thing: connect KM to the technologies and systems that make KM clickable for the end users. In order for a true KM transformation to take hold within an organization, yield consistent value, and be felt by the average end user, the transformation must include a clear strategy for KM systems.

This book bridges the gap between knowledge management and technology. It embraces the complete lifecycle of knowledge, information, and data from how knowledge flows through an organization to how end users want to handle it and experience it. Whether your intent is to design and implement a single technology or a complete collection of KM systems, this book provides the foundations necessary for success. It will help you understand your organization's needs and opportunities, strategize and prioritize features and functions, design with the end user in mind, and finally build a system that your users will embrace and which will realize meaningful business value for your organization.

In this book, we answer three major questions:

- What is KM, and how do I understand what it can do for my organization?
- What are KM systems, and what will they do (independently and collectively) for my people and my organization?
- How do I actually run a KM systems project from start to finish?

This book is the culmination of our collective careers, a combined 60 years of experience doing exactly what is detailed in this book. Our guidance has been honed by our own successes and failures as well as many others we have researched in order to provide a comprehensive study on KM transformations and the systems that help to enable them. We have successfully applied this knowledge as the founders and leaders of the world's largest dedicated knowledge management consultancy, which runs these projects for some of the world's largest and most complex organizations. We are writing as practitioners directly to you with the intent you will be able to apply the knowledge and experience herein.

KM only works when it is practical for both organizations and end users, so we have endeavored to detail real-world stories and actionable guidance in this book. We also detail outcomes, tell stories of successes and failures, and describe what an organization can do with a fully realized and integrated enterprise KM ecosystem.

With these examples and guidance, the reader will be armed with the knowledge to drive the strategy, design, implementation, and operations of KM systems within their own organization.

Arlington, VA   Joseph Hilger
                                                                            Zachary Wahl

Contents

Part II   Understanding KM Systems

About the Authors

Joseph Hilger is a graduate of Boston College and has over 30 years of experience leading and implementing cutting-edge, enterprise-scale IT projects. He has worked with an array of commercial and government clients in a wide range of industries. He was an early pioneer in the use of Agile techniques for knowledge management systems design, implementation, and integrations projects. Joe is an expert in implementing enterprise-scale content, search, and data analytics solutions. He consults on these areas with organizations across the world and is a frequent speaker and instructor on topics including enterprise search, enterprise content management, Agile development, and knowledge graphs.

Zachary Wahl is a graduate of Dickinson College and has over 20 years of experience leading programs in the knowledge and information management space. Early in his career, he defined the business taxonomy concept to address the need for human-centered taxonomy designs. He has worked with more than 200 public and private organizations in over 40 countries to successfully strategize, design, and implement knowledge management systems of various types. Zach has developed his own taxonomy design methodology, has authored a series of courses on knowledge management, and is a frequent speaker and trainer on information governance, knowledge management strategy, and taxonomy design.

Joe and Zach founded Enterprise Knowledge (EK) in 2013 and presently serve as COO and CEO, respectively. EK has been listed on the Inc. 5000 List of Fastest Growing Companies in the USA every year from 2018 to 2021. EK is now the world's largest dedicated knowledge management consultancy, having won a myriad of awards not just for its leadership in the KM field, but also as a best place to work in the region and across the USA. Their philosophy regarding EK carries through their approach to knowledge management detailed in this book; well-designed KM systems lead to happier employees, and happy employees are more likely to embrace and support KM as a result.

Knowledge Management Primer

1

This section defines what knowledge management is, or rather, how we define it. It then discusses a detailed and proven approach to understanding where your organization is regarding KM (what is working and what is not), where it could and should be, and how to define a path to get there in a realistic and achievable manner. This section goes beyond just KM systems and technologies in order to ensure you have got a clear foundation from which to start your KM systems efforts. As we stress throughout, a KM systems effort is about a lot more than just software and IT. This section provides a complete level of enterprise thinking around KM to establish how you should approach any KM engagement, regardless of whether it is an enterprise-wide transformation or a business-level KM system implementation.

1.1 Knowledge Management Defined

There are many different definitions of knowledge management. They diverge markedly in their definitions of knowledge and the inclusion of terms like data or even technology. Our one-sentence definition of KM is purposely broad to ensure it covers everything necessary for an organization to be truly successful in designing, implementing, and maintaining a KM program or office that adds real business value.

Knowledge management involves the people, process, content, culture, and enabling technologies—necessary to Capture, Manage, Share, and Find information.

When we unpack this definition, it covers a great deal of ground. When explaining it, we tend to focus on the verbs first. Simply put, effective KM is about enabling organizations and the individuals within and between them to take actions: to do things that will help their knowledge last within the organization, be shared, and therefore be leveraged by others. We want them to be able to *capture* their knowledge in reusable forms, *manage* it so it is consistently reliable and improving, *share* it so others may benefit from it, and *find* it so we can further act

© The Author(s), under exclusive license to Springer Nature Switzerland AG 2022
J. Hilger, Z. Wahl, *Making Knowledge Management Clickable*,
https://doi.org/10.1007/978-3-030-92385-3_1

Fig. 1.1 The KM action
wheel. © 2021, Wahl/Hilger,
reused with permission

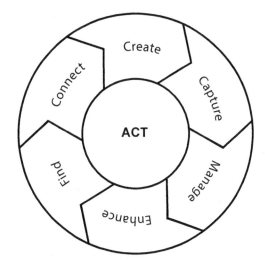

upon it. We further explain this using our KM Action Wheel in Fig. 1.1, which
expands on the concept of verbs in greater detail.

The wheel allows us to define KM based on what it enables an organization to do
with its knowledge and information.

Create

The generation of new knowledge, either by transferring tacit knowledge into
explicit knowledge or through combining, improving, or updating existing explicit
knowledge. Create recognizes that a key element of good KM is not only the capture
of existing knowledge but also the creation of new knowledge. This can take a
number of forms, from allowing knowledge creation by an individual via innovation
forums or social reporting, to group knowledge creation via better and improved
collaboration systems.

Capture

The placement of knowledge into a format and system where it can be stored and
maintained. Capture entails all the forms in which knowledge and information
(content) move from tacit to explicit, unstructured to structured, and decentralized
to centralized. This ranges from an expert's ability to easily share his or her learned
experience to a content owner's ability to upload a document he or she has created or
edited.

Manage

The maintenance of captured knowledge to ensure it remains current, accurate, and
accessible. Manage involves the sustainability and maturation of content, ensuring
content becomes better over time instead of becoming bloated, outdated, or obsolete.
This is about the content itself: its format, style, and architecture. Manage also covers

the appropriate controls and workflows necessary to protect content and the people who may access it.

Enhance
The improvement of knowledge by combining it or relating it to other knowledge, adding additional information such as context or adding metadata. Enhancement focuses on the fact that effective KM will lead not just to the creation and capture of knowledge but to the sustainable improvement of that knowledge. This means creation and stewardship of the leadership, processes, and technologies to make information "better" over time rather than having it fall into disrepair. Content's natural state is entropy, and good KM will counteract that. Enhancement also covers the application of metadata, comments, or linkages to other information in order to improve the complete web of knowledge.

Find
A broad term to express that the right people are able to locate and access the right information. Though findability is often linked to search, for our purposes, it means much more than that. Find covers the capability for knowledge and information to be easily and naturally surfaced. The concept of findability goes well beyond traditional "search," and it includes the ability to traverse content to discover additional content (discoverability), connect with experts, and receive recommendations and "pushes."

Connect
The development of a web of relationships between content, people, and systems. Connect hones in on the "find" action mentioned above, recognizing that beyond access to knowledge and information in paper or digital forms, KM is also about direct access and formation of connections with the holders of that knowledge. This concept is even more critical with more and more well-tenured experts leaving the workforce or switching jobs and taking their knowledge with them. The more KM can connect holders of knowledge with consumers of knowledge, the smarter an organization is and the more effective it can be about transferring that knowledge.

The most successful KM initiatives are those that are organized in terms of these (and other) verbs. What is the organization trying to do? What are end users within the organization wanting to do but finding it difficult to accomplish? By speaking in terms of verbs, KM initiatives become action-oriented and value-focused. Being able to define KM in terms of what the organization will be able to do (or do better and more effectively) is critical to the success of any KM initiative. This is particularly important in the early stages of KM system initiatives, where large capital expenditures may be required.

The other key component to our definition of KM is the list of five KM elements represented in Fig. 1.2: People, Process, Content, Culture, and Technology.

People

- Flow of knowledge through the organization
- Knowledge holders and knowledge consumers
- Understanding of state and disposition of experts

Process

- Existence and consistency of processes
- Awareness of and adherence to processes
- Quality of processes

Content

- State and location of content
- Consistency of structure and architecture
- Dynamism of content
- Understanding of usage (analytics)

Culture

- Senior support and comprehension
- Willingness to share, collaborate, and support

Technology

- Maturity of KM Systems suite
- Integration with and between systems
- Usability and user-centricity

People refers to the individuals who hold the knowledge, the individuals who need knowledge to grow and perform, and the flow of knowledge between them. The flow of knowledge includes how easily knowledge is transferred, the availability and accessibility of experts within the organization, and awareness of who experts are. Organizations that are mature when it comes to the people category know who their experts are, have easy and effective means of transferring their knowledge to those who need it, reward people for sharing their knowledge, and maintain strategies to consistently spread and transfer their knowledge.

Process refers to the policies and procedures, roles, and responsibilities governing the capture, management, and maintenance of knowledge and information. This entails not just whether the appropriate policies and procedures exist but how well they are being followed and how consistently they are being applied. The most mature organizations have built these policies and procedures into their knowledge management systems so that they are easy to follow, or even better, nearly impossible not to follow.

Content refers to the full breadth of an organization's knowledge, information, and data. This includes both unstructured information, such as files, e-mails, documents, and images, as well as structured information, which is typically data and appears in databases, data lakes, and other transactional systems like Customer Relationship Management (CRM) tools. Virtually every organization has a myriad of content types that exist in multiple formats, systems, and repositories. An assessment of content does not just cover the quality of the content, but also the state and structure of it, allowing it to be effectively captured, managed, and shared. Mature organizations do not necessarily have all of their content consolidated into a few repositories, but they do have a strategy in place leveraging their knowledge management systems to integrate their content and surface it consistently for their end users.

Culture refers both to an organization's leadership supporting good KM practices and the overall willingness of individuals within it to share their knowledge. Leadership support entails modeling good behavior, rewarding staff who exercise good KM, and supporting KM initiatives with funds and communications. For the most mature organizations, culture also includes the integration of rewards and incentives for good KM with human resources, including job responsibilities and official employee reviews.

Technology refers to the KM systems themselves: what they are, how well they are designed, how they are operated and maintained, and the extent to which they are aligned and integrated with each other. We always mention technology last, for although it is largely how KM becomes real to the average end user and it is the thrust of this book, it typically proves worthless if the other factors of people, process, content, and culture are not adequately addressed and considered. Technology, therefore, is both the most critical factor as well as the least important. Mature KM organizations will have a focused suite of KM technologies that are integrated, that work with each other, and that have been designed with the end user in mind. The most mature organizations will achieve a KM suite that feels natural to end users and maximizes good KM actions in a way that consistently results in greater knowledge capture, sharing, and use/reuse of the right information. In this book, we focus on how to ensure your organization can achieve these goals.

According to Frank Leistner, a former Chief Knowledge Officer at SAS Institute, knowledge management is composed of around 70% people and culture, 20% process, and 10% technology (Leistner 2010). We tend to approach KM from a more balanced perspective, considering it equal parts people, process, content, culture, and technology. All five of these factors are necessary for success, and minimizing any of the five will put your entire initiative at risk.

1.2   The Value of Knowledge Management

The field of knowledge management has consistently struggled with quantifying value and return on investment (ROI). Much of this challenge stems from historically overly academic approaches to KM, which focus on theoretical concepts and overly optimistic human-to-human programs. These often result in failure, or, at best, their success is difficult to quantify and measure.

Incorporating a Knowledge Management System (KMS) into the equation makes it much easier to demonstrate KM as a whole and measure value. Knowledge Management Systems, by definition, are meant to add value to how an organization does business. This, of course, means that we should be able to measure the impact of the KMS and translate that into real ROI for the organization.

There are two ways to talk about KM value: KM Outcomes and Business Outcomes. Too frequently, KM value is discussed solely in terms of what we call KM Outcomes. These are important, but they are very difficult to tie to ROI. That is why discussing the value of KM, and Knowledge Management Systems, in particular, should be done in the framework of Business Outcomes. These Business Outcomes can be tied directly to ROI. Examples of both Business Outcomes and KM Outcomes are listed in Fig. 1.3.

KM Outcomes
- Improved content findability and discoverability, and therefore less time waiting, searching, and recreating knowledge.
- Increased use and reuse of information.
- Decreased knowledge loss.
- Improved organizational awareness and alignment.
- Enhanced quality, availability, and speed of learning.

Business Outcomes
- Improved productivity.
- Decreased costs (and cost avoidance).
- Increased employee satisfaction and retention.
- Faster and better up-scaling of employees.
- Improved customer satisfaction and retention.
- Improved delivery and sales.
- Increased collaboration and innovation.
- Future readiness.

Fig. 1.3 Comparison of KM Outcomes and Business Outcomes. © 2021, Wahl/Hilger, reused with permission

KM Outcomes are the result of KM transformations and the successful implementation of KM Systems. The following are the most common and important KM Outcomes.

Improved Content Findability and Discoverability, and Therefore Less Time Waiting, Searching, and Recreating Knowledge

This tends to be the number one driver for KM efforts as well as the dominant use case for KM Systems. In short, organizations possess the appropriate knowledge, but the right people are not finding it (or finding it easily). Our internal research has found that an organization's employees may spend up to 40% of their time looking for information, waiting for answers from others, or recreating information that already existed but of which they were unaware. In short, a great deal of time is wasted, and KM can play a major role in addressing this issue. This wasted time and effort is addressed by improving findability and discoverability. Findability means an end user's ability to find what they are looking for. Discoverability goes beyond findability by surfacing content for the user that will help them do their job or answer their question, but of which they were potentially unaware.

Increased Use and Reuse of Information

As a critical benefit of improved findability and discoverability, organizations see that more of their knowledge is leveraged by those who need it. End users are also able to leverage content generated by others, which saves the time it would take to recreate something. This reuse of content also creates the potential to enhance source material, creating new knowledge from which still others may benefit.

Decreased Knowledge Loss

A common concern of organizations is that their critical knowledge is "walking out the door" when an employee leaves. This concept of the brain drain has been an important topic in KM and spawned major programs to counteract knowledge loss to varying degrees of success. In short, the benefit of decreased knowledge loss is that more knowledge has either been translated into a sustainable (commonly digital) format so that it remains even if the original holder or creator of that knowledge has departed or has been transferred to others within the organization in order to maintain it and continue to pass it to others.

Improved Organizational Awareness and Alignment

Many organizations, especially those that are large, topically diverse, and geographically distributed, suffer from a lack of internal collaboration, awareness, and alignment, commonly referred to as siloing or stovepiping. By defining common vocabularies, helping share content across the enterprise, and connecting people that are organizationally or geographically separated, KM can help organizations operate more cohesively, sharing knowledge and working together at the enterprise level rather than group or team level. Another benefit of organizational awareness and alignment can be that with a more diverse set of people working together to generate ideas and address organizational challenges, innovation, and problem-solving will be improved.

Enhanced Quality, Availability, and Speed of Learning
In this context, learning does not necessarily mean going to a class or getting a certification, but also includes learning how to perform or develop. This fits together with the concept of the Learning and Performance Ecosystem, defined by Marc Rosenberg and Steve Foreman as "enhancing individual and organizational effectiveness by connecting people, and supporting them with a broad range of content, processes, and technologies to drive performance" (Rosenberg and Foreman 2014). Good KM offers a wide range of content and people to learn from, meaning your people will be upskilled faster and will be able to perform at a higher level of consistency and quality.

No one would argue with the fact that each of the above elements is of major value to most any organization, and C-levels would certainly find these benefits appealing. That said, the problem is that they are largely intangibles when it comes to value for an organization. Though they clearly spell out benefits, none of them can be directly translated to return on investment that can be measured in dollars and cents. As a result, speaking solely in these terms often leads to a lack of executive support for or interest in KM, and in some cases means that KM programs are the first to get cut when an organization is struggling financially.

To counteract this perceived lack of value, KM needs to be put in terms of business outcomes. The clear fact is that KM transformation can be hugely valuable to an organization and can often yield a complete return on the initial investment within 2–3 years of commencing the transformation. The following are the most meaningful and most easily measured Business Outcomes.

Improved Productivity
Almost any conversation regarding the business value of KM begins with productivity. If your people are spending time looking for information, waiting for answers, recreating information, struggling to perform, and duplicating effort, a massive amount of time is being wasted. As mentioned above, for a large enterprise, our research pegs this at as much as 40% of staff's time wasted. Even a more conservative estimate, an average of 20% of time wasted due to overall poor KM, has the potential to yield a major productivity increase for organizations. That said, many organizations incorrectly express the potential ROI for this by simply taking their average salary, multiplying it by number of employees, and then factoring the 20% to 40% savings from that number. That calculation will almost always be incorrect for three reasons:

1. The math only works if the organization intends to reduce their staff by the percentage of time saved. Though some organizations do use productivity increases to reorganize staff, resulting in reductions in force (a pretty term for terminations), this does not tend to be the case in most organizations. Even if there is a reduction in force, it would infrequently be as sweeping as the time

savings yielded by improved productivity. That said, there are in some cases focused staff reductions that can result from KM, largely in help desk agents, technical writers, or other support staff.

2. Not everyone in an organization will actually realize an increase in productivity to the same extent. In fact, typically, the most highly compensated individuals will see the least productivity improvement, as they are no longer the primary consumers of an organization's knowledge and have already, to a large degree, accessed the organization's knowledge.

3. Even if an organization is focused solely on the value of productivity, there is no guarantee that employees will apply their time saved in a productive manner. In other words, a KM transformation may indeed free up 20–40% of an employee's time, perhaps even more, but that does not translate to that freed up time being spent serving customers, innovating, or creating more widgets. There is no guarantee improved productivity, by itself, means cost savings or cost reductions.

Notwithstanding these previous points, for most organizations, there are some cost savings resulting from improved productivity. Though the specific formula varies from organization to organization, this can be a significant cost savings over time.

Decreased Costs (and Cost Avoidance)
One of the most tangible and easily quantifiable benefits for an organization is decreased costs. This can take many forms, some of which we explore in additional detail below, including decreased recruiting and training costs, decreased marketing costs, and decreased staff, license, and consulting costs to acquire or reacquire lost information. Specific to KMS, there are two major cost savings: 1) Decreased software license costs through the elimination of redundant or obsolete systems and the improved integration of the KM suite, and 2) Decreased administrative burden related to the maintenance and management of multiple systems, often holding duplicate content and working at odds with each other. These two elements alone consistently result in the necessary business case to realize ROI within a measurable period of a few years or less.

Increased Employee Satisfaction and Retention
Employees that feel supported in their job with easy to access information, the right guidance to perform, and a clear path with the right resources for how to move up are simply happier employees. The top reasons employees leave a company consistently include lack of opportunities for career advancement, lack of support, and feeling disconnected from their company or the company's mission. Statistics supporting this abound. According to Gallup, millennials rank the opportunity to learn and grow in a job above all other considerations, and 69% of non-millennials say it is important to them (Gallup 2021). A recent Salesforce study, "The Impact of Equality and Values Driven Business," found that employees who feel their voice is heard at work are nearly five times (4.6×) more likely to feel empowered to perform their best work (Salesforce Research 2017). O.C. Tanner finds that 60% of employees are

more likely to stay at a job for 3 years or more if they have a good onboarding experience (O.C. Tanner n.d.). The math on this is simple. The Society for Human Resource Management estimates that direct replacement costs for a lost employee can reach as high as 50%–60% of the employee's annual salary, with total costs associated with turnover ranging from 90% to 200% of annual salary (Allen 2008). Moreover, the Work Institute estimates (conservatively) that the average cost of turnover is $15,000 per employee. In short, good KM leads to higher engagement and employee satisfaction, directly negating costs to replace and retrain employees (Work Institute 2019).

Faster and Better Up-Scaling of Employees
According to Training Magazine, in 2019, the average cost of training an employee was $1286, with over 40 hours per year spent on training by each employee (Training Magazine 2019). Effective KM systems will house a variety of knowledge that may serve as learning content, delivering learning at the point of need, which is more effective and less time intensive. Rather than taking a long class where employees may retain only 10–20% of what was taught, consuming learning as smaller chunks of knowledge when needed allows employees to retain more and immediately act upon the knowledge. With knowledge and learning delivered at the point of need, training costs and time may decrease, while overall employee skills and development will increase. Of course, it is also notable that employees who have developed faster and have attained more expert skills are more likely to stay with the organization and provide effective and consistent customer service, adding additional returns to this concept.

Improved Customer Satisfaction and Retention
Effective KM systems can a) make self-service content easier to find, easier to read, and easier to access; b) arm help desks, call agents, and other customer-facing staff with better, more consistent, and more complete knowledge to support customers; and c) leverage analytics to identify themes and gaps in customer-facing information in order to fill those gaps. All of these elements result in greater customer satisfaction and higher retention of existing customers. Just as employees who feel supported stay with an organization, the same is true for customers. The cost of acquiring new customers can vary greatly from industry to industry, but higher customer retention means either greater growth (and growth in revenues), or lower cost to acquire replacement customers. In either case, the ROI is clear.

Improved Delivery and Sales
In the same way that customers and customer service staff can be armed with the right knowledge, an organization can also leverage KM systems to provide better and more consistent knowledge to other types of employees, including those in delivery and sales. Improved delivery is more likely to result in customer retention as discussed above, and of course improved sales will lead directly to growth and increased revenues. The reason we call this out separately is that these two areas often benefit from advanced KM systems features, including advanced search,

knowledge graphs, and machine learning. Sales in particular can benefit when an organization's system is automatically spotting trends in customer behavior and making recommendations to sales staff. For instance, if your KMS has the ability to "understand" what types of customers are purchasing which widgets, the tool can make recommendations to the sales staff on which customers should be offered which new widget. These same employees can also benefit from knowledge assembly tools that would even configure the appropriate pitch materials on the recommended widget, thereby saving them time that can be spent on closing the next deal.

Increased Collaboration and Innovation
KM systems enable increased collaboration and innovation by breaking down silos and creating paths for people to connect, share, and discuss information, thereby enabling them to create new knowledge. In some cases, this new knowledge yields an idea to improve a process, better serve a customer, eliminate a risk, or even create a new revenue stream. Though more difficult to quantify than some of these other business outcomes, creating safe and efficient means of employee collaboration and innovation exposes the potential for significant cost savings and increased revenues.

Future Readiness
Finally, designing and implementing effective KM systems will ensure the organization is future ready for the next stage of technology within their organization. A recent study from Appen found that while nearly three out of four organizations said AI is critical to their business, nearly half feel their organization is behind in where they want to be with AI (Appen 2021). Many of these organizations are finding that although they are willing to invest in AI technologies, that is not sufficient. Knowledge AI only works when the systems can make sense of the data and information they find. Without the appropriate structure to this organization, AI will fail. Moreover, AI technologies may surface an organization's content, but if that content is out of date or inaccurate, or if the critical knowledge is in the heads of employees rather than in a digital format, the AI technology will not offer the necessary value and results for the organization. KM provides structure to the content and governance that ensures the content is formatted, so it can be leveraged and accurate, so it can be trusted. In many cases, basic KM practices are the foundation to make AI work, and moreover, advanced KM systems leverage AI to best serve the users, as we'll detail throughout this book. To this end, KM offers major value to an organization that sees AI as a competitive advantage or avenue to cost savings or growth.

Taken as a whole, for most organizations, these business outcomes mean that a clear case with measurable return on investment can be made for a true Enterprise KM transformation that includes real capital investments in a KM suite of technologies. Regardless of the size or scope of your KM initiative, defining the real business outcomes and putting the right governance and analytics in place to measure and report on results will be critical to long-term success.

References

Allen D (2008) Retaining talent: a guide to analyzing and managing employee turnover. SHRM Foundation. https://www.shrm.org. Accessed 28 Jul 2021

Appen (2021) The 2021 state of AI and machine learning report. https://appen.com. Accessed 16 Jul 2021

Gallup (2021) Workplace learning and development programs. https://www.gallup.com. Accessed 15 Jun 2021

Leistner F (2010) Mastering organizational knowledge flow: how to make knowledge sharing work. Wiley, New York

Rosenberg M, Foreman S (2014) Learning and performance ecosystems: strategy, technology, impact, and challenges. The eLearning Guild, Santa Rosa

Salesforce Research (2017) The impact of equality and values driven business. Special Report. https://c1.sfdcstatic.com. Accessed 02 Jun 2021

Tanner OC (n.d.) Employee engagement strategies for new employees. https://www.octanner.com. Accessed 16 Sept 2021

Training Magazine (2019) 2019 training industry report. The Industry Report. https://trainingmag. com. Accessed 19 Aug 2021

Work Institute (2019) Trends, reasons, and a call to action: insights from over 250,000 employee interviews. 2019 Retention Report. https://info.workinstitute.com. Accessed 15 May 2021

Part I
Knowledge Management Transformation Strategy and Planning

With the foundations of what KM is (or can be) and the value it offers understood, the next step in a comprehensive KM transformation and attainment of high-value KM systems is to understand where you are, where you should be, and how to get there. This section defines the proven methodologies to understand and document your organization's KM current state and transformation roadmap. The part details what each of these products should look like, what detail they should contain, and how best to communicate them to different audiences for different purposes. The effective outcome of achieving the direction in this section is that all of your stakeholders will have a shared vision and understanding of what KM should look like for your organization, what value the organization can attain by achieving that vision, and what it will take to get there. In short, these are the steps to getting a KM transformation supported, approved, and funded.

Assessing Your Organization's KM Strengths and Weaknesses (Current State)

2

One of the most important aspects of a successful KM transformation is an awareness of your baseline. What is working within your organization and what is not? Where are your people struggling to perform good KM behaviors, or where is it too difficult or impossible to effectively complete the right KM actions? Having a clear understanding of your organization's KM strengths and weaknesses is important for four reasons:

1. If developed properly, it is a critical tool to communicate the value of KM. Knowing the current state of KM within your organization is the first step to defining the cost of immature KM, which in turn can evolve into an ROI assessment.
2. KM, as we discussed earlier, is esoteric and easily misunderstood. By defining a clear picture of your organization's current state, you will be able to paint the picture using specific use cases and anecdotes of pain points, wasted hours, and missed opportunities.
3. Developing a clear current state is the first and most critical piece of a true KM transformation strategy. Too frequently, organizations will jump to the technical solution or attempt a series of uncoordinated or disjointed KM projects. An enterprise current state assessment will help to provide a comprehensive view of the organization, making way for an accompanying target state definition and KM transformation roadmap.
4. Part of preparing for a KM transformation is determining which KM strategy will best work within your organization, based on the strengths/weaknesses and scope that you will determine in the planning process. The American Productivity and Quality Center (APQC) identifies six broad knowledge management strategies that an organization may adopt: enterprise-wide, transfer of knowledge and best practice, customer-focused knowledge strategy, personal responsibility for knowledge, intellectual asset management, and innovation and knowledge creation (Gamble and Blackwell 2001). These strategies are not mutually exclusive, and we will touch on each at some point in this book, but we emphasize an

© The Author(s), under exclusive license to Springer Nature Switzerland AG 2022
J. Hilger, Z. Wahl, *Making Knowledge Management Clickable*,
https://doi.org/10.1007/978-3-030-92385-3_2

enterprise-wide approach as the most comprehensive and most critical to long-term growth and competitive development.

2.1   Top-Down Analysis

The most effective approach to conducting a KM assessment is what we refer to as a hybrid approach, consisting of both top-down and bottom-up activities.

Top-down activities are those that are human based. They are important to capture opinions, priorities, and stories directly from stakeholders and end users. Though the process can be time intensive in large organizations, there is no viable alternative to truly understanding the state of KM (and the potential for improvements) within an organization. The most common examples of top-down knowledge gathering activities are:

- Executive sponsor interviews to understand business drivers, priorities, and pain points.
- Workshops (typically ranging from 12–18 people for a half-day to a day) that cut across an organization to define personas, use cases, and other design elements that will help to understand the users, their needs, and their priorities.
- Focus Groups (typically ranging from three to six people for one to three hours) that detail a specific business area, business process, or KMS.

Typically, within an organization, a combination of these different types of top-down business activities will be most effective in extracting a true and complete understanding of an organization's current state for KM. There is no magic percentage for how many people should be engaged within an organization. It varies widely; in small organizations of hundreds of people, you may choose to engage nearly everyone, while in large and global organizations, you will be lucky to get one percent.

What matters more than headcount, by far, is representation. There are three key factors that are critical to get representation right when it comes to top-down knowledge gathering activities specifically.

1. Organizational Area: An effective current state analysis will obtain a broad understanding from all business areas and functions within the organization. The level of granularity required will be heavily dependent on the homogeneity of the business. Regardless of size, if an organization has a relatively focused mission and set of services or products, it will require less granularity than an organization that is highly diverse, siloed in nature, or divergent regarding products or services. The most challenging organizations tend to be those that span a wide array of activities and topics of expertise and have grown largely through acquisition. Global services organizations and complex manufacturing, sales, and distribution organizations are two examples of the level of complexity

that requires a great deal of granularity to ensure a full understanding of the business is acquired.

2. Seniority: The level of seniority within an organization has a major impact on how an individual leverages KM. The most junior and senior people within an organization will typically be consumers of knowledge more often than creators of knowledge. The junior people will consume knowledge in order to learn and upskill themselves into experts and more independent performers (thereby growing into creators of knowledge). The most senior people within the organization, based on their roles as leaders and executives, will typically be acting on the knowledge created by others or directing others to generate new knowledge, but they do not independently tend to be creators of knowledge. Even when an organization's senior people do create knowledge, they do not tend to be the person publishing it or directly loading it into a KM system. This leaves a wide band of people in the middle of the organization as the primary creators and publishers of knowledge. The different perspectives gained from different levels of seniority also go well beyond just whether someone is a primary consumer or creator of knowledge. Different levels of seniority mean different priorities, perspectives, and missions, all of which need to be understood and weighed in order to obtain an understanding of an organization's current state.

3. Tenure: The third factor for knowledge gathering is the length of time an individual has been with an organization. For the sake of simplicity, we tend to look at tenure in terms of new (less than a year), relatively new (a year to three years), relatively tenured (three years to eight years), and very tenured (more than eight years). Of course, these categories will absolutely vary from organization to organization (We recently worked with an organization whose average retention was 18 years and another whose average retention was 9 months), so what qualifies as tenured in one organization may not in another. Nonetheless, these different perspectives will ensure you are obtaining an understanding from those deeply familiar with the organization's processes, structures, and secrets to success (As in, who are the go-to people and where can the right information be found), versus those who are still struggling to figure it out.

Another important type of top-down activity is an employee survey. Surveys, ideally as wide reaching as possible, can draw out statistically significant themes regarding KM needs and wants and also define a baseline of performance and satisfaction from which to track progress. These are four benefits to running a survey as part of a current state assessment.

1. Whereas the aforementioned interviews, workshops, and focus groups are critical tools to obtaining a deep understanding, in large organizations, it would be prohibitive to run such in-person sessions with a representative sampling of the organization, taking undue time that most organizations cannot afford. A well-designed survey, on the other hand, can reach your entire organization (or a carefully chosen sampling) in order to gain a complete representative sample at a much lower cost of time.

2. Given the prominence of a company-wide survey, conducting a KM-specific survey for your organization can raise the profile of the KM initiative, developing interest and potentially support for it. (Of course, this can be a double-edged sword if people within your organization may be wary of or against such an initiative.)

3. If the survey is properly conducted and yields statistically significant results, it can become an important baseline to capture KM trends and report on ROI. For instance, the survey could capture inputs regarding average time spent searching or waiting for information, levels of employee frustration, and feelings of employee support in their learning journeys. If these survey questions are repeated over time, they should demonstrate ROI by revealing positive trends in these and other factors.

4. The survey can help to prioritize early adopter groups, as well as KM features and functions, not just at the enterprise level but at the division or group level. If one's organizational entity is captured as one of the survey questions, sub-trends within a particular group can be analyzed and understood, resulting in an understanding of which groups have which needs and helping to suggest potential pilot entities. This level of granularity will also help determine if the KM challenges you are identifying are enterprise-wide or exist more commonly within specific groups.

Tip:
If your organization is like many, you may not be able to get approval to run a comprehensive KM survey. All is not lost. Is there an existing employee survey that is scheduled for imminent release? Consider whether you can get a couple of questions added to it. Of greatest import, we recommend the following to be answered on a 10-point Likert scale from Strongly Disagree to Strongly Agree.

- I have access to the right information to perform my job.
- I have guidance from the right people to perform my job.
- I have access to the right resources to expand beyond my role and do my job better.

Given the targeted topic of KM, a KM survey should generally take no more than 15 minutes to answer (And we have squeezed several in under 10 minutes). A well-designed and succinctly written survey should generally yield high response rates and provide a great deal of granular insight as part of an assessment.

Though there are many benefits to conducting a survey as part of a KM assessment, we have found that many organizations balk at this, as surveys are considered carefully as precious time asked of employees. Many organizations express concerns regarding too many surveys already sent to employees and therefore employees showing fatigue in answering them (or answering them completely). The arguments in favor of a survey are clear, as expressed above, but many organizations will still

Table 2.1 Survey questions to ask in order to understand the interviewee

Understanding the Interviewee	
1	What is your role in the organization?
2	What does a typical day look like?
3	How much of your role has to do with using [the organization]'s technology/systems?
4	How long have you been in the organization?
5	How did you learn to perform your role?

Table 2.2 Survey questions to ask to understand the foundation of the KM systems

Foundational KM Systems Understanding	
1	Where do you currently go looking for information?
2	How hard/easy is it to find what you are looking for?
3	If you have created or updated a new piece of information, how do you share it with others?
4	Do you know where to go looking for the information you need?
5	Do you know how to find the right people to help you answer a question?
6	How long would you say you typically spend looking for something?
7	What do you do if/when you cannot find it?

resist. In these cases, consider whether past surveys regarding HR, Customer Service, or Learning and Development are available. These and others are likely to offer some level of value to a KM assessment.

Tables 2.1, 2.2, and 2.3 show the most important questions to get answered specifically in regard to KM systems. Note that many of these questions are more qualitative than quantitative. The top-down elements of a KM assessment are often more about how a user feels and perceives rather than hard facts and figures. These elements of the assessment are nonetheless critical when we remember that KM, at its core, is a human endeavor, and we need the individual's understanding and support to make a KM transformation stick. The bottom-up approach described in Sect. 2.2 will round out the assessment with more concrete data and quantitative analysis.

Table 2.3 Survey questions to ask to understand the features of the KM systems in place

KMS Features	
1	What systems do you like using the most (because they are easiest or work the best)?
2	What features or tools of these systems do you like the most?
3	Are you aware of any pilot initiatives or projects that might offer new capabilities?
4	What do other organizations have that you wish you had?

You should also note that all of these questions are written plainly, with minimal jargon or KM terminology. This is very purposeful and critical to remember that the vast majority of people with whom you will be speaking are not familiar with the ins and outs of KM and, at best, may be skeptical of such an initiative.

Taken as a whole, in addition to obtaining the findings necessary for benchmark scoring, the common findings regarding KM systems yielded by top-down activities tend to include:

- Current systems, uses, and general likes and dislikes.
- Specific pain points regarding KM actions users are trying to take but find difficult or impossible.
- Prioritized wish list of features and functions end users are seeking.
- Primary business problems users are dealing with and envisioning where KM systems can potentially help.
- Inputs regarding costs in terms of lost time and frustration with the functionality and usability (or lack thereof) of current systems.

Another important element of these top-down activities is the collection of anecdotes. Though not as compelling as a statistically significant data analysis, anecdotes from real end users can be incredibly important to make KM less esoteric for decision-makers and paint a picture of the costs of a missing or poor KM solution. These anecdotes do not necessarily need to be tied to specific names, but it is helpful to characterize the individual in ways that will provide greater context and make their quote all the more clear. Here are some real-world examples of such anecdotes.

I know there's good stuff out there, but we've got so many places to go looking for it, I honestly don't know where to begin.
  –Associate with six years of experience

I never know where to begin. It is far easier just to e-mail [more tenured manager] in order to get the right starting material than to go looking for it.
  –HR Manager in their first year

I've lost deals because I didn't have the right intelligence on a specific customer. We've actually tried to sell a customer something they already bought from us because there's no easy way to see their history.
–Sales Associate in the Midwest Region

We're always changing versions and the look of our materials. I spend hours trying to figure out if I am using the right version so I don't get my wrist slapped.
–Pre-Sales Specialist with over five years of experience

We're a big company so it is bound to happen, but the number of times I've found out someone else was working on the exact same thing as me is embarrassing. What a waste!
–Senior Scientist in Research and Development

Collectively, top-down activities create a narrative of what is working and what is not and help to surface wants or needs that do not exist within the organization but should. Top-down collection activities are particularly important for understanding what would change a stakeholder's behavior. In terms of KM systems, top-down activities often surface the "killer app," the features that users are clamoring for and will actually make them willing to change their behavior in order to get it.

2.2 Bottom-Up Analysis

As opposed to human-based top-down activities, bottom-up activities are content- or system-based. Bottom-up activities still require participation and guidance from humans, but they function more as guides to an organization's content, documentation, and technologies. Bottom-up activities ensure you are leveraging the time of your constituents as effectively as possible, exhausting other sources of information and what they can offer you before taking an undue amount of time from the actual stakeholders and end users in an organization. The key types of bottom-up knowledge gathering activities are described below.

2.2.1 Documentation Review

Reviews of past or existing project plans and project charters related to knowledge, information, and data (i.e., content management, enterprise search, customer relationship management, knowledge graph, taxonomy design, or content migration/cleanup projects). Even though many of these documents may not outright mention KM, such documents often have previous research and findings regarding KM challenges or issues. Of particular value as starting points in such documents are:

- Identification of personas and their motivations for design purposes, including persona wants, needs, frustrations, and goals.
- Previous research or survey findings regarding common KM action challenges, such as issues with findability and discoverability, ability to adequately capture and manage content, or ability to find and connect with colleagues or experts.

- Past functional or feature backlogs for KM technologies that may guide prioritization of new systems or identify potential functionality and features being sought by users.
- Identified risks and issues that had previously surfaced from planned or conducted projects. Such project charters and risk registers can often provide important insight on future challenges.

2.2.2 System Review

Reviews of existing systems that manage knowledge, information, and data. As mentioned above and detailed in the subsequent sections, many of these systems might not be known or considered specifically as KM systems, but any technologies where information is stored can provide important insights into the organization's current state, and they may also provide starting points for future design where a particular system may be especially effective or advanced. In these cases, such systems and their design may be foundational components of the future state of the organization's KM systems. Blackwell and Gamble observe that "the key to sustainability is to establish systems and choose a standardized platform" (Gamble and Blackwell 2001). When dipping your toe into KM systems, the key is to keep it simple. By integrating existing systems and technologies into the KM initiative, users and creators will have a shared point of reference and familiar framework to build upon, upholding the importance of standardization. When reviewing systems, the following items are often of particular value.

Information Managed
Understanding what information is managed in each system is an important way to identify a map of where knowledge is stored across the enterprise. Many organizations share the same information in multiple systems, or they have gaps in which information is stored. We typically use these information maps as a way to simplify what information goes where and how to look for it.

Information Architecture
Reviewing the state of the system's page layout and overall organization (both from the front-end navigation perspective and back-end administrative perspective) can quickly provide indications of the overall complexity of the system and the content therein. In addition, effective page layouts and navigation may be a valuable starting point for future taxonomy and metadata design.

User Types
Assessing whether the system provides customized experiences for different types of users will again help to understand the overall complexity of the system, as well as the flexibility and dynamism of the user experiences. Systems with different user types, each with customized views and interfaces, are also more likely to provide

insight into the various wants and needs of those different user types, serving as a potential input for better understanding users and their desired future state.

User Permissions

Just like User Types, the number of different permissions within a system can be an important indicator of a system's complexity and the granularity of the user experience. For purposes of a baseline Current State/Target State analysis, it is not necessary to index the complete assortment of permissions for different User Types but rather the number of different activities or capabilities built into a system.

Taxonomy

Going beyond simple Information Architecture, many systems may have an existing taxonomy (or taxonomies). The state of these taxonomies (how well they are designed and maintained) can be an important indicator as to the maturity of the system and the organization as a whole. In addition, systems with well-designed and well-maintained taxonomies may serve as good candidates for the future state. A well-designed taxonomy that has evolved in a particular system, moreover, may be a starting point from which to build and expand into an enterprise taxonomy design that may be applied across multiple systems.

Metadata

In addition to the existence or state of taxonomy within the system, the level to which that taxonomy has been applied as metadata and the level to which other metadata are being applied is both a strong indicator for the management of the system as well as the content within it. Systems with consistent, correct, and complete metadata typically have successful content governance and well-designed workflows to publish content. This governance and these workflows are both foundational elements of an enterprise KM system and may serve as good starting points for enterprise design. Kimiz Dalkir describes in his book *Knowledge Management in Theory and Practice* how the current stage of KM emphasizes the description and organization of content above all else, "characterized by the advent of metadata to describe the content in addition to the format of content, content management, and knowledge taxonomies" (Dalkir 2017). Metadata, like the other items on this list, contribute to the overall goal of KM: allowing individual end users to easily identify, access, and apply content.

Content Types and Templates

For content management and digital asset management systems, in particular, the most mature systems will have clearly defined content types that describe the format, metadata requirements, and entry fields necessary to generate, maintain, and publish consistent content. Assessing how existing systems are using content types, determining how many there are, and evaluating whether they are being used for their intended purpose will help to determine an organization's current state of maturity. If a system is employing content types, a key watch element is whether the majority of content published is leveraging a generic or catch-all content type or whether the content is more evenly distributed across multiple fit-for-purpose content types. The most mature systems will leverage an array of content types for specific purposes, each generating a different type of content. As with other elements like taxonomy and personas, existing content types that have been proven to work for the business can serve as important starting points for consideration when designing an enterprise KM system.

Governance and Workflows

Any mature KM system will have a governance plan that clearly identifies the roles and responsibilities, policies, and procedures governing who can do what within the system (regarding, for instance, functional changes, user changes, navigation changes, content changes, etc.). The more mature KM systems do not just have documented system governance but also have more detailed governance plans over content, taxonomy, and other critical elements. The *most* mature systems will not just have detailed governance, they will have it designed into the system as workflows. In other words, governance will not be a separate plan one has to read and choose to follow or one that administrators must actively enforce. Instead, it will be designed into the KM system itself as permissions, workflows, analytics, and notification tools that collectively "force" the correct behavior. When reviewing systems, it is important to assess whether a governance plan exists, whether it is being followed, and whether it is integrated by design into the system.

Search

An organization's assorted search tools are often the most visible element of KM within an organization. When reviewing search within systems, the first step is to understand whether the organization has any semblance of enterprise search (A search tool that searches across multiple systems where content is held) or whether search only exists within specific tools. Few organizations have mastered enterprise search, so in organizations that do possess an enterprise search tool, do not assume it is connected to all content repositories or that it is surfacing content in the appropriate way. The most mature organizations will possess an enterprise search that covers all content repositories, both structured and unstructured, and surfaces results in a customized and ordered way that allows for easy filtering and action-oriented results. In most organizations, however, search is deemed one of the biggest issues, with "I can't find what I'm looking for," one of the most common cries for help. Baseline assessments of search should include 1) Does the KM system actually have a functioning search? 2) Is it working, meaning, is it actually returning meaningful results? 3) Are those results able to be refined to encourage improved findability and discoverability using techniques like filtering? Beyond this baseline, organizations that have designed more mature searches may be employing action-oriented hit types that build two-way features directly into the technology. If a specific system or group has designed and implemented advanced search, that typically places them in the minority, and that search effort should be considered for expansion beyond its current use.

Lastly, reviews of existing systems can help to identify leading groups that are leveraging innovative designs and technologies, such as ontologies, knowledge graphs, natural language processing, and machine learning. Any groups using these more advanced building blocks of KM have strong potential to be early adopters and support foundational pilots. The mere existence of advanced capabilities, of course, does not indicate KM maturity. It will be important to assess whether such practices and technologies have actually been thoughtfully deployed, applied to business challenges, and proven to add business value within the organization. In other words, do not be fooled by an organization that has purchased and installed the shiny new tool. Ensure you understand how it has actually been configured, integrated, and used in order to assess the organization's actual maturity in these areas.

2.2.3   Content Analysis

Content (the data, information, files, or other digital assets maintained by the organization) is a critical indicator of the organization's overall KM maturity, and specifically, an indicator of how well the organization's various KM systems may or may not be working. Poor content capture, management, and findability are amongst the most visible signs of a struggling or nonexistent KM effort, and specifically, poorly designed and/or governed KM systems. Therefore, taking a clear look at the state of an organization's content is a key component of a KM assessment. It should be noted, however, that a KM assessment typically does not and should not require a complete and detailed content analysis wherein each individual piece of content held within the enterprise is inspected and documented. On the contrary, such a content analysis would potentially take longer than a normal KM assessment itself. Instead, a content analysis for purposes of a KM assessment and strategy should address the following four questions.

1. *How much content (roughly) is the organization managing?* The overall amount of content an organization possesses is one of the single most important indicators of the KM challenges that the organization possesses. An organization managing tens of millions of pieces of content requires drastically different KM systems and supporting processes than an organization that is only managing thousands or even hundreds of thousands.
2. *Where is the content?* A characterization of where that content is being stored also provides an important view of complexity. Organizations that have dumped scores of content on old file drives or in antiquated document management systems are in a much more challenging starting position than an organization that has kept up with technology trends and is managing their content in current technologies. In addition, an organization that has consolidated their content into a few targeted systems, each with a discrete purpose, is in a much more mature state than an organization that has content spread across dozens of repositories, many of which may be redundant or conflicting in nature and design.

3. *What type of content is it (generally)?* This, again, does not require a piece-by-piece logging of the content's file type or format but rather a broad characterization of what comprises the content. For instance, can you identify that a majority of content is related to client deliverables, sales, engineering, or some other purpose or function? Is more of your content internal or external to the organization? Roughly what percentage are reports, meeting minutes, presentations, or other types? What amount comprises working documents versus finished products? These types of characterizations help to understand the complexities of content management and maintenance for your organization and may also shed light on the potential redundancies of systems. For instance, if you find you have multiple systems that seem to be housing content of the same type, purpose, and audience, it is likely there are efficiencies that can be realized by eliminating the redundancy. Characterizing content in this way is also an important first step in understanding requirements for a future search solution in your organization. The more heterogeneous your content is, the more complex the future state search solution will likely be.

4. *How dynamic is the content?* This may be difficult to ascertain in its entirety, but a key indicator of KM system complexity and health is how dynamic the content is. There are two sub-metrics to this: 1) How much new content is being added, and 2) How much and how frequently is existing content being edited or replaced? Getting a sense of content dynamism will help to inform the usability of these systems (usable systems tend to be more dynamic), as well as the complexity of the content management challenge (Content that changes frequently is more difficult to manage). Especially dynamic stores of content will also potentially identify areas that require improved collaboration technologies and processes. Identifying a specific type of highly dynamic content is also a potential focal point for a pilot regarding improved content management or governance, and such content may hold an ideal pilot for consideration as part of a new KM system effort.

Tip:
In many organizations, obtaining access to analytics can be a rigorous process with a fair bit of red tape involved. If you are conducting an assessment, make sure to request access to analytics data as early as possible to ensure you will be able to obtain it.

2.2.4 System Analytics

When available, system analytics of various types can help to form the picture of what is working and what is not as part of a current state assessment. Since it is based on concrete data, it also tends to be a highly regarded source of information and should be considered as such when prioritizing actions for a target state, as well as discussing your findings and recommendations. In other words, people trust analytics as "real" data, and their prominent inclusion in your analysis and findings will lend additional credibility to the overall KM analysis. There are, of course, several different types of analytics in multiple types of systems. The following tend to be the most valuable as part of a KM assessment.

Basic Counts

Analytics should help to quickly ascertain the counts of users and amounts of content within any given system. Taken as a whole, this provides indicators towards complexity of a redesign, content cleanup, or content migration, as the more users and the more content, the more time and complexity of redesigning, migrating, and implementing a new or improved system. Of course, basic counts alone typically do not tell the complete picture. Basic counts of users do not actually indicate the number of active users in a system, just like basic counts of content do not indicate how much content is typically being accessed, leveraged, or worked upon within a system. Years ago, a CTO from a globally recognized brand proudly approached us after a conference talk we gave, excited to share his successes. He pronounced his organization's success in creating an intranet and knowledge base, with his proofpoint being that the system contained over 2,000,000 pieces of content in their system! Our question, of course, was how many of those 2,000,000 pieces of content had actually been accessed or otherwise interacted with since their launch? To be clear, loads of content dumped into a system is not an indicator of KM maturity and might very well indicate the opposite.

Active Counts

To that end, active counts are a much more valuable indicator of what is actually happening in any given system. An active user is typically identified as one that has logged in or performed any action in the system within a given period of time. The standards for that length of time vary greatly from system to system and use case to use case, but for standard KM purposes, if a user has not logged in within the last month, they should not be considered an active user. For content, we typically define active content as that which has been accessed at least once over the last year. For some organizations, depending on their industry and overall size, the time period may be increased or decreased. Government agencies tend to define active content over a longer period, whereas smaller and more dynamic organizations that focus on current events and rapidly changing concepts may define active content in months rather than years. More specifically, it is important to note that active content will vary from content type to content type. For instance, a policy will be active, in most cases, until it is replaced, regardless of when it was last accessed or changed, whereas a sales presentation or news item will typically become inactive much faster than other content types. Overall, identifying active content and active users creates a much clearer picture of the current state, both as a measure of complexity for a transformation to a target state or migration to a new system, as well as creating a baseline of the overall current state. For instance, we have stated previously that organizations, on average, are managing roughly five times more content than they need to. If your measure of active content represents more than 20 percent of all content, that means you are typically ahead of the curve. The opposite is also true: if your measure of active content is vastly outweighed by your total content, that is a good indicator your content cleanup and content migration challenge will be a major one.

Content Dynamism

Many systems may also be able to provide a running count of the new content being loaded into the system or the amount of existing content that is being edited. Both of these factors speak to content dynamism. Systems with low content dynamism, or churn, may indicate there is poor usability in the system, and it is too difficult to publish or edit content within it. Of course, there may also be a valid reason for low content dynamism, such as the purpose of the repository is to house infrequently changing content like established corporation policies and procedures. Make sure to determine the intended use cases for the system before making conclusions in cases such as these. However, in general, when you see low content dynamism, this should serve as an indicator that a system and the associated content management and publication processes require redesign. If, on the other hand, you see a system with extremely high levels of content dynamism, you will want to determine whether this is by design, expected, and yielding the appropriate results or whether it represents a system with poor content governance where the content is running out of control and users have co-opted the intended purposes of the system. If you determine the system is highly dynamic, users are providing positive feedback on it, and the content within is of the quality anticipated, you have likely identified a well-designed and governed system that may serve as a strong model for the enterprise.

Search Activities and Paths

The last key type of analytics to obtain a good understanding of your current state, specifically the state of your KM systems, is related to search. There are some simple and some more advanced approaches that can be taken to understand how search is working. The simple reports can come from any web analytics tool. This includes things like top search terms, empty searches (searches with no results), most common facets selected, and the average depth of the selected search result (How far down the list the searcher went to select a result). There are also some more advanced analytics that many systems do not offer, but if you can obtain them, even in a subset of systems, they can offer great insights. The first search analytics is the simplest. What is the ratio between searches and clicks (clicks meaning results of the search that a user chose to open)? A very low search ratio (under 0.9) means that your users are not finding any meaningful results they wish to explore when searching. A very high ratio (over four) may be positive, but more often, it is actually an indicator that the search results are not clear enough to allow a user to discern from the results page whether the results are actually going to be valuable for them. Between those two numbers, we typically see the healthy zone where users are understanding the search results and finding content that is valuable to them. As with other analytics, there are, of course, caveats, where these ratios are just a starting point, and specific industries, content types, and system purposes might show a different healthy zone. However, in general, low and high ratios mean there is a problem with your search, the content, or the metadata on the content. If your analytics cannot derive this search ratio, there is another simpler analytic that may be obtainable. How many searches result in no further action (what we call a dead end)? Ideally, you want to see no dead ends, but for our purposes here, anything over five percent of total searches showing a dead end suggests your system has problems. As we move into even more advanced analytics, a system may also be able to show the navigational path a user has taken through a system. Again, if those navigational paths are ending with a dead end where no document or piece of content has been opened, that suggests there is a clear problem with your system and/or the content therein.

Time Spent

The amount of time spent in KM systems or spent looking for information in such systems may be useful, especially for trending purposes, but we generally do not consider it as a key metric to collect for two reasons. The first is that it is notoriously inaccurate to capture time spent. Though a system may be able to capture how much time you are logged in, it is much more difficult to consistently capture active time in these systems (where you are actually doing something, rather than just logged in as a background tab on your browser). The other reason time spent is not a key type of analytics is because it is not a true indicator of much at all. What does it mean if your users are spending more time in a system than they used to? Does it mean they are finding more value there and therefore dedicating more time to it, or does it mean that the system is increasingly convoluted or clogged with obsolete content, forcing them to spend more time looking for what they need? For that reason, we do not tend to prioritize a generic value of time spent as a key metric. However, time spent can be useful in specific systems and for tracking changes to specific features or functions. For instance, if you can cleanly link time to a positive action, increased time spent does become a useful indicator. An example of this is a positive trend of people spending more time in an online community of practice. In this case, more time means people *want* to be there and are getting value out of it. For changes to specific features or functions, improvements to a publishing workflow, redesign of a taxonomy for tagging, or integration of a new auto-tagging tool as part of a content management system would all be examples where tracking the amount of time to publish a document could offer important information to determine if your changes have saved the user time (on average). In this case, less time means higher value and success of the change.

Tip:
Though analytics can play an important role in informing your current state status, especially for KM systems, be wary of interpreting too much from analytics alone. Is your search ratio a perfect one because each of your users is finding exactly what they want on the first try, or is it because the first document they have clicked was so far off the mark they abandoned their quest? Is your system generating so much new content because your users are actively sharing their knowledge and engaging in the experience of content sharing, or is it because your governance is out of control, and your users are filling the system with junk content?

Capturing good analytics as part of an assessment will often serve a secondary purpose if your KM assessment graduates into a KM transformation, and you get the opportunity to transform the organization. Each of the captured metrics, especially those on enterprise systems that serve the entire organization, will serve as a baseline for how your KM transformation may change the organization. Improved active users, active content (and ratio of active content), and improved search ratio activity, in particular, will be critical indicators to prove the business value of the KM transformation. Each of these analytics trending in the right direction will serve as proof that the KM transformation is serving its intended purpose.

2.2.5   Past Surveys

In our discussion on top-down activities, we discussed the value of running an employee survey. In many organizations, however, running a discrete employee survey specifically for the KM analysis may not be feasible. Many organizations raise the complaint of "death by survey," where their employees have been barraged by too many surveys, and they are averse to subjecting them to yet another. In these cases, not all is lost. The odds are good that many of the already-run recent surveys can offer insights or provide potential baselines. For instance, common questions in employee satisfaction surveys cover overall satisfaction, such as likelihood to stay with the recommendation or recommend employment to a friend (both valuable as a baseline to measure trends and to understand the current state challenge), as well as more detailed questions that may be useful. Topics including learning and development, access to experts, and availability and quality of the tools and information necessary to perform are all valuable inputs to capture and analyze as part of a current state assessment.

2.2.6   Advanced Technologies

As a final point of bottom-up analysis, it is important to take special note of past or current projects related to advanced knowledge technologies, such as knowledge graphs, auto-tagging, ontology management, natural language processing, graph search, and machine learning. In many cases, these technologies are collectively described as Artificial Intelligence (AI). AI has been hot for some time, and it will continue to be so. In the remainder of the book, we cover a great deal on these technologies, including how they can be successfully designed, integrated, and implemented to achieve real Enterprise AI within an organization.

There are several reasons why it is important to understand what your organization is doing with AI, even if such projects are not completely being considered as knowledge or information projects. At this point, effective KM organizations are vastly more prepared to adopt and implement AI than other organizations that have not achieved the necessary KM maturity. In other words, KM maturity is a critical precursor to effective knowledge AI. That being the case, the efforts your organization may have made in AI, as well as its relative successes and factors, will be strong indicators regarding your organization's KM current state. Organizations that have successfully completed AI projects, ranging from prototype to full-scale enterprise implementations, are not just indicating they have the appropriate KM foundations, they are also demonstrating overall technical maturity, forward-thinking strategy, and willingness to work on the technical leading edge. As a result, again, these organizations are likely to be more ahead on their KM current state.

There are likely many organizations that have tried AI and failed. Our own experience shows a vast majority of organizations have attempted to implement AI at some level, but they have failed due to their lack of KM foundations as well as a lack of strategic vision and leadership regarding what their AI efforts are actually for, what business cases they would solve, and what capabilities they would actually provide to the organization. For our purposes, identifying attempted but mediocre or failed AI initiatives is extremely valuable to understanding the organization's KM current state. For these projects, you will want to understand:

- What was the intended goal of the AI initiative? Who was the audience, and what would it do for them?
- Is there remaining documentation or design work that can be leveraged (i.e., personas, use cases, architecture designs, etc.)?
- What were the sources of knowledge, content, and data from which the AI would pull?
- Why did the project fail/struggle? Can you draw the link between those struggles and a potential lack of KM foundations (i.e., poor starting content, lack of structure, lack of governance, etc.)?
- What is the perceived reason the project failed?
- Is there continued interest in iterating the project or trying again?

Understanding past and present AI initiatives can also provide two important indicators. If AI has been a failure, has it left your organization with undue skepticism or a sense that the organization is not ready for AI? Understanding the sense of this will be important to determine if the organization is culturally prepared for major change due to a KM transformation and whether the organization is open to advanced technologies as a part of that transformation. The opposite also holds true. Regardless of whether the AI initiatives have been successful or not, there may exist project or product owners within your organization that may be blockers to future initiatives. This may be due to a sense that if they have not been successful, they do not want others to be, or it may be due to a sense of protectiveness and ownership of their own initiatives and a worry that AI is being taken away from them. Regardless, identifying potential human blockers and adversaries to future efforts and transformation will be a valuable input to log and understand.

Collectively, these bottom-up activities will work alongside the top-down activities in order to score your organization on the benchmark. In addition, common findings and takeaways gathered from these activities should include:

- An index of existing KM systems, with an understanding of who is using each system as well as the understood system purpose. This should also include an understanding of which have design elements that may be leveraged to move forward.
- Identification of target state "starting points," such as personas, information architecture, taxonomy designs, and content types designed or currently in use.
- High-level content analysis, including understanding of amount of content, content dynamism, and types of content within each system.

2.3   The Enterprise Knowledge Proprietary Benchmark

For organizations that require a very clear definition of their target state, employing a benchmark, when chosen wisely and completed thoroughly, can offer a great deal of value as part of a KM transformation and/or KM systems update. Specifically, the right benchmark will:

- **Provide a standard to compare against**. In many cases, organizations do not know where they stand when it comes to KM. Though they likely have the sense they are struggling or at least have room for improvement, they often cannot detail why that is or what it would mean to the organization. A benchmark should concretely identify where the organization is and whether they are ahead or behind what is considered standard for organizations.
- **Serve as a starting point to define and prioritize KM.** There are many different definitions of KM out there. Some focus solely on tacit knowledge, the knowledge held by people. Others focus more on digital content that is unstructured (i.e., files and documents), and yet others, like our definition, take a very proud definition that traverses content from structured to unstructured and includes the complete aspects of people, process, content, culture, and technology. Many organizations struggle to define what KM means to them. A good benchmark will offer enough detail for the organization to identify what matters to them and then build a meaningful organizational definition of KM from that.

- **Deconstruct KM into its parts.** As we have already established, KM is complex and can contain a number of other disciplines, concepts, and technologies. An effective benchmark will pull KM apart into a more concrete set of components, allowing the organization not only to be scored on each one, but for the organization to understand each component and determine the value it could gain by making improvements.
- **Apply math to an otherwise esoteric concept.** Even with a good understanding and basis of comparison, KM can still feel overly fuzzy. An effective benchmark will allow the organization to do the math of KM in two ways. By scoring on different factors, an organization should be able to measure clearly where it stands. It is one thing to say, "We seem to be behind on this element of KM." It is another to know that your organization is in the lowest 5% when it comes to a particular factor. The latter is quantifiable. It is a lot more meaningful to understand specifically where you are rather than simply knowing you have got room to improve. This idea of knowing you are far behind can also serve as an important tool to gain executive support in your organization. No executive wants to be told his or her organization is a laggard compared to competitors or the world of other organizations. Being able to provide those numbers can be a critical motivator to ensure your KM initiatives receive the attention and funding they deserve.

EK's own proprietary KM benchmark is the culmination of decades of observation and analysis of real organizations from all over the world, ranging from global to local, large to small, and spanning hundreds of industries and business model types. The benchmark deconstructs the key elements of KM into five categories: People, Process, Content, Culture, and Technology. It also offers over 40 clearly measurable, scored factors on a five-point Likert scale. Each of the factor scores is arrayed on a bell curve, as shown in Fig. 2.1, with roughly 80% of organizations scoring between

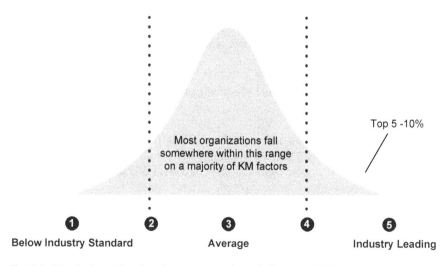

Fig. 2.1 Distribution of benchmark scores arrayed on a bell curve. © 2021, Wahl/Hilger, reused with permission

a two and four on any given factor. A score of one on any given factor means your organization is well below average. Note, however, that is not necessarily a bad thing. For instance, if your organization is small and all staff are collocated, there is perhaps no reason for your organization to score highly on asynchronous collaboration or communication technologies. A score of five on any given factor means that you are, to put it simply, doing it right. As a whole, when the factor scores are all averaged, only 5–10% of organizations will score above a four, with that score indicating they are operating as a world-class KM organization. There can of course still be room for improvement, but we find it is typically organizations that are scoring between a 1.5 and 3 that are most consistently seeking to transform their organization via an extensive KM transformation.

Critical and unique to our benchmark is that it is not based on opinion or undefined requests to agree/disagree with a concept. On the contrary, it is constructed to be consistently scored based on clear observations of organizational realities. Whether you employ EK's benchmark or a different one, ensure this is the case. An effective benchmark should not be left to opinion or the whims of the respondent.

The benchmark has gone through many iterations over the last decade, with Version 7 included at the end of this chapter as Tables 2.4, 2.5, 2.6, 2.7, and 2.8. The various iterations have updated language to be cleared and have added over ten additional factors since the first version, responding to changing approaches to KM, offering additional clarity, and incorporating advanced technologies including knowledge graphs and machine learning.

A completed current state assessment can take many forms, depending on what you are trying to do with it. If you are conducting a current state assessment in order to identify organizational gaps or priorities to address on a piecemeal basis, a relatively informal set of deliverables is likely fine. If, on the other hand, your current state analysis is the beginning of an intended transformation for your organization, especially one that will carry significant capital costs, you will want to create a more formalized set of artifacts. Of course, this depends on your organization and the formality of products, but generally in these cases, an official current state analysis will include a current state report and an executive summary report.

Current State Report
A detailed analysis that combines the findings of the top-down and bottom-up analysis to:

- Review methodology and approach. This should include a detailed count of all the ways findings were gathered, with a focus on the number of people internal to the organization who were included. There is a great deal of power in expressing that you interviewed hundreds of people across business lines, geographic areas, and functions, for instance.
- Detail the KM strengths and weaknesses of the organization. The formats for this vary, but a Strengths, Weaknesses, Opportunities, Threats (SWOT) Chart that cuts across the KM elements of people, process, content, culture, and technology is an effective way to organize and visualize this.

- Score the organization against a benchmark, providing specific data and supporting anecdotal evidence to justify the scores.
- Call out specific quotes and stories to provide business-specific examples regarding pain points.
- Identify starting points for a transformation based either on greatest need (where there is a burning requirement for something to be addressed) or greatest potential (where a part of the organization or specific system therein is doing things well and has the potential for expansion).
- Summarize the cost of the current state, meaning, the negative impact the current state of KM is having on the organization.

Executive Summary Report

One of the most important uses of a current state analysis is to ensure executive support and stakeholder buy-in to continue with a transformation and fund the complete initiative. To that end, an executive summary report should be created to express the key findings of the current state analysis. We generally consider these to be the most important elements. Our rule of thumb is that this report should be expressed in no more than ten slides and be presentable in less than 30 minutes. The report should include:

- A high-level summary of methodology and approach, making sure to include the aforementioned counts of people engaged.
- A summary of major KM challenges and issues within the organization matched to the impacts or costs of each of these challenges.
- A rolled-up benchmark score with a brief explanation of the benchmark employed.
- A summary of next steps to ensure executives understand that this is the first step in a potentially long initiative.

> **Tip:**
> Beware of the "so what" factor. Sometimes, the executive summary view of a current state will be delivered at such a level that the findings and results will seem obvious. Be sure to explain the richness of the supporting material (oftentimes hundreds of pages) and that this is the first step in the process for alignment and prioritization, leading to a future state plan and roadmap that will help to transform the business. In short, the current state step is not always the most exciting, but it is critical to the process in order to establish a baseline and ensure everyone knows what they are working with.

The successful completion of a current state analysis should result in your own ability to concisely express the core KM challenges within the organization as well as their impacts. The desired outcome of a current state analysis is a shared recognition by executives and stakeholders that there are KM deficiencies within the organization and changes need to be made, yielding their support to proceed with the definition of a target state.

Table 2.4 EK's KM Maturity Benchmark Version 7, "People" section

People					
	Score—1	Score—2	Score—3	Score—4	Score—5
Engagement	Staff do not engage in new initiatives within their team, departments, or at the enterprise level.	Staff are engaged in their own team's initiatives, but there is not engagement across departments.	Staff engage in some initiatives outside of their team or department (e.g., process improvement efforts) but, otherwise, there is limited and siloed engagement in terms of initiatives across the organization.	Staff engage in cross-functional initiatives, but initiatives lack a clear plan, executive support, and scalability.	Staff are engaged and proactive at the enterprise level in cross-functional initiatives; there is executive support and planning.
Organizational Awareness	Staff do not have an understanding of how their role contributes to organizational goals, and do not have insight into how each department contributes to the organization's mission.	Staff have an understanding of how their role and everyone in their department contributes to the organization's mission, but do not possess insight outside of their department.	Staff are aware of how other departments with whom they work regularly contribute to the organization's mission, but do not possess a holistic understanding of every department's work and interdependencies.	Staff are aware of how all departments contribute to the organization's mission, but do not have mechanisms to regularly communicate with or stay informed of happenings in departments outside of their own.	Staff at every level of the organization possess a holistic understanding of the organization's operating environment and the interaction between departments, and internal processes support transparency and timely communication across departments.

(continued)

Table 2.4 (continued)

Intradepartmental Communication	Staff do not communicate within their department. This leads to speculation, the perpetuation of misinformation, suspicion, misalignment, and/or gaps in organizational awareness.	Information flows from top leadership to management, but trickles down inconsistently to non-supervisory staff and/or is released on a need-to-know basis.	Leadership communicates regularly to all levels of staff, but offers few, if any, opportunities for staff to provide input or feedback.	In addition to top-down communication, information flows from employees to leadership and between employees but occurs unplanned and irregularly.	Within a department, leadership and staff communicate frequently, directly and transparently, invite questions and feedback at all times, and proactively address information gaps before they widen.
Interdepartmental Communication	Staff do not communicate across departments. This leads to speculation, the perpetuation of misinformation across the organization, suspicion, misalignment, and/or gaps in organizational awareness.	Information flows among leadership of departments, but trickles down inconsistently to management and non-supervisory staff and/or is released on a need-to-know basis.	Leadership across departments meet regularly, and there are defined mechanisms in place to ensure information flows down to all levels of staff. However, there are few opportunities for information to flow between employees of different departments, with the exception of those departments that work together on a regular basis.	In addition to top-down communication, there are opportunities for information to flow between employees of different departments, but these occur unplanned and irregularly.	There is strong internal connectivity across departments. Staff at all levels communicate frequently, directly and transparently, invite questions and feedback at all times, share information widely, and proactively address information gaps before they widen.

(continued)

Table 2.4 (continued)

Individual Roles	The organization does not communicate a vision for KM nor incorporate KM-related organizational goals and initiatives into staff's roles. Staff do not understand how their role contributes to the organization's KM goals nor display a sense of responsibility for KM.	The organization has defined a vision for KM, but leadership has not articulated how staff can contribute to advancing the organization's KM goals. Staff have a limited understanding of how their role might align to the organization's KM goals.	The organization has incorporated KM goals, responsibilities, and initiatives into some staff member's performance evaluations as part of the organization's vision for KM, but the practice is not universal. Only a limited number of staff understand how their KM efforts impact the organization's overall success.	The organization has incorporated KM responsibilities into job descriptions and performance evaluations for all roles within the organization but does not clearly communicate expectations for team members nor track progress.	The organization communicates their vision for KM effectively for all roles, and staff recognize the value KM brings individuals and teams. KM responsibilities are incorporated into job descriptions and performance evaluations for all staff, and supervisors use KM indicators to actively evaluate the performance of their teams.

(continued)

Table 2.4 (continued)

Access to Expertise	Staff are somewhat aware of the expertise of their immediate co-workers and find it difficult to discover experts beyond their immediate team.	Staff are aware of and can access the expertise available within their own department AND have the encouragement of their supervisors to make use of it. Outlets are available regularly across the department. Staff are unaware of the expertise of others across the organization.	Staff are aware of expertise available in other departments with whom they regularly collaborate with but struggle to reach across the rest of the organization. Staff gain access to expertise through resources with moderate knowledge of how to connect to experts in other departments.	Staff are aware of expertise available in other departments across the organization. Staff gain access to expertise through designated resources (e.g., contact lists) and/or points of contact with organizational knowledge who can connect them to experts in other departments.	Staff are well-informed of the expertise available to them and have access to resources that can connect them to experts who they may not be aware of. Management is unified across the organization in making experts more accessible outside organizational boundaries and communicating their presence and methods to connect with them to staff.
Strategic Alignment	KM efforts are not clearly aligned with any wider team or organizational objective.	KM efforts are only planned in alignment to a single, immediate initiative within a department.	KM efforts are planned in alignment to a single, immediate organization-wide initiative.	KM efforts are planned in clear alignment to the organization's wider strategic objectives.	KM efforts are planned in clear alignment, and regularly revised to maintain alignment to the organization's wider strategic objectives

(continued)

Table 2.4 (continued)

KM Leadership	No formal or informal KM leadership is present in the organization.	There are informal KM leaders in the organization who advocate for KM best practices at a departmental level.	There are formal roles for KM leaders within the organization who advocate for KM best practices at a departmental level.	There are formal roles for KM leaders within the organization who advocate for KM best practices at the organizational level.	There are formal roles for KM leaders in the organization who can leverage their influence to embed KM practices and resources at a strategic level.

Table 2.5 EK's KM Maturity Benchmark Version 7, "Process" section

Process					
	Score—1	Score—2	Score—3	Score—4	Score—5
Knowledge Retention	The organization does not possess the processes or tools necessary to retain knowledge from staff leaving or retiring and has not identified the need and the type of information that should be retained.	The organization does not possess processes and tools to retain knowledge from staff leaving or retiring but has identified the need and the type of information that should be retained.	The organization possesses minimally defined processes to retain knowledge from staff and possesses tools that are only occasionally utilized to retain such knowledge.	The organization possesses well-defined processes, roles, and responsibilities for retaining knowledge from staff leaving or retiring and tools are frequently utilized to support these functions.	The organization possesses well-defined processes, roles, responsibilities, and tools for knowledge retention and formally applies these processes and tools to retain, reuse, and evolve knowledge from staff leaving or retiring.
Explicit Knowledge Capture and Sharing	The organization does not possess processes and tools to capture and share explicit knowledge and has not identified the need and the type of explicit knowledge that should be captured and shared.	The organization does not possess processes and tools to capture and share explicit knowledge but has identified the need and the type of explicit knowledge that should be captured and shared.	The organization does not possess well-defined processes to capture and share explicit knowledge but possesses some tools to capture and share such explicit knowledge.	The organization possesses well-defined processes to capture and share explicit knowledge and possesses tools that are occasionally utilized to capture and share such explicit knowledge.	The organization possesses well-defined processes, roles, responsibilities, and tools for explicit knowledge capture and sharing AND applies the right tools to capture and share explicit knowledge.

(continued)

Table 2.5 (continued)

Tacit Knowledge Capture and Sharing	The organization does not possess processes and tools to capture and share tacit knowledge and has not identified the need and the type of tacit knowledge that should be captured and shared.	The organization does not possess processes and tools to capture and share tacit knowledge but has identified the need and the type of tacit knowledge that should be captured and shared.	The organization does not possess well-defined processes, roles, and responsibilities for capturing and sharing tacit knowledge, but tools to support these processes are informally established.	The organization possesses well-defined processes to capture and share tacit knowledge and possesses tools that are occasionally utilized to capture and share such tacit knowledge.	The organization possesses well-defined processes, roles, responsibilities, and tools for tacit knowledge capture and sharing and applies these processes and tools to capture and share tacit knowledge.
Content Governance	The organization does not possess a framework (e.g., policies, processes, practices) nor roles and responsibilities to maintain and evolve its content.	The organization possesses a loosely defined, informal framework to maintain and evolve its content.	The organization possesses a defined framework to maintain and evolve its content, but does not have clearly defined roles and responsibilities to enforce the framework.	The organization possesses a defined framework to maintain and evolve its content, and has formally defined roles and responsibilities to enforce the framework.	The organization leverages its content governance framework and roles to strategically and proactively shape content strategy and oversee content operations in alignment with the organization's strategic priorities. .

(continued)

Table 2.5 (continued)

Learning, Training, and Development	The organization does not possess any tools, processes, or programs dedicated to learning and does not support staff in their training efforts.	The organization possesses some learning tools, processes, or programs, but does not actively support staff in their training efforts.	The organization possesses learning tools, processes, or programs, and informally supports staff in their training efforts.	The organization possesses learning tools, processes, or programs, actively supports staff in their training efforts, and possesses a standardized and formal training plan for employees.	The organization possesses clearly defined, widely adopted learning tools, processes or programs with rich content, and a fully articulated and formal training plan for employees, catered to their specific needs.
Personalized Learning and Training	The organization offers limited or no training and learning opportunities for staff, and those few that are available are generic and are not customized for specific roles or audiences.	The organization offers some customized training and learning opportunities for staff members, but the majority of the training that is available is intended for a universal audience, lacking personalized or customized options.	The organization offers both generic training and learning opportunities for a universal audience and more personalized training and learning opportunities, however, the amount of personalized training options that are available is not enough to meet the breadth of staff's needs.	The organization offers a wide range of personalized training and learning opportunities for staff that is geared towards specific roles, business functions, or other identified staff groupings.	The organization offers staff members personalized training and learning opportunities and is able to recommend content to individuals that meets the needs of their specific role, desired opportunities, and business function.

(continued)

Table 2.5 (continued)

Taxonomy Governance	The organization does not possess processes to maintain and evolve its taxonomy.	The organization possesses loosely defined, informal processes to maintain and evolve its taxonomy.	The organization possesses defined processes to maintain and evolve its taxonomy but does not have clearly defined roles and responsibilities to enforce the processes.	The organization possesses defined processes to maintain and evolve its taxonomy and has formally defined roles and responsibilities to enforce the processes.	The organization possesses and effectively applies collaborative taxonomy governance processes with clearly defined roles and responsibilities.

Table 2.6 EK's KM Maturity Benchmark Version 7, "Content" section

	Content				
	Score—1	**Score—2**	**Score—3**	**Score—4**	**Score—5**
Content Creation and Contribution	Staff create content locally without the intention of who their audience will be.	Staff create content on shared drives with the intention of sharing it with others on their team.	Staff create content on shared drives with the intention of sharing it with others in their departments.	Staff create content on collaborative CMS platforms with the intention of sharing it enterprise-wide.	Staff create content on collaborative CMS platforms with the intention of sharing it enterprise-wide in a way that could be modified and reused.
Duplicate Content	Employees and users perceive that the organization possesses a high amount of duplicative content with no established versioning.	Employees and users perceive that the organization possesses a moderate to high amount of duplicative content with ad hoc version control processes.	Employees and users perceive that the organization possesses a moderate amount of duplicative content across systems, with informal version control processes.	Employees and users perceive that the organization possesses a low to moderate amount of duplicative content and semi-formal version control processes per system(s).	Employees and users perceive that the organization possesses a low amount of duplicative content and utilizes formal version control processes across systems.
Outdated or Obsolete Content	Employees and users perceive that the organization possesses a high amount of outdated or obsolete content.	Employees and users perceive that the organization possesses a moderate to high amount of outdated or obsolete content.	Employees and users perceive that the organization possesses a moderate amount of outdated or obsolete content.	Employees and users perceive that the organization possesses a low to moderate amount of outdated or obsolete content.	Employees and users perceive that the organization possesses a low amount of outdated or obsolete content.

(continued)

Table 2.6 (continued)

Defined Content Types and Templates	Content types and subsequent templates are not defined for any systems within the organization.	Content types and subsequent templates are defined for some systems within the organization but are not aligned at the organization level.	Content types and subsequent templates are defined for most systems within organizational functions but are not aligned at the organization level.	Content types and subsequent templates are defined for most systems within the organizational functions and are aligned at the organization level.	Content types and subsequent templates are clearly defined across systems at the enterprise level of the organization.
Taxonomy	The organization does not possess a formalized taxonomy OR content is tagged with free terms.	The organization possesses formalized but fragmented taxonomies across various systems.	The organization possesses a formalized enterprise taxonomy but has not yet implemented it in content repositories across the organization.	The organization possesses and utilizes a formalized enterprise taxonomy to tag content in repositories.	The organization possesses and utilizes a comprehensive enterprise taxonomy/thesaurus with term definitions, synonyms, and alternate terms to tag content in repositories.
Ontology	The organization does not possess a formalized ontology.	The organization possesses formalized but fragmented ontologies across various systems.	The organization possesses a formalized enterprise ontology but has not yet implemented it in content repositories across the organization.	The organization possesses and utilizes a formalized enterprise ontology to tag or relate content in repositories across the enterprise.	The organization possesses and utilizes a comprehensive enterprise ontology with term definitions, synonyms, alternate terms, and semantic relationships to tag and relate content across organizational repositories.

(continued)

Table 2.6 (continued)

Content Deconstruction				
The organization possesses a high number of large files and unwieldy documents that need to be broken down, but there are no considerations for breaking down said content to be more user friendly.	The organization possesses a moderate to high number of large files and unwieldy content that should be broken down and has considered a process for breaking down content.	The organization possesses a moderate number of files and unwieldy content that it needs to break down but has established a basic process for determining what content needs to be broken down and breaking that content down to be more accessible.	The organization possesses a low to moderate amount of large, unwieldy content that it needs to break down and has implemented and utilized a successful process for determining what content should be broken down and breaking that content down in a timely manner.	The organization possesses a low to moderate amount of large, unwieldy content that it needs to break down, and such content has been thoughtfully and consistently broken down to be more user friendly through a well-established process across the organization.
Data Integration				
The organization has no formal data organization in place and data is handled at the individual level.	Organizational teams or projects have shared data resources, but no other alignment.	The organization has established data repositories at departmental/business unit level dedicated to different types of data.	The organization has established integrated data repositories that integrate data across organizational departments/units.	Data is fully integrated at the enterprise level, allowing access to organizational data from a single resource or platform.
Data Awareness				
Staff make exclusive use of data they have personally produced or collected to inform their decisions.	Staff make exclusive use of data produced or collected by their own organizational unit to inform their decisions.	Staff make sparing use of data available across the organization to inform their decisions.	Staff are actively using data available across the organization to inform their decisions.	Staff are actively using data available across the organization to inform their decisions and are proactively engaging to improve and enhance the data.

Table 2.7 EK's KM Maturity Benchmark Version 7, "Culture" section

Culture					
	Score—1	Score—2	Score—3	Score—4	Score—5
Incentives	Staff receive no recognition or rewards for knowledge management best practices.	Staff receive some informal recognition or rewards for knowledge management best practices.	Staff are informally recognized and rewarded for knowledge management best practices on an ad hoc basis.	Staff are formally recognized and rewarded for knowledge management best practices.	Staff are formally recognized and rewarded for knowledge management best practices and recognition is built into performance reviews or standard processes.
Innovation	The organization discourages innovation efforts by staff, and staff do not put effort into innovation.	The organization does not encourage innovation, but there are fragmented innovation efforts.	The organization encourages innovation, does not tangibly recognize such efforts, and there are only fragmented innovation efforts.	The organization encourages staff innovation, and there are more structured innovation efforts but does not tangibly reward these efforts.	The organization encourages staff to innovate and recognizes/rewards innovation initiatives.

(continued)

Table 2.7 (continued)

Sharing and Collaboration	The organization does not share information or collaborate on information creation.	The organization has fragmented information sharing and collaboration on information creation.	The organization lacks KM leadership and/or budgetary support to achieve information sharing and collaboration but shares and collaborates on an ad hoc basis using individually identified methods.	The organization possesses KM leadership support and budgetary support to achieve information sharing and collaboration but has not yet implemented the necessary components.	The organization is actively promoting people, practices, and technology necessary for sharing information and collaborating on information creation at the enterprise level.
Openness to Change	The organization is strongly averse to change.	The organization is not open to change, lacks executive sponsorship for change, and does not have a change management plan.	The organization is somewhat open to change, there is fragmented executive sponsorship, but lacks a clear change management plan.	The organization is open to change, possesses executive sponsorship for the change, but does not have a clear and defined change management plan.	The organization embraces change, possesses executive sponsorship for the change, and there is a defined change management plan.
Measurable Success Criteria	The organization has no defined metrics or milestones for KM.	The organization has defined milestones for their KM initiatives but has not identified a way to support them with metrics.	The organization has defined milestones but has limited metrics to demonstrate progress and value of KM initiatives and is not measuring or communicating any results.	The organization has defined milestones and metrics to demonstrate the progress and value of KM initiatives and is measuring and communicating results to stakeholders.	The organization has defined milestones and goals for its KM initiatives, which are aligned to corporate objectives, and is learning and adapting their initiatives based on feedback from stakeholders.

(continued)

Table 2.7 (continued)

Trust				
Staff are afraid of capturing and sharing knowledge because they fear potential repercussions.	Staff share and communicate some knowledge with each other but possess some fear that sharing will lead to repercussions.	Staff share and communicate knowledge with each other or recognize that they can share without fear.	Staff share and communicate knowledge with each other and are informally rewarded for doing so.	Staff are formally rewarded for sharing and communicating knowledge and they know that they can do so confidently and consistently without fear.

Table 2.8 EK's KM Maturity Benchmark Version 7, "Technology" section

	Technology				
	Score—1	Score—2	Score—3	Score—4	Score—5
Source of Truth *Knowledge Portal*	Content is not centrally managed, and staff do not know where the most recent version is stored when faced with choosing between multiple systems.	Minimal business and technical processes are in place to centralize content in specific locations but efforts are not effective.	Content is centrally managed, but versioning is not clear or intuitive to users. Version management requires extensive training to operate effectively, and the training is not consistently provided.	Content is centrally managed and version control is set up in an easy and intuitive way to manage. However, all staff do not use it consistently or according to the same governance processes.	Content is centrally managed so that staff from across the organization can leverage the information to accomplish individual, department level, and organizational level objectives. Staff and organization systems utilize this source of truth to maintain consistency and centralize governance processes.

(continued)

Table 2.8 (continued)

Management Systems *Repository Layer*	The organization lacks systems to manage the visualization, creation, and modification of digital content (Web Content, Multimedia Content, Documents, etc.).	The organization possesses systems to manage the visualization, creation, and modification of digital content but they are segmented across different lines of business.	The organization possesses systems to manage the visualization, creation, and modification of digital content but one or more are insufficiently configured or lack functionality to support critical processes, such as workflows, versioning, reporting, application of metadata, etc.	The organization possesses department-level systems to manage the visualization, creation, and modification of digital content and all are well configured and capable of supporting all critical processes, such as workflows, versioning, reporting, application of metadata, etc.	The organization possesses enterprise-level systems to manage key digital content and all are well configured and capable of supporting all critical processes, such as workflows, versioning, reporting, application of metadata, etc.
Search *Findability Layer*	The organization possesses no search tools or low-functioning search tools that are segmented across multiple repositories.	The organization possesses defined search tools that are segmented across multiple repositories.	The organization possesses centralized search with inconsistent indexing across systems and affecting relevant results.	The organization possesses centralized search with indexing of key content from prioritized systems returning relevant results.	The organization possesses centralized search with a complete index of critical content and well weighted / accurate results.
Ontologies and Knowledge Graphs *Findability Layer*	The organization does not control their vocabularies, instead leverages free-text tags within their ecosystem.	The organization has tools and practices in place to leverage controlled lists within the organization's ecosystem.	The organization has an established set of tools and practices to leverage taxonomies and their hierarchical structure within the organization's ecosystem.	The organization has an established set of tools and practices to leverage ontologies and expanded relationship types within the organization's ecosystem.	The organization has an established set of tools and practices to leverage ontologies and knowledge graphs to serve as the semantic layer within the organization's ecosystem.

(continued)

Table 2.8 (continued)

Artificial Intelligence (AI) *Findability Layer*	The organization does not recognize or understand the value of Artificial Intelligence (ML, NLP, etc.)	Some business areas across the organization recognize and understand the value of AI.	Some business areas have launched pilot projects to test use cases and tools for AI.	Some business areas have an established set of tools and initiatives to leverage AI to help them realize their goals.	The organization leverages concepts of Artificial Intelligence (ML, NLP, etc.) to support the capture, management, presentation, and recommendation of information.
Collaborative Authoring and Editing *Collaboration Layer*	There are no systems that support collaborative authoring and editing. Collaboration is done over email or in person.	Collaborative authoring and editing tools are used on an ad hoc basis within departments but are not standard practice.	Collaborative authoring and editing tools are used within departments but are not well integrated into formalized processes or departmental systems.	Collaborative authoring and editing tools are well integrated into departmental systems and are part of formalized content creation processes.	Collaborative authoring and editing tools are well integrated into organizational systems and are part of formalized content creation processes.
Social, Communication, and Collaboration Tools *Collaboration Layer*	The organization does not possess any social, communication, and collaboration tools or capabilities and collaboration is siloed.	The organization possesses basic and fragmented functionality to enable social, communication, and collaboration tools but relies primarily on in-person processes.	The organization possesses social, communication, and collaboration tools with limited integration and mobile access.	The organization possesses unified social, communication, and collaboration tools that are integrated with key systems including mobile access.	The organization possesses unified social, communication, and collaboration tools that are integrated in day-to-day platforms across the enterprise, are available on mobile devices, and are being utilized by staff.

(continued)

Table 2.8 (continued)

Metadata Infrastructure *Metadata Layer*	The organization does not possess a metadata strategy or the systems to manage metadata for structured or unstructured data.	The organization possesses a metadata strategy but does not possess the systems to manage metadata for structured and unstructured data.	The organization possesses an enterprise-level metadata strategy but does not consistently enforce it or leverage systems to manage department-level metadata for structured and unstructured data.	The organization possesses an enterprise-level metadata strategy and has started to enforce it using systems to manage department-level metadata for structured and unstructured data.	The organization possesses and enforces its enterprise-level metadata strategy using systems to manage metadata organization-wide for structured and unstructured data.
Text Mining/Auto-Categorization *Metadata Layer*	The organization does not possess text mining or auto-categorization capabilities.	The organization possesses basic functionality that analyzes and categorizes content.	The organization possesses text mining and auto-categorization capabilities to produce low accuracy results or simple reporting. These efforts are department or system specific.	The organization possesses text mining and auto-categorization capabilities to produce medium accuracy results and actionable reporting for organizational systems used by multiple departments.	The organization is leveraging entities, controlled lists, taxonomies, and ontologies in order to analyze unstructured content and categorize and analyze its use organization-wide.
Auto-Tagging *Metadata Layer*	The organization does not possess auto-tagging capabilities and applies content metadata manually.	The organization possesses basic functionality that applies content tags such as based on content location, author, etc.	The organization possesses an auto-tagging functionality which produces low accuracy results or is implemented in select systems only.	The organization possesses and utilizes a high accuracy auto-tagging functionality across main enterprise systems.	The organization is leveraging entities and tagged content as ways to perform trend analysis and problem detection within unstructured information.

(continued)

Table 2.8 (continued)

System Analytics *Analytics Layer*	KM platforms have no known capabilities to collect, aggregate, or report data analytics.	KM platforms have limited analytics generation, collection and reporting capabilities. These are minimally configured in alignment to KM success criteria.	KM platforms have the capability to generate user behavior, content use, and adoption analytics on a system-by-system basis. There are reporting capabilities to visualize and communicate the collected data. Analytics collection and reporting are configured in alignment to KM success criteria.	KM platforms have the capability to generate user behavior, content use, and adoption analytics. Some, but not all of this data is aggregated in a single system which offers further analysis and reporting capabilities. Analytics collection and reporting are configured in alignment to KM success criteria.	KM platforms have the capability to generate user behavior, content use, and adoption analytics. All data is aggregated in a single system for further analysis and reporting capabilities. Analytics collection and reporting are configured in alignment to KM success criteria.
Content Publishing Strategy *Content Creation Layer*	Staff responsible for creating content do not have access to authoring tools with the capabilities to manually publish content in different formats.	Staff responsible for creating content have limited access to authoring tools with the capabilities to manually publish content in different formats.	Staff responsible for creating content have limited access to channel specific authoring tools that are not configured to automatically publish content to multiple formats.	Staff responsible for creating content have access to omni-channel and multi-channel authoring tools, but the tools are not configured to automatically publish content to multiple formats.	Staff responsible for creating content leverage omni-channel and multi-channel authoring tools with user centric interfaces capable of publishing content to multiple formats.

(continued)

Table 2.8 (continued)

Automated Knowledge Curation *Governance Layer*	Procedures for capturing, sharing, updating, auditing, preserving, archiving and disposing of knowledge content are manually executed.	Procedures for capturing, sharing, updating, auditing, preserving, archiving and disposing of knowledge content are mostly manually executed, but some are embedded as automated workflows in technological systems.	Procedures for capturing, sharing, updating, auditing, preserving, archiving and disposing of knowledge content are executed to equal extent through manual processes, and as automated workflows in technological systems.	Procedures for capturing, sharing, updating, auditing, preserving, archiving and disposing of knowledge content are mostly embedded as automated workflows in technological systems. A few are still carried out manually.	Procedures for capturing, sharing, updating, auditing, preserving, archiving and disposing of knowledge content are fully embedded as automated workflows in technological systems.
Knowledge Connectivity	The organization's KM systems are not integrated with other systems.	The organization's KM systems are rarely integrated with other systems.	The organization's KM systems are primarily integrated with other department-level KM and non-systems.	The organization's KM systems are inconsistently integrated with other enterprise-level KM and non-KM systems.	The organization's KM systems are seamlessly integrated across the enterprise with other KM and non-KM systems.

References

Dalkir K (2017) Knowledge management in theory and practice. The MIT Press, Cambridge
Gamble P, Blackwell J (2001) Knowledge management. Kogan Page, London

Understanding Your Organization's Future KM Needs (Target State)

3

Whereas the current state is critical in order to ensure you understand your organization and can develop a baseline to track whether your KM transformation is yielding the appropriate results, the target state is essential to setting your KM transformation on the correct path, prioritizing the right elements, and defining an accurate and meaningful vision for what a successful KM transformation will mean to your organization.

More specifically, a fully formed target state definition will include Changes to the Organization, Changes for the People, Changes to the Systems, Business Case and/or ROI Analysis, and a Future State Vision, which are explained in detail below.

Changes to the Organization
The target state will clearly identify what will have changed within the organization across the KM factors of People, Process, Content, Culture, and Technology. This includes the elements listed in Table 3.1 which are broken out by these factors.

Changes for the People
The target state should clearly express what will change for different types of people (based on the personas identified previously). The types of changes expressed should largely be in terms of benefits but should also cover major behavior changes that will require a concerted change management effort to effect. There are a number of tools to express these changes for people/personas, but the following are some of the most effective.

Journey Maps
One excellent way to express major changes in the organization is via before-and-after journey maps, an example of which is in Figs. 3.1 and 3.2. The first journey map would show the current experience for a KM action, e.g., looking for an answer to a question, and the second shows how this experience would change (ideally, markedly positively). These journey maps should convey time savings and also chart the positive/negative sense of the experience.

© The Author(s), under exclusive license to Springer Nature Switzerland AG 2022   59
J. Hilger, Z. Wahl, *Making Knowledge Management Clickable*,
https://doi.org/10.1007/978-3-030-92385-3_3

Table 3.1 Target state changes broken out into the categories of people, process, content, culture, and technology

People	• Organizational changes including new roles and responsibilities specific to the maintenance and decision-making of KM within the organization (i.e., KM Organizational Definition). • New or changed roles and responsibilities related to knowledge and information, KM processes, and KM systems.
Process	• New or changed policies, processes, and procedures for the creation and management of content and the systems that hold that content. • New or changed processes for knowledge capture and knowledge retention, specifically to ensure knowledge flows more effectively throughout the organization and consequently is not lost when individuals leave.
Content	• The cleanup of content such that old, obsolete, or duplicate content has been addressed. • The consolidation of content from competing or antiquated systems and repositories. • The standardization of content via templates and content types. • The enhancement of content via metadata and other features. • Integration of different types of content.
Culture	• Changes in leadership support and attention for KM. • Changes in rewards or incentives for KM. • Improved understanding of the value of KM. • Improved willingness to share knowledge.
Technology	• The modernization and consolidation of systems. • The addition of new technologies to fill gaps. • Design (or redesign) of systems to be more consistent and leverage KM design practices. • The integration of technologies to work together, resulting in a true KM suite. • Implementation of advanced technologies to aid in automation and customization.

Current State Challenges Mapped to Future State Capabilities

In the section on the current state, we discussed the importance of documenting current challenges regarding KM actions that are hard or impossible to do. Revisiting these with a corresponding view of how employees/users will be able to more easily perform this action is a simple and clear way of expressing the future state. A table form often works well for this.

New Process/Workflows

Graphic depictions of new processes, which include detailed steps that show how previously complex, inconsistent, and duplicative actions are now improved, can provide not only a quick reference to understand the changes to the current state, but also a valuable starting point for the design of new KM systems.

Future Quotes

As the real quotes from actual employees are an important part of evaluating the current state, an excellent way of portraying the intended future state is to craft

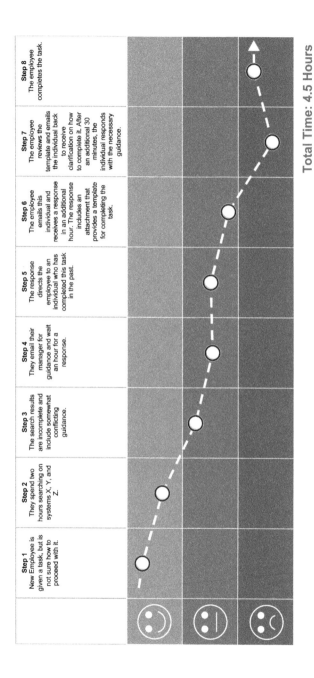

	Step 1	Step 2	Step 3	Step 4	Step 5	Step 6	Step 7	Step 8
	New Employee is given a task, but is not sure how to proceed with it.	They spend two hours searching on systems X, Y, and Z.	The search results are incomplete and include somewhat conflicting guidance.	They email their manager for guidance and wait an hour for a response.	The response directs the employee to an individual who has completed this task in the past.	The employee emails this individual and receives a response in an additional hour. The response includes an attachment that provides a template for completing the task.	The employee reviews the template and emails back the individual to receive clarification on how to complete it. After an additional 30 minutes, the individual responds with the necessary guidance.	The employee completes the task.

Total Time: 4.5 Hours

Fig. 3.1 Example journey map of the current experience for a KM action before KM systems changes occur. © 2021, Enterprise Knowledge, LLC, reused with permission

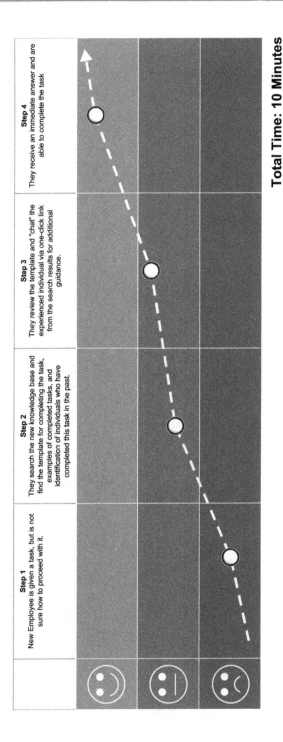

Fig. 3.2 Example journey map of the experience for a KM action after KM systems changes occur. © 2021, Enterprise Knowledge, LLC, reused with permission

fictional quotes based on personas to express how people will ideally talk about the future state once it is realized. For instance:

> I wish this existed when I was new! I remember how many hours I spent trying to figure out how to do this. Now, our new employees have a single place to go to connect with their colleagues and get all the information they need to learn and perform.
> –Division Manager based at Headquarters

> My time to sales has improved markedly. It takes me less time to craft sales decks, less time to get the right customer and industry information, and less time to get approval from my leadership.
> –Sales Specialist

> For the first time ever, I feel like a part of this company. I know what is happening at HQ, and I have a way to connect with and learn from other folks in the field like myself
> –Remote Resource Working on Client Site

Changes to the Systems

Detailing the changes to the organization's technology set is a critical piece to the future state for several reasons. First, as this book expresses, technology is the way much of KM value becomes "clickable" to the organization. In other words, technology is the avenue through which most organizations will experience and realize the value of KM. To that end, getting the technology right, and clearly understood, is a must. In addition, the potential technology investments are where much of the upfront cost will come from (through licenses, but also design and implementation). Equally, much of the realized hard ROI will come through technology savings, as detailed previously. Detailing technology, therefore, will be necessary for the overall justification of the KM transformation as well as the potential ROI to accompany it. Key elements to include as part of the future state of Technology/Systems should include:

- **Logical Architecture of the Future State:** The most important place to begin is a logical architecture diagram, which details the entire set of KM technologies that will comprise the future KM suite. The logical architecture should include the tools that will be involved in the KM suite along with some designation as to how these tools will speak to one another, what information each system will store, and how people will interact with them. This logical architecture allows senior IT people to understand at a quick glance how the systems will fit together. It also allows the team to explain to business users what they will see.
- **System Consolidation:** As we expressed in our earlier discussion on the value of KM, most organizations have a myriad of redundant and even competing systems. The consolidation of these systems is not just good for KM usability and findability, it is good for the organization's bottom line. Technology consolidation can deliver decreased software license costs through the elimination of redundant or obsolete systems and decreased administrative burden related to the maintenance and management of multiple systems. The cost, complexity, and risk

of consolidating systems, however, cannot be underestimated. Therefore, it is critical to identify a mapping of how current systems will be consolidated into future systems, in order to have a tool to plan and ensure buy-in from your organization's IT group.

- **Gap Analysis:** Most organizations will also find they are lacking some pieces of their KM technology puzzle. In these cases, potential technology evaluation and selection efforts, followed by cost justification for capital expenditures, will be required. The first step required as part of the future state documentation will be the list and justification of gaps to be filled.

Business Case and/or ROI Analysis

Depending on the size of the organization and the projected cost of the anticipated KM transformation, the target state should define the benefits to the organization in as clear terms as possible. For smaller organizations that may not require seven-figure investments in their KM transformation, a Business Case that simply expresses positive outcomes may be sufficient. This will largely be a consolidation of the other target state deliverables we have discussed above. However, in most cases, a large organization preparing for an enterprise KM transformation can anticipate significant capital and operating costs as part of a multi-year, iterative KM transformation. In these cases, a true and robust ROI Analysis will likely be necessary in order to convince your organization's leadership to fund the engagement. In most cases, as covered in the Value of KM chapter, some of the most important ROI calculations and factors will be:

- **Decreased Costs from Consolidation of Software and Licenses and Reduction of IT and Administrative Support for Redundant Systems:** These numbers will be highly specific to the organization, depending on the number of systems, potential consolidation, and license and personnel costs of supporting them. For many organizations, this calculation alone can provide the complete return on investment for a KM transformation within 2–5 years. It is also attractive because it is the most concrete, requiring little to no assumptions in order to derive.
- **Employee Retention:** Regardless of the calculation you use, it costs money to replace an employee who leaves, most tangibly in recruiting costs and retraining. If you take the average at $15,000 per employee and project a conservative estimate that the KM transformation will result in 2–3% higher retention (we have witnessed as much as a 12% improvement), the annual savings can be significant. Brent Hunter notes in *The Power of KM* that one Fortune 500 company was able to raise employee retention by 20% through exit interviews, essentially gaining and leveraging knowledge from departing employees in order to perform more effectively as an organization (Hunter 2016).
- **Employee Learning and Development:** The training costs per employee can vary widely between companies and industries. If you take a conservative estimate of $1000 per employee and recognize a KM transformation can reduce this by making distributed learning resources available at the point of need, the

annual savings can add up quickly. We generally estimate 5–25% reduction in costs, with those on the upward end of that spectrum being organizations presently heavily reliant on in-person training where employees are being taken "off the line" and traveling to training locations.

- **Customer Retention:** Again, the cost to acquire a new client varies greatly in different organizations and industries. A telecom company, for instance, might have a relatively low cost of $50 per new customer, whereas an industrial construction company's customer acquisition cost could be 1000 times that. Regardless, a KM transformation can improve customer retention from 0.05–10%, yielding major savings in some circumstances.

The above, as detailed previously, tend to be the key elements of an ROI calculation for many organizations. Of course, depending on the industry, other metrics will also play an important role. In organizations with major customer service wings, creation of knowledge bases and improved learning and development for call agents can result in improved Tier 1 call resolution and improved customer self-service, both of which can yield significant ROI. In product or service-oriented organizations, improved sales success rates or speed to close will be major factors. In manufacturing, fewer errors, fewer accidents, and less downtime will all be measurable factors with meaningful results.

Future State Vision

Weaving the complete future state together is a succinct vision that expresses how the organization will have changed and what benefits for employees and the organization as a whole will be gained. The future state vision can be considered a rollup or summary of the four previous artifacts/deliverables, but with more of a marketing bent. In short, the Future State Vision should be crafted to be easily consumed and understood, resulting in organizational executives and stakeholders understanding the value and prioritizing the initiative. An effective Future State Vision is often no more than a few pages or a handful of slides. A successful future state vision will result in executive approval and projecting funding.

> **Tip:**
> The approval of your KM transformation often rests on a clear and compelling Future State Vision, which clearly articulates the anticipated value to the organization and its employees. Though it must be accurate and direct, ensure you have also approached it from a marketing perspective, adding compelling details and exciting prospects that will get the attention and support of decision-makers.

Supplemental Techniques

In order to deliver the following elements, most of the inputs will have already been collected through the process described in Chap. 2 for the current state top-down and

Table 3.2 Survey questions to ask in order to understand the interviewee, repeated from Table 2.1

Understanding the Interviewee (Repeated for Target State)	
1	What is your role in the organization?
2	What does a typical day look like?
3	How much of your role has to do with using [the organization]'s technology/systems?
4	How long have you been in the organization?
5	How did you learn to perform your role?

Table 3.3 Survey questions to ask to gather foundational target state inputs for the KM systems

Foundational KM Systems Understanding	
1	What would you change about how you find information if you could?
2	How would you like to be recognized or rewarded for sharing your knowledge and expertise?
3	After you have created a new piece of information, how do you wish you could share it?
4	How would you like to be able to find and connect with your colleagues?
5	How much time and effort would you anticipate these changes would save you?

bottom-up analysis. The following are supplemental techniques to round out your understanding of the organization's KM needs and ensure you have got the comprehensive understanding of priorities and anticipated outcomes needed to define the target state.

Supplemental Interviews, Focus Groups, and Workshops
To supplement the vast amount of information already collected, additional interviews, focus groups, and workshops can be effective for brainstorming key elements of the future state.

The questions in Tables 3.2, 3.3, and 3.4 are a valuable script to capture target state inputs. Note that these questions can be used during the same meeting where the current state questions were asked or can be asked to the same or other interviewees as a second round of questions once the current state has been established. Both approaches can be successful, with the simultaneous approach requiring slightly longer interviews, and the two-round approach taking more time and scheduling overall but potentially enabling engagement with more stakeholders.

Table 3.4 Survey questions to ask to gather target state inputs for KMS features

KMS Features	
1	What would you change about your knowledge and information management systems if you could?
2	What features or tools do you wish you had?
3	In an ideal world, how would you: • Find information? • Connect with colleagues? • Share documents you have created? • Share your expertise/knowledge? • Learn what is changed in your organization? • Learn how to do a new task (learn something new)?
4	If you could make one change to your organization's knowledge and information systems, what would it be?

Group Journey Mapping

Another valuable input for future states is to task small groups (generally three to six people each works best) with envisioning the ideal future state way an existing task could be completed and performed by a specific persona. For instance, you might offer the following inputs:

> Persona: Sam the Sales Professional, 3 Years with the Organization, 12 Years of Overall Experience

> Task: Create/Assemble a Pitch Deck for a New Prospective Client

Another example of a user persona is shown in Fig. 3.3.

For each of these Persona and Task scenarios, instruct the group to document the ideal way the persona would complete the task, with as much detail as possible. An exercise like this takes practice; in the first round, group participants often will not offer sufficient detail and may be limited in their creative thinking. To ensure you obtain value from this exercise, conducting multiple rounds with the same people is ideal, with brief outs between each round where the facilitators can ask leading questions, suggest more innovative solutions, and seek greater detail. Through this process, each successive round should be more valuable. This exercise is also valuable when done with multiple different groups working simultaneously but separately on the same personas and tasks to identify whether there are themes that run across different groups, potentially helping to focus discussions or prioritize a particular element of the future state.

Though not all journey maps will yield a practical or actionable element for inclusion in the target state, the process as a whole generally offers clarity on how the organization wishes to approach KM, where they see the greatest needs for

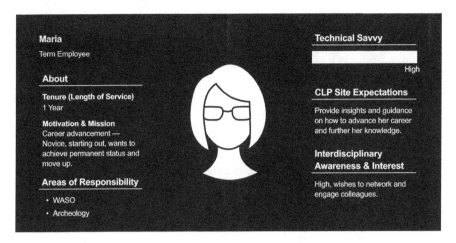

Fig. 3.3 Example of a user persona. © 2021, Wahl/Hilger, reused with permission

improvement, and what technologies they believe will be important to their overall future state solution.

Competitive or Collegial Analyses

A look at what other organizations in the space/industry are doing can be another valuable input. In some cases, an organization will be stuck in what they are currently doing. More conservative organizations will sometimes be bogged down by naysayers or lack the insights to ask for something truly innovative. Of course, that your job is to coax the innovation out of them, but without "seeing it" some organizations will struggle. In these cases, a competitive or collegial analysis will be valuable. Showing what other organizations have done with their KM transformations helps to make it real by showing it is practical and achievable. In some cases, these other organizations may have collected outcomes or conducted an ROI analysis, which is even more valuable to help make the case. In the case of competitive analyses, the notion that "Competitor X" is ahead of "us" may also be a crucial incentive for executive support.

The challenge to competitive or collegial analyses, of course, is that many organizations do not share what they have done for KM, either because it is proprietary or because they simply have not thought to publish it. Luckily, however, a vast amount of research and presentation is out there, which should provide at least a starting point on where to go looking for more. As a particular note, seeking an organization in your exact industry that is willing to share details on the KM transformation may prove challenging. Do not get too bogged down in finding the perfect industry match; rather, seek out organizations with similar size, models, and geographic complexities to obtain a broader, but still applicable, cross-section of examples.

KM Tools Gap Analysis

A mature target state will typically entail the addition of new tools and technologies, as well as the integration of various tools and technologies to better connect and present a cohesive user experience. A KM Tools Gap Analysis will likely be necessary to support the future state elements of a logical diagram, technology consolidation plan, and identification of missing tools, technologies, and features. We use the diagram in Fig. 3.4 to express the potential of an exhaustively complete collection of KM systems.

It should be noted, again, that all organizations are different and many or most will not require all the elements expressed in this diagram. However, it can be a good starting point or checklist to ensure you are considering all of the potential technologies that may come into play and methodically eliminating them if there is not a clear need, use case, or business case.

This approach will likely surface not only technologies that may belong in your target state plan, but also opportunities to better integrate existing and new technologies.

Prioritization Exercises

As the future state begins to come into focus, the depth and the breadth of the challenge may begin to feel overwhelming. Recognizing that many KM transformations take place over 2–5 years, you can imagine there is a great deal of effort wrapped up in an enterprise transformation. At this point, it becomes extremely valuable to leverage your organization's individuals to help you prioritize what matters the most. There are any number of techniques to prioritize the pilots, projects, tasks, and features that make up a KM future state. Leveraging a combination of these techniques will allow you to transform your future state vision into an actionable roadmap.

Regardless of your technique, the first step to successful prioritization is to ensure you are comparing apples to apples. Many organizations make the mistake of trying to compare and prioritize different things. This is common when dealing with something as complex and big as a KM transformation. For instance, do not compare the addition of a new feature against the purchase, installation, and configuration of a brand-new tool. Do not compare a pilot project for a group against an enterprise project for the entire organization. Moreover, do not compare an expected outcome (like improved search or higher retention) against a project (like designing and implementing search). This will only lead to confusion and frustration. For each prioritization exercise, make sure that you are prioritizing a corresponding set of things, be they expected outcomes, needs, pilots, features, tasks, or projects, in order to get the most out of the exercise and ensure you are approaching your decision-making consistently.

When you have identified your collection of similar "objects" to prioritize, we recommend leveraging different groups of stakeholders and different prioritization techniques in order to identify themes to plug into your roadmap. If you are looking for guidance on prioritization techniques, Agile approaches are a great place to start. For those not familiar with the concept of Agile, it is a highly iterative methodology

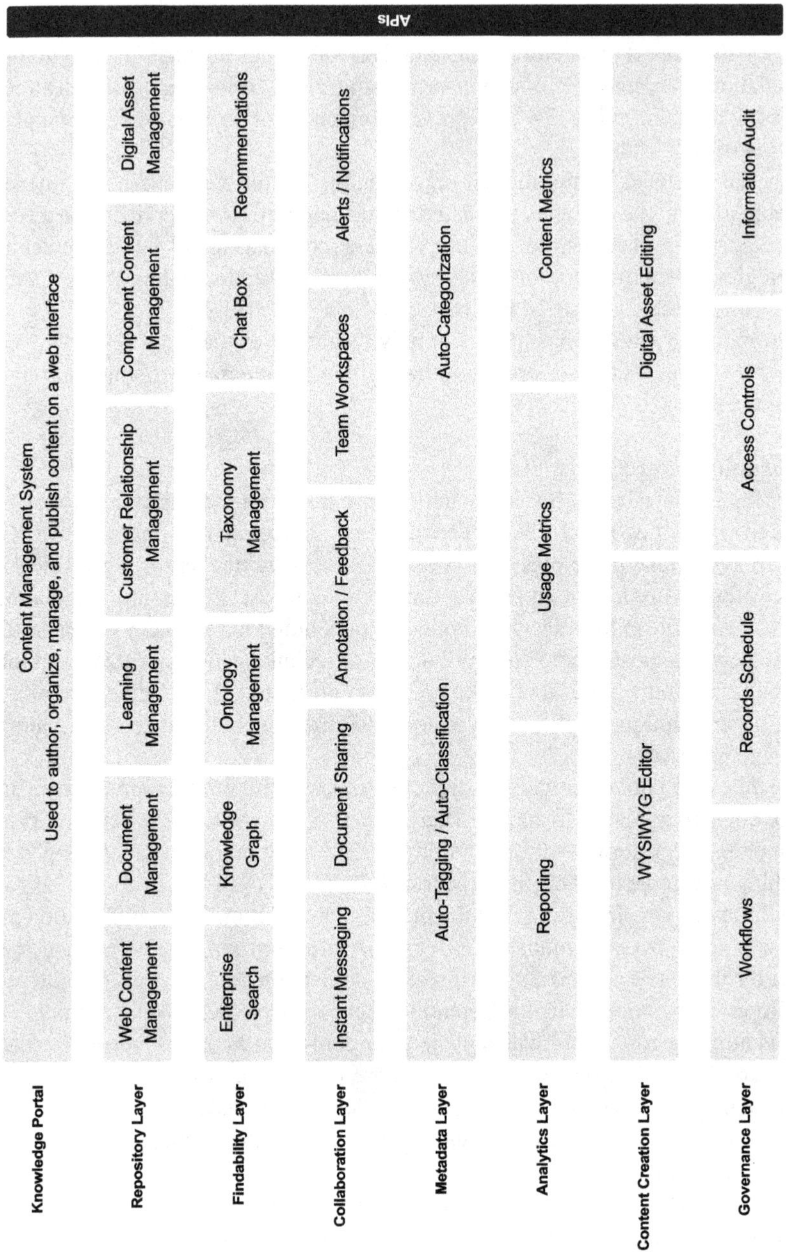

Fig. 3.4 Extensive view of potential technologies in a complete KM suite. © 2021, Wahl/Hilger, reused with permission

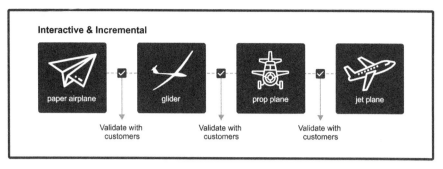

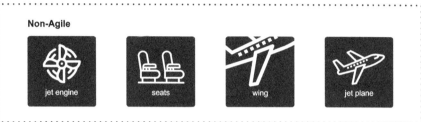

Fig. 3.5 Agile Project Approach. © 2021, Wahl/Hilger, reused with permission

that leverages prioritization techniques and specific approaches to segment big projects into smaller tasks, arraying work in such a way that each period of work (called a sprint in Agile terms) offers a testable product or something real to have stakeholders react to. Figure 3.5 provides a representation of this, in that each segment of work generates a "complete" and testable product where customers can see it, touch it, and react to it. This creates much greater opportunity for end user engagement, allowing end users and stakeholders to provide more meaningful feedback and guidance.

A few of the most common options, all of which we have proven to work well with KM, include the following:

- MoSCoW is a dynamic systems development method that asks individuals to classify all options into one of four categories:
  - Must: The must requirements are given the top priority. In KM terms, these would be the items that are foundational in nature, meaning other work cannot proceed without the completion of these, or KM systems will not function without these features and functions.
  - Should: The next priority is given to the requirements that are highly desirable, though not mandatory. Again, in KM terms, these would be options that would encourage buy-in and demonstrate business value, but are not technically necessary to the success of the KM transformation.
  - Could: The next priority is given to the options that are the nice-to-haves. For KM systems, these are often the "wow" features that stakeholders have

identified as things they would want and are potentially majorly transformative to the business, but would almost be considered bonus features if they were attained.

  – Won't: The final category is given to the requirements which were identified during the current and target state analyses, but are broadly considered non-starters for the KM transformation, either because they are cost or time prohibitive, or because they would not actually yield the desired goals for the transformation. In short, these are the "bad" ideas.

• Dot Voting is a simple, democratic means of identifying themes in priorities. The process here is to list a series of options, talk through them, and then distribute a set number of dots (in most cases, small round stickers) to all participants. Participants are then directed to place their dots on the items that they individually rank as highest priority. This is simple and fast, allowing for multiple rounds in a short period of time, and tends to yield actionable outcomes that are clearly ranked.

• A variant of dot voting, inspired by Planning Poker, provides each participant with a certain amount of cash (as in fake money, ideally with my face printed on it). Participants are then directed to spend their money on the items they wish to prioritize. In this case, they can choose to spend all their money on a single critical option or spread it around amongst many options. Another variant of this option is preceded by a valuation of each option, wherein certain options, based on time and resources, would cost more to vote on or "buy."

Overall, prioritization techniques can be as simple as plotting options into a single matrix, such as Fig. 3.6 inspired by Stephen Covey.

Fig. 3.6 A simple prioritization technique. © 2021, Wahl/Hilger, reused with permission

Such a simple prioritization approach is good for small groups and simpler transformation but is likely to have everything jammed into the upper right box for more complex considerations.

Organizations can also define their own weighting and prioritization matrix to consider, weight, and vote on the factors that matter most to them. Figure 3.7, for instance, is one we have often used when we wish to consider multiple factors and impacts on multiple functions (or personas).

The problem with a detailed technique like this, however, is that it will be easy to get lost in the math of it all, spending too much time trying to decide on granular scores and not enough time actually developing a logical set of priorities.

Regardless of the technique, our weighting and consideration typically come down to a combination of three simple factors:

- Business Value: Options that will provide the most meaningful and measurable business value (and ideally hard ROI) should receive the highest prioritization.
- Technical Complexity: In short, options that are easiest and fastest should receive the highest prioritization. Of course, technical complexity can be considered in many ways (i.e., use of proven or new technologies or concepts, requirement for external expertise, requirement for IT involvement, etc.), so it will be important for an organization to clearly define what they mean by technical complexity.
- Foundational Value: This tends to be the factor that is most important, but in fact least used by organizations. Options that are necessary predecessors to a KM transformation should receive the highest value, in order to ensure the subsequent tasks have the right building blocks. Being able to rank foundational value effectively requires KM expertise, not just a knowledge of the business, so special attention should be paid to this criteria. Consider tasks like content cleanup, content governance, creation of a KM governing organization, development of enterprise personas, piloting of various knowledge transfer techniques, and design of an enterprise taxonomy all as examples of likely high foundational value efforts.

Combining these three primary criteria of Business Value, Technical Complexity, and Foundational Value typically yields the clearest view of priorities as in Fig. 3.8, which can then be translated into the actual roadmap to achieve the target state.

Of course, with all considerations like this, there will be "real world" factors to weigh. Do your executives have a specific interest in a technology or area of change? Is there a burning need that is extremely complex, but will itself ensure the attention of executives and approval of budget? If so, you will likely want to show that as higher priority than it might otherwise score. Is there something that would normally score very high, but is associated with a major past failure, or treads on the territory of a senior potential blocker? In these cases, lowering the overall score and priority may be in order.

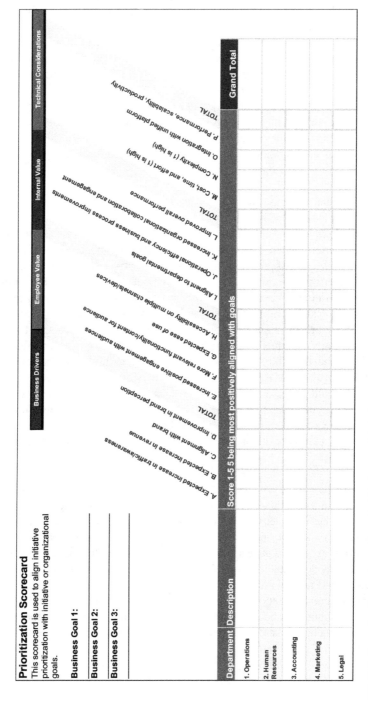

Fig. 3.7 Example of a more complex prioritization matrix. © 2021, Enterprise Knowledge, LLC, reused with permission

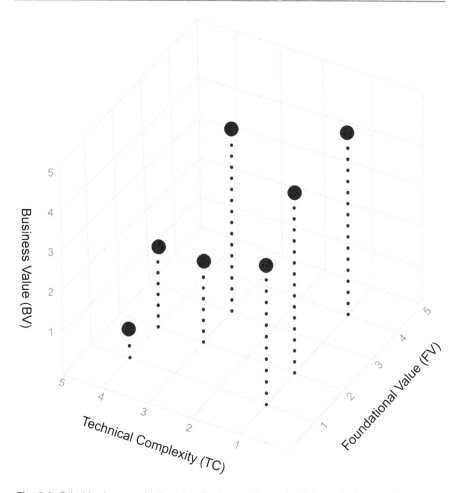

Fig. 3.8 Prioritization exercise based on business value, technical complexity, and foundational value. © 2021, Wahl/Hilger, reused with permission

Reference

Hunter B (2016) The power of KM. Spirit Rising Productions, San Francisco

Creating the Target State Vision

4

At this point, you will have gathered what should be a thorough understanding of the organization. Leveraging the range of hybrid approaches detailed previously, you should understand where the organization is, what the potential changes are that should comprise the target state, and their relative value and importance to the organization. From here on, the task becomes the development of the actual target state, defining specifically what it will include (and what it will not), what KM systems it will be composed of, and how the collective people, process, content, culture, and technology changes will work together to impact the organization.

Defining the target state (Deciding what will be included and what will be left out) is a big thought exercise. If you have got a white board, you are going to want to use it. There are three different approaches you will want to consider in order to define your target state: building up from components, breaking down from solutions, and spidering out from a known need. Though these are three very different approaches, they each can play a role in helping you to formulate the true vision of the target state; in fact, for complex organizations, all three approaches should be used in order to ensure a comprehensive vision for the target state has been defined.

4.1 Building Up

In the first approach, your thought process should begin at the individual needs and wants you have identified from your various research techniques thus far. In this case, your job is to find themes in what those various top-down and bottom-up approaches revealed. For instance, you are likely to have identified many separate search, discovery, and findability challenges.

When building up, your task is to collect all of the "like" needs, wants, and requirements and combine them into a consolidated concept, which can become an anchoring element of the target state.

The following are examples of inputs from the current state and target state analyses, along with the source of the input:

© The Author(s), under exclusive license to Springer Nature Switzerland AG 2022
J. Hilger, Z. Wahl, *Making Knowledge Management Clickable*,
https://doi.org/10.1007/978-3-030-92385-3_4

- Initial Interviews: Ability to find information was a common and consistent frustration.
- Focus Groups, Journey Mapping Exercises: A new search technology was a consistent component of exercises.
- Interviews and Focus Groups with New Employees: Clear frustration in ability to find learning content or "how to do my job" content.
- Interviews and Focus Groups with Sales: Strong agreement that it is difficult to find the latest version of sales materials and customer intelligence data.
- Survey: 72% of employees agree or strongly agree that it is difficult to find the information they need to do their job.
- System Review, KM Tools Gap Analysis: No enterprise search tools, content management possesses internal search which consistently returns poorly weighted results.

All of these data points, when combined, paint a very clear picture of the need for a search solution. However, stopping at that point would generally yield only part of the picture. Once you are on the theme of search and findability, go back to your inputs and find other elements on that theme:

- Focus Groups, Brainstorm Activity: Wish to find people that were responsible for creating or editing content.
- Focus Groups, Brainstorm Activity: Wish to see a visual of who people are, where they are, what they are experts in, and how to connect with them.
- Interviews and Focus Groups with New Employees: Desire to connect with and learn from people who have held a similar position in the past.
- Interviews and Focus Groups with New Employees: Desire for automated match-making to find a mentor for certain skills or topics.
- Survey: 68% of employees agree or strongly agree that it is difficult to find people that can show them how to do tasks.
- Survey: 83% of employees agree or strongly agree that it is difficult to find a mentor from whom they can learn.
- System Review, KM Tools Gap Analysis: No expert finder capabilities, several limited communities of practice with insubstantial activity.

This additional set of inputs is now pointing toward a broader theme of an advanced enterprise search solution. In order to accommodate the inputs above, the advanced enterprise search solution would need to:

- Index multiple systems and repositories, covering a mix of structured and unstructured content types.
- Manage a range of result views or search hit types for search results, including different content types, people, and data.
- Leverage ontologies and graph search to allow a searcher to traverse content of different types and people in order to discover additional pertinent results.

That level of detail is enough, then, to use a section of the target state definition. The above also acts as a guide to additional questions that should be answered in the target state definition. For instance, what systems will be indexed, what types of content may be surfaced in search, what types of content should be traversable as part of a graph? Also, remember that not every question needs to be answered in excruciating detail as part of a target state; you must plan for flexibility and additional learning as a project proceeds, recognizing you will learn more and will need to adjust to additional learnings and the changes of the business.

For this approach, you would then repeat the thought process for other themes that can be rolled into a major requirement and definition as part of the target state. Reference back to the KM Action Wheel and the five elements of KM to ensure you are thinking about all of the components that should go into a successful target state.

The building up approach is best for organizations that have collected a number of inputs but do not yet have a clear vision of what their target state should actually look like and do not have strong impressions of what some of the key elements of their target state might be. This approach can be very effective, but it requires the expertise of knowing what to look for in order to forge the right connections and identify appropriate themes.

4.2 Breaking Down

In other organizations, your analysis will have surfaced a much firmer concept of what the KM target state should look like. Generally, this would include a driving theme of the problem statements the organization wishes to address, and it typically includes an identification of a major technology component or two that the organization has self-diagnosed as a requirement for success. For instance, an organization may have consistently stated that its two primary issues are 1) knowledge retention and transfer from more experienced staff to less and 2) ability to share information and collaborate on documents remotely and asynchronously; as a result, the organization has consistently stated the need for a state-of-the-art content management solution to address these issues.

There are two things to keep in mind when you receive such a clear diagnosis from an organization. First, in our experience, the organization tends to be correct about 75% of the time, which is a fine percentage, but it still means you need to ensure you have done a thorough current state and target state analysis to ensure it is in fact correct. Secondly, and more importantly, in 100% of the cases where the organization's self-diagnosis is correct, it is only part of the actual problem, never the complete set of KM challenges that need to be considered and solved. This will be most important when an organization seems to have a predetermined course for a particular type of software, like a search tool or content management system. In these cases, it will be your job to help the organization avoid rushing into a purely technical solution without understanding the dynamics of the organization. In other words, no matter how certain the organization is, ensure you have done the work to understand the entire organization and make confident recommendations.

Going back to our example, you may encounter an organization that identified knowledge transfer and knowledge sharing issues as their burning challenges and has self-diagnosed a new content management system as the fix. In a case like this, your recommended approach is, to begin with the assumption that this is, in fact, a central element of the target state, but apply a level of skepticism to ensure your inputs from the current state and target state analysis actually support this conclusion. We refer to this as "breaking down," as your job is to break down the assumptions of an organization like this by applying your knowledge and expertise to challenge whether the prescribed solution will actually address the challenges and needs of the organization, resulting in a mature target state.

As we described above, in many cases, you will find there is in fact a place in the target state for their new content management system, but that is likely only part of the solution and perhaps not even the highest priority part. By breaking down the conclusion the organization had come to, you may instead find that the existing content management technology itself is fine, but the user interface, workflows, or training around it instead are the culprits of the challenge. Similarly, you may find that the organization does indeed have an issue with knowledge retention and transfer, but the primary driver culprit for this is not the supporting technology. Instead, it may be a lack of leadership support or personnel incentives for knowledge sharing or perhaps even a lack of awareness of who knows what within the organization, requiring a different overall solution like an expert finder or communities of practice.

It is important to note that all of these new or additional findings come from a place where you have listened to the organization and started from its self-diagnosis conclusion, but you have leveraged the current state and target state research and findings to challenge it, validate it, and expand upon it. This approach of breaking down, therefore, will respect the organization's thinking and foregone conclusions but also allow a path to move beyond them in the best interest of the organization.

4.3   Spidering Out

If you are going to use just one approach, this is the way to go. This approach requires strong experience in the KM space to think holistically, but it will yield the most comprehensive target state, covering the right aspects of people, process, content, culture, and technology. Using this technique, your first step will be to identify one of the anchor elements of the target state. Perhaps you have got strong hints at what this is, as suggested in the breaking down method above, or perhaps you need to leverage some of the building up concepts and approaches in order to discover what anchoring elements you can surface. In either case, your first step in the spidering out approach is to find the central element of the enterprise user's experience. Yes, in a true KM transformation, there will be a myriad of ways an average employee's work day will change, but increasingly, there is a technology component of these changes around which most of the new or different interactions will be centered.

The key to the spidering out approach is to find what the center of the new KM experience may be. In most cases, what we are seeing is that this new element will take the central form of a new enterprise search, knowledge base, or intranet/portal. Once you have identified what you think this anchoring feature is (The place where KM will become real to the average employee), list out the actions that will occur within it. For instance, employees will be able to:

- Go to one place and find all the "stuff" they need to do their job.
- Find people to connect with and learn from.
- Get quick answers to questions about how to do their job.
- Identify resources in order to learn and develop.
- Ask questions and receive answers from experts.

This, in five bullets, is the makings of a compelling KM system that will yield a great deal of the business value and return on investment any organization would be seeking. However, it is just the beginning of a comprehensive target state. A system like this does not just happen. As we have been expressing throughout the book, technology is just one piece of the puzzle, an enabling factor, and generally, it will fail if not powered by a comprehensive KM program. However, by envisioning the end state of that piece of technology, you are able to extrapolate, or spider out, from that starting point in order to identify a host of other changes to the organization that would need to be present within the target state. In other words, with this view of an anchor KM system, you are able to extend the capabilities and functions expressed simply in bullets to identify the other elements necessary to make it happen.

Let us take one of the bullets as an example of this. When you consider, for instance, the feature of "finding people to connect with and learn from," it seems simple at face value. However, when you look at it through a systems lens and apply KM expertise, several different questions arise, each spawned by the previous question:

1. If we are seeking to connect people and learn from them, what factors will we be using to connect people?
2. If we use topics or subject competencies to connect people, how will we derive these topic/competency taxonomies?
3. If we have derived these topic/competency taxonomies, how will we relate them to people within the organization? Will we allow people to do this themselves, or will we manage this centrally?
4. If we are managing this centrally, what will be the threshold to consider someone an expert and therefore be tagged with the appropriate topic/competency?

The above questions are just one line of questioning that can stem from the feature. Another line of questioning would be more focused on system design and technology:

1. Do we already possess a tool where each person's profile is captured?
2. If not, can we leverage an existing tool, or do we need a new one?
3. If we need a new one, should we buy it or build it?
4. If we build it, what current systems should it connect to in order to extract existing employee data?

The list goes on, and if your head is not spinning yet, you are not paying attention.

Another way to think about this approach, which offers more structure, is a table like Table 4.1 that breaks apart each feature or capability across the five KM elements of people, process, content, culture, and technology. This approach helps to challenge your thinking and consider all the elements that will be required to make that anchor KM system actually work.

Tip:
Are you getting to the right level of detail for your main consolidated concepts/anchoring elements? A good test is whether each of the components of your target state has an element of people, process, content, culture, and technology in it. In almost any case, anchoring elements of the target state will require organizational changes within the categories of people, process, content, culture, and technology in order to yield the anticipated value.

Through the use of extended logic or Table 4.1, the spidering approach quickly establishes the range of activities and foundational elements that will be required in order to make the anchor KM system actually add value to the organization. This approach also quickly paints the picture of how complex a true KM effort can be. Even Table 4.1 only begins to approximate the level of depth one could go into for such an effort.

Regardless of the approach used, or whether you used both approaches, the work is not done once you have created the first draft of your target state. A second pass at target state definition must focus on integration and alignment of your defined vision.

Table 4.1 Using the spidering out technique to map features and capabilities across all five KM elements

	People	Process	Content	Culture	Technology
Go to one place and find all the "stuff" they need to do their job.	Experts sharing their content, loading it, and tagging it correctly.	Expert and organization reviews to ensure content is accurate (content governance).	Content governance plan. Content cleanup to ensure old, obsolete, and incorrect content is not included in search results. Identification of the right content repositories.	Improve the culture of knowledge sharing. Create incentives and rewards for loading correct content.	Search connectors to correct systems. Design and implementation of search hit types to deliver contextualized and action-oriented search.
Find people to connect with and learn from.	Organizational definition of expertise and clear listing of competencies. Definition of knowledge sharing approach.	Governance process to determine how experts are identified for each topic/competency. Process for identifying and rewarding potential mentors. Processes for what can and should be shared in People profiles.	Strategy for capturing content from existing sources and migrating it to people profiles. Strategy of People Content Type and Hit Types.	Incentives and rewards for employees to create and maintain their people profile. Marketing and communications campaign to encourage all users to complete their People profiles.	Design and implementation of People Hit Type for search.
Get quick answers to questions about how to do their job.	Identify who should be identified experts to answer given topics and competencies.	Develop a review process for organizational reviews and vetting of new answers. Develop a maintenance process to regularly review past answers and ensure they are still accurate.	Seed Questions and Answers with materials migrated from other Q&A sources.	Develop rewards/gamification strategies for people to answer questions.	Implement workflows and input technology for Questions and Answers, including upvoting capability for most liked answers.

(continued)

Table 4.1 (continued)

	People	Process	Content	Culture	Technology
Identify resources in order to learn and develop.	Engage Learning and Performance group to support the migration process.	Develop an iterative process and plan to migrate and tag learning content.	Review existing learning content and explore expanding on-demand learning resources. Expand learning content into more short answers and video formats. Tag learning content with appropriate topics and competencies tags.	Work with Learning and Performance and Human Resources functions to design, test, and support integration of learning resources.	Design and implement a range of Learning Content Hit Types for search.
Ask questions and receive answers from experts.	Identify who should be identified experts to answer given topics and competencies.	Develop a review process for organizational reviews and vetting of new answers and determine which should be promoted to official corporate knowledge.	Mine existing FAQs for initial questions and answers with which to populate the system.	Incorporate answering questions into job description and performance evaluation for identified experts. Develop incentives and rewards for experts to answer questions.	Evaluate technologies to enable questions automatically routed to correct experts based on topic/competency. Explore use of communities of practice or chat functionalities.

In defining the target state, regardless of your approaches, keep these key concepts in mind:

1. Build for your organization—Do not rely too heavily on benchmarks, and certainly do not try to force your organization into the highest state of maturity for any and all aspects of KM. Build for your organization, and only transform the elements that are not working and will result in value to your people and the organization as a whole. Essentially, make sure you know why you are suggesting a particular change.
2. Ensure you have a reason—To the previous point, you must be able to answer the "why" for each element you are putting within the target state. Part of the answer to the "why," of course, is that it will yield value to your organization and its people. Do not stop there, though. Ensure you can specifically explain the value of each element of the target state, ideally in terms of business value and hard ROI. Beyond immediate impact to the business, the other major "why" that will exist in your target state is if something offers foundational value. An example of this might be the design of an enterprise taxonomy. Without it being implemented, it will not do much for the organization, but it is nonetheless of major value and importance to your target state as people finders, enterprise search, content management, and other core components of the KM system will heavily rely on it.
3. Consider your starting point—Not every organization needs to be bleeding edge or even has the capacity to absorb that much change. If your organization is currently well behind the curve, do not attempt to create a target state that turns it into a world-leading organization across all factors. That much change would either take too long, be too expensive, or simply be rejected by the end users of the organization. Instead, focus on what will produce the greatest impact for the organization in a manner that is practical to achieve.

> **Tip:**
> Feeling stuck? If you are looking for inspiration on what a mature target state should look like, go back to the benchmark and look at the definitions for scores of four and five. Weaving these together will create a generic mature target state. Be warned, however, that every organization is different. Ensure you are using the inputs from your organization to focus on what will yield true business value.

The successful completion of a target state analysis should result in your ability to paint a picture of what the organization will look like, what it will be able to do, and the resulting value (and ideally ROI) of these changes. The outcome of a successful target state analysis is buy-in from executives and stakeholders that the transformed state of the organization is not only desirable, but business critical, resulting in their continued support and willingness to proceed with the transformation plan.

Typically, at this point, budgets for the actual transformation should be getting estimated, with you and the organization's executives collaborating to seek approval and plan for the subsequent design and implementation effort. In the meantime, a roadmap is being created to accurately express the timeline, major priorities, and anticipated iterative outputs.

Getting from Here to There (KM Transformation Roadmap)

5

At this point, you should have a very clear picture of what KM is and should be within your organization. Note that at this point, we are no longer saying what KM *could* be but rather what it *should* be. That wording is purposeful, and it speaks to the point that a KM transformation plan or roadmap cannot be completed without understanding where the organization should get to and what value it will reap from KM. If you are still guessing at what should be in the target state, you are not ready to plan out your roadmap of how to get there. Possessing this level of clarity is critical to formulating a KM transformation roadmap with an adequate level of detail.

Whereas the goal of the current state is to express where the organization is, and the target state is to represent where it should be and value that will result from achieving it, the roadmap is where ideas and concepts get translated into timelines and actions. A complete KM transformation roadmap will include:

1. A timeline or project plan that arrays all the tasks that must be completed in order to achieve the target state.
2. Details regarding each task on the roadmap that ensure a complete and consistent understanding of what should be done, why it should be done, and how success (or task completion) will be verified.
3. Identification of the pilots that should occur toward the beginning of the roadmap in order to demonstrate business value and engage business stakeholders in the early stages of a KM transformation.
4. Clear indicators of milestones and outcomes, portraying what the organization will get (the benefits it will realize) at each stage of the roadmap.

The overall goal of a roadmap is to deconstruct the transformation to the point where tasks can be measured in weeks and months, not years, and each individual task is achievable and understandable with measurable outcomes and business impacts. This structure is incredibly important for a few main reasons:

J. Hilger, Z. Wahl, *Making Knowledge Management Clickable*, https://doi.org/10.1007/978-3-030-92385-3_5

- KM transformations fail when they take too long to show business value, are too difficult to understand and measure the outcomes, or are too hard to adopt from the business user's standpoint. By breaking an otherwise complex roadmap up into smaller tasks, the transformation effort can demonstrate value and introduce iterative change, rather than wait too long to show value and introduce overt change all at once.
- Many organizations will have previously tried KM and failed. Executives may agree about the what, but they may still not believe it is practical or achievable in reality. In these cases, showing incremental progress and demonstrating value in weeks and months will be critical. With this, the "ask" for funding becomes easier. Your total required budget might be two million dollars, but you may only need 50 thousand before the first checkpoint where you will prove that the KM transformation has begun to work and offer value.
- There will be surprises. No matter how thorough your current state and target state assessments are, there will be surprises either from something that was missed, something that has changed, or something new that has been introduced. It may be that a particular task, design, or system does not yield the intended results or rate of adoption. In any case, a deconstructed roadmap is much more flexible than a long and complex Gantt chart with multiple complex dependencies. An Agile roadmap that leaves room for flexibility and reprioritization, as well as the discovery of where changes need to be made, will help progress the organization along the transformation.

5.1   First Steps for Roadmap Development

KM transformation roadmaps can look drastically different depending on the transformation effort and the organization it is for. Some roadmaps will be relatively high-level, not showing a great amount of detail or including too much background documentation, while others will require significant granularity and tomes of backup materials. The first step in developing your KM transformation roadmap is to consider your organizational culture and project management standards, as well as the rough order of magnitude (ROM) for the total cost of the transformation and current understanding of overall transformation complexity. Each of these elements will weigh on the look and style of the roadmap, the level of detail it contains, and the overall length (in time) of the roadmap. Here is how you should consider each of those factors that will play into your decision-making:

- Organizational Culture—If your organization is particularly risk averse, consensus driven, or cautious regarding decision-making, a more detailed roadmap will likely be necessary. Other organizations, typically those that are smaller and less hierarchical, will prefer a less granular view of the roadmap that is easier to digest and avoids committing the organization to too specific a path. Organizational culture will also help you determine the overall timeline/length of your roadmap. There are two considerations here. First, is your organization adept at embracing change, or is it change averse? If the latter is true, you will want to design a longer roadmap to provide more time for the organization to absorb the change and adjust to doing business iteratively. If the former is true, you may be able to aim for a faster and shorter transformation time period. The second consideration concerns whether the organization has other major changes taking place. If the KM transformation will be the primary focus of the organization, it can likely take place over a shorter time period. However, if the KM transformation is happening concurrently with other major organizational changes (e.g., reorganizations, sales or acquisitions, strategic changes, major product releases, shifting to remote work, and/or changes in leadership), you will want to plan for a longer roadmap.

- Project Management Standards—The look and style of your roadmap should be heavily impacted based on whether your organization leverages more traditional, waterfall project management methodologies or has made the transition to more flexible and iterative Agile approaches. As we discuss in further detail in Part III, "Running a KM Systems Project," KM transformations typically are more successful when approached with an Agile mindset. That said, how you help your organization visualize the transformation can be impacted by your organization's project management standards and levels of comfort. In more traditional, waterfall-type organizations, you will want to adopt more of a Gantt chart style for your roadmap. In more agile organizations, you will want your roadmap to look more like a product backlog. In actuality, the ideal KM transformation roadmaps will borrow from both disciplines in order to completely portray the approach, and a happy medium between the two is often the right approach if you are lacking other direction.
- ROM Transformation Costs—As with organizational culture, the ROM Transformation Cost should have a significant impact on the level of granularity you show in your roadmap. If the vast majority of your costs are sunk costs within the organization, or if the transformation can be accomplished with a small budget, a relatively high-level roadmap is likely to suffice. However, if your transformation costs will be in the millions or make up a significant portion of your organization's budget, more detail should be included to ensure you are portraying what the organization will be spending its money on and, most importantly, what it will get as a result. Though all roadmaps should clearly express business value and ROI, the transformations that require the greatest budgets will be those that focus the most on measurable ROI.
- Transformation Complexity—If your transformation will consist of sweeping changes for the organization, including several new technology components (Each of which requires a procurement process) and dramatic changes to business processes, a longer overall timeline is needed to accommodate this activity. To reference the benchmark, if you are seeking to move the organization over two points (say, from a 1.5 to at least a 3.5), your roadmap will likely require at least 2 years. More minor changes that are not as technically complex or do not introduce as much change into the business can be accomplished in a shorter period. Overall, we see two to two and a half years as the sweet spot for the length of a KM transformation. This tends to be the right fit for many organizations as it:

- Does not introduce too much change at once, but it still allows for marked improvements on a quarterly basis (at least).
- Spreads the costs out over 3 or 4 years, making the budget required more attainable.
- Fits within the constraints of most strategic plans for a business, meaning it does not stretch on for an interminable period where the business will have gone through other unpredictable changes that might inadvertently change the organization's KM needs.

With these considerations in place, you should have an understanding of the rough time frame, level of detail, and overall approach required to build the roadmap from your current state to your target state.

Tip:
Thinking of a KM transformation roadmap as a project plan will, in most cases, be too limiting. In reality, most KM transformations would better be described as a combination of several aligned projects, spanning the strategy, design, implementation, and operations of multiple different technologies, introduction of sweeping new business practices, and overall change in communications and organizational culture. No single project can adequately encompass such expansive change or integrate so many different disciplines and business areas. To that end, consider your KM transformation as the alignment and integration of multiple projects. Indeed, each project may have a different manager and even different business sponsors. The key to KM transformation is not that all work is centralized, but that it is coordinated, aligned, and integrated to achieve the KM target state.

5.2   Workstreams in Roadmaps

An effective roadmap will not just convey the tasks, outcomes, timelines, and dependencies of a KM transformation; it will also be easy to understand. Whereas KM transformations are frequently considered too complex and difficult to understand, a good roadmap will demystify the complexities of KM and make it easy for anyone to easily understand what it will take, what will happen, and what the business will get out of it at any given time.

When you consider that some roadmaps might comprise hundreds of tasks, the idea of simplifying the complex quickly becomes somewhat of a lofty goal. One approach to helping individuals understand and quickly consume the roadmap is to break it into workstreams. The idea of workstreams needs to be approached carefully. The intent is not to overly segment the transformation roadmap or make it seem as though different workstreams are completely independent or discrete. On the contrary, care should be taken to show how each workstream supports the others toward the achievement of the target state.

There are several different configurations of workstreams you might want to consider for use in your roadmap, each with potential value given your circumstances and what is most important for you to convey:

- KM Element Based—One option is to have a separate workstream for each of the five elements of KM (people, process, content, culture, and technology). This approach is helpful as it maintains the definition of KM we have set previously and allows individuals within your organization to focus on the elements of KM that are most important to them or will impact their function within the organization the most. The challenge with this approach is, though these five elements work well when it comes to defining KM, they can be tricky when it comes to implementing KM. This is for the simple reason that there is overlap between them, and there will typically be a web of dependencies between them.
- System/Technology Based—Another option is to focus each workstream around one of the main technology elements of your target state. For instance, if your target state includes the implementation of a new search, upgrade of a content management system, and implementation of an ontology management tool, you would create one workstream for each of these three technology components. This approach often works well as it focuses on the most visible (and typically most expensive) elements of a transformation. However, care must be taken to ensure, even though the workstreams are organized based on technology, they cover the full gamut of KM tasks. For instance, the workstream for a new search could include non-technical tasks like cleaning up target content for the search to ensure it is accurate and up to date, designing a taxonomy for use as filters and recommendations, applying the taxonomy as tags to content, developing a governance plan for taxonomy iterations and search-weighting decisions, and creating a change management and communications plan to ensure everyone understands and uses the new tools and associated processes.
- Product/Outcome Based—In most cases, the ideal method of expressing workstreams is based on the main product or outcome of the work. This is similar in many cases to a system/technology-based approach but has a fundamental difference: each workstream should be put in the context of the business product or outcome. So, rather than a workstream titled "Enterprise Search," it could instead be titled "Findability," and a workstream that is centered around the implementation of an Enterprise Content Management system could instead be titled "Content Improvement" or "Information Management." Though these are perhaps subtle nuances, they are nonetheless important as they keep the focus on business outcomes rather than technologies, and they put things in terms of the business value that will appeal to the stakeholders. This also opens up a greater sense that some workstreams might not possess a major technical component at all (for instance, one dedicated to KM Organization or Tacit Knowledge Transfer, both of which would be more human and process driven).

Overall, leveraging workstreams will help to improve the understandability of your roadmap and can also help to segment responsibilities. In many large and complex organizations with intensive KM transformations, workstreams allow for each workstream, in a way, to be run as a separate project, thereby dividing responsibilities and allowing more ownership of and focus on separate elements of the overall transformation. For instance, in a recent multi-year roadmap for a global pharmaceutical, we defined a 3-year roadmap with seven different workstreams. Each workstream was given a different project manager and a different business owner who best matched the business lines priorities. At the same time, a single program owner was hired to "own" KM within the organization. This model allowed coordination of the entire transformation while still ensuring sufficient focus on each highly detailed and complex workstream.

Tip:
Defining workstreams can help simplify your roadmap and provide options to divide overall KM transformation and management responsibilities within the organization. However, make sure you do not overdo it. Too many workstreams can actually make your overall roadmap too complex and, worse yet, may generate unnecessary divides in your overall KM transformation effort. If you are looking at a complex transformation, five to seven workstreams may be necessary, but do your best to avoid going beyond that without a very clear reason for doing so.

5.3   The Building Blocks of a Roadmap

At its core, the KM transformation roadmap will consist of a collection of tasks that, collectively, build off of each other in order to iteratively allow the organization to achieve the KM target state. Each of these tasks will have the same purpose, and we define the elements that should be considered for each further on in this chapter. For purposes of designing a better roadmap, however, you can consider three different types of tasks that will make up each roadmap: foundational tasks, pilot tasks, and extension tasks.

5.3.1   Foundational Tasks

Foundational tasks are those that must be completed early on in a roadmap as predecessors to more visible and user-facing tasks on the roadmap. This makes the foundational tasks of critical importance, but they are also some of the most difficult to accomplish as they lack the visibility and interest of other roadmap elements.

Foundational tasks will be the most difficult for which to receive executive support or business line interest. They are called foundational for a reason, however, and they must be completed early on to get value out of the other elements on the roadmap. An example of this is content assessment and cleanup as foundational tasks to making enterprise search or findability work. Most organizations are maintaining at least five times more content than they should be, with 80% of the leftovers including a great deal of duplicate, old, obsolete, and incorrect content. What good is designing a new and powerful search solution if it is indexing and returning this 80% of "bad" content as a result? In this case, making content more findable may actually hurt the organization if the vast majority of that content contains unhelpful, incorrect, and potentially risky content.

Unfortunately, we have all too many examples of this in practice. One large aerospace company introduced a new search solution without considering the content it was indexing. On day one of the search launch, user after user found unsecured HR documents that listed the salary of every executive in the company. That content had been sitting undiscovered on a server for years, but the introduction of the new search tool surfaced it, much to the chagrin of all involved. The search worked perfectly, but the company suffered a major embarrassment because of the lack of foundational task work.

Taxonomy design is another example of a foundational task. Before a taxonomy is implemented in systems, it can feel unnecessary and esoteric, making it an unfortunate absence from many projects that require it to be successful. One large government agency project serves as a key example of this. After purchasing a leading-edge content management system and launching a multi-year effort to migrate their legacy content from secondary systems and file drives to the new system, the project leaders left out any consideration of an enterprise taxonomy design. Instead, they allowed each business group to organize its content however it saw fit. A year in, the project was canceled because users said their content was unfindable. They largely knew where it used to be, so they had made things work. When their content was moved to the new system with no ability to find it, they were left lost in a sea of newly consolidated content with no ability to navigate through it.

What these examples show is that foundational tasks are absolutely essential to ensure you achieve the outcomes you are planning for your KM target state or even that you reach that target state! Since these tasks lack the excitement or immediate business value of many of the tasks that will follow them, they run the risk of being skipped or minimized if you are not careful. Ensure these foundational tasks are clearly understood and intertwined with the more enticing tasks for your business users to guarantee they receive the support and focus necessary to make your whole roadmap work. Running these tasks incrementally can also help to spread out the cost and effort that is required, but ensure you plan for them nonetheless, as no KM transformation will be successful without them.

5.3.2 Pilot Tasks (and Projects)

Pilot tasks are those that make up pilot projects early in the roadmap. As we note regarding foundational tasks, their challenges are that they lack immediate business value and impact for business lines. Pilot tasks and projects are largely meant to counteract that issue by giving the business something specific in relatively short order to serve as proof and interest that KM will add value and support business users.

The value of pilots is clearly established. Pilots can be used to test business value, validate an approach or methodology, test assumptions, and generate buzz or interest in a particular solution. We often use pilots in skeptical organizations to prove that KM can actually help them and will yield the features and outcomes as promised. In one recent organization, all but one of the business lines was largely resistant to a new comprehensive KM system we were putting in place. We piloted with the one supportive group, careful to define and track success metrics, and developed a reporting and communications plan to share with the complete organization. The pilot group gained immediate value from its participation in the pilot, realizing noted efficiencies and improved performance, which was highlighted by the COO in an all-hands meeting. The other business lines quickly lined up to participate, pushing to avoid being left off subsequent iterations of the system.

In another organization, there was a strongly held agreement that the organization needed to improve its knowledge transfer capabilities to avoid knowledge leaving the organization, but the company's executives disagreed on how (or if) this could be done. To help move this effort forward, we developed a shortlist of different knowledge transfer techniques ranging from technical to non-technical and piloted each with a different group. These pilots proved which techniques could be successful within the organization and also generated valuable lessons on how to improve the process moving forward. With this information, the stakeholders were able to agree on which knowledge transfer solutions to implement enterprise-wide.

The ideal pilot tasks are those that will:

- Show demonstrable progress in months, if not weeks. This is not to say the overall problem needs to be solved that quickly, but progress must be visible to the average end users in no more than 3 months in almost any case.
- Fit together to form a concise pilot project that will quickly demonstrate KM value in a way that is compelling and will cause other stakeholders to participate.
- Prove an approach or methodology to allow decision-makers to proceed with confidence or provide enough information to adjust their approach.
- Lay the foundation for further expansion by creating a framework for design, a repeatable process, and/or the instantiation of technology.

Pilot tasks are often where a roadmap will succeed or fail. Carefully chosen pilot tasks that meet the above criteria typically generate proof of KM value, continued executive support, and increased business line interest and engagement. Choosing the tasks, as well as the appropriate parts of the business to run pilots with, is of the utmost importance.

Pilot group participants should have at least one of these three criteria, but the ideal pilot groups and projects will have all three:

1. A burning problem, which they agree on and are keen to solve. This problem can be as broad as "we can't find what we're looking for" or as specific as "this particular document is continuously out of date." The agreement part of this is most critical. A great deal of time can be spent trying to align stakeholders on the problems they want to solve if you are not careful. An ideal pilot group is one that is aligned in its problems and priorities. It is a bonus if the members are also in broad agreement regarding the solution to the problem.
2. Leadership buy-in and engagement to serve as the leader. Any KM effort takes time, and the best and most impactful KM efforts will demand time and attention from business stakeholders. This requires leadership support, demonstrating that the project is a priority and that time should be spent on it. Ideally, this means the group leader will be an active participant, modeling the right behavior and clearing roadblocks, but at the very least, this means the leader is endorsing the effort and ensuring business stakeholders are giving it the necessary time and attention.
3. Interest in a technical leap. Many of the most impactful pilots will have a technical component, so groups that are willing to learn and test a new technology make strong pilot group candidates. This technical component for pilots is often a new search tool, knowledge group, or taxonomy management and auto-tagging, but virtually any technology form can help move the organization forward. In many cases, this early adopter group will not be the group that could benefit the most from this new technology, but it is the one willing to take the step and dedicate the time to introducing the new technology. This is more than sufficient, as active and willing participation and a willingness to innovate and explore new technologies are all qualifiers for a successful pilot. With success and buy-in demonstrated by this first pilot group, others will be sure to follow.

Pilot tasks are where you will find your champions. These are the executives and senior stakeholders who will fight for your budget and ensure the KM transformation continues to get support from above. Choose your pilot group participants quickly. You seldom get more than one chance to succeed, so the first few pilot projects and pilot groups are of the utmost importance. If chosen correctly and completed with demonstrable value, the pilot participants will become not just stewards of the KM transformation but marketers to help ensure the entire enterprise falls in behind them, convincing more skeptical individuals and groups within the organization that the KM transformation holds meaningful business value. This marketing will always be more meaningful from them, as business leaders, than you, as a KM leader.

5.3.3   Extension Tasks

The third type of tasks to populate the roadmap are extension tasks. These are effectively the expansion of foundational tasks or pilot tasks, extended to work for the entire enterprise. When you consider your complete roadmap and all the tasks therein, most of them will be extension tasks, meaning the vast majority of a complete KM transformation is taking the initial designs and systems from the early stages, learning from them, and replicating them across the enterprise. There are three main types of extension tasks:

1. Extending Along Organizational Lines—The most common type of extension task is along organizational lines. The concept is simple. The pilot proved the value of a specific KM transformation element to one business group, which is ideally now using it to realize business value. In theory, other business groups are now asking for the same or similar features. In the case of extension tasks along organizational lines, the tasks are basically replicated from the pilot for different groups. Each one will require new design activities (i.e., extending the taxonomy design or adding content types), but the goal should be to leverage as much as possible from the pilot to keep the system design in sync and avoid rework. The concept with extension tasks along organizational lines is that, with each new business group, the collective whole should have more content, features, and functionality from which to benefit, and through this process your organization can iteratively design and implement an enterprise solution. This is a great and clear-cut approach in most organizations as long as the designers and implementers guard against creating business silos through the process of designing group by group. After each new business group is added, a review should be conducted to ensure the overall system design is as aligned as possible, encouraging an enterprise view and cross-business collaboration to the greatest extent possible.

2. Extending Along Content Lines—A pilot project will not typically take on the full spectrum of content, ranging from the many different types of structured and unstructured information. One of the primary functions of extension tasks is to add additional content and content types to expand from a pilot to an enterprise system. Extending along content lines adds a richer experience for the pilot group and can create an additional foundation to then replicate along organizational lines. Examples of this include adding additional target indexes (or source content) to a search system or migrating additional content into a content, records, or digital asset management system. Though this may sound simple, in each of these examples, the tasks include much more than just indexing or moving content. In the case of the search example, there would be a cascade of activities, including extending the taxonomy, cleaning up the target content, designing and implementing new content types and/or hit types, and potentially even extending an ontology in the case of a graph search. For the content, records, or digital asset management example, many of these same activities would also be required, as well as content governance and publishing and approval process designs. This becomes even more complex when making the leap between drastically different types of content or different back-end technologies, like a transition from incorporating unstructured content to structured content or a transition from standard file types to unique or obscure types. In short, defining extension tasks based on additional stores and types of content is easily explained and pictured, but as with all KM transformation tasks, it is more complex than it initially sounds, and you must plan accordingly.

3. Extending Along System or Feature Lines—The third and last major type of extension task is along system or feature lines. In this case, if the pilot tasks introduced a core product, or in Agile terms a Minimum Viable Product (MVP), an additional set of tasks could be applied to add new features or integrate additional systems with the pilot. For instance, a pilot project might have established a knowledge graph, and these new extension tasks might introduce natural language processing capabilities to it. Or perhaps a pilot designed and implemented a basic knowledge base, and these new tasks would add auto-tagging capabilities to the knowledge base. Extending along system or feature lines ensures the initial pilot can be short and relatively simple, but you can also promise your pilot groups new features and functionality in short order. Like extending along content lines, this adds a richer overall experience for your early-adopting pilot groups and creates a more robust solution to replicate along organizational lines after it has been further built out.

For each of these types of extension tasks, you will also need to decide whether to extend all at once, meaning moving from a pilot design immediately to an enterprise rollout, or whether to continue iterative expansion. In most cases, we have found iterative expansions are lower risk and allow for greater flexibility. There are some cases, especially where you can leverage economies of scale to get a job done or where the overall outcome will be stronger if the design is considered from the enterprise view, where it will make sense to have a larger enterprise extension task that leaps from a pilot to an enterprise implementation. Even in these cases, look for opportunities to divide the effort into smaller tasks or simpler increments.

Tip:
Feeling stuck getting started with your roadmap task creation? If you are struggling to get started, begin at the end. Consider the end product or organizational state for each workstream, and work backwards from there. The breaking down and spidering out techniques described in Chap. 4 can be used to identify tasks. Also, consider using a top-down approach to task creation. Begin with big tasks, and if they are too large or complex, simply divide them into smaller tasks. Experimentation and iteration will be critical here. You are not going to design the perfect roadmap in your first go of it. Make an attempt, and share it with colleagues who can offer a critical eye of what seems too complex or unachievable. Do not rush out a less than perfect roadmap. Though you can (and should) certainly iterate a roadmap once you move into implementation, the better your starting roadmap, the smoother the transformation.

5.4   Task Creation in Practice

To illustrate the process of task creation, let us focus on a workstream based on the goal or outcome of Enterprise Search and Findability. The first step is to reference your target state and understand what the organization will possess at the end of the roadmap. Let us assume that this workstream is an enterprise search tool connected to all core systems and a knowledge graph that powers the search and also powers a chatbot and recommendations engine. Let us further assume we know that these findability tools should primarily surface unstructured content but also cover a people finder and some structured data currently housed in a CRM.

Breaking down from that end state, the following inputs and components would likely be required:

- Enterprise Taxonomy
- Enterprise Ontology
- Content Audit and Cleanup
- Content Types Design
- Content Governance
- Populate People Profiles
- Tagging Approach
- Content Tagging
- Search Hit Types

For each of these components, a series of foundational, pilot, and extension tasks could be placed on a roadmap, as shown in Fig. 5.1.

In addition, a series of technical tasks specific to the KM systems would require product selection, installation, training, configuration, and population for Enterprise Search, Knowledge Graph, and Taxonomy/Ontology Management. Figure 5.2 shows the placement of these additional tasks.

At this point, the roadmap is looking complex and cluttered. To that end, it may make sense to divide the tasks into two separate workstreams, one for Content Readiness and Quality and one for Enterprise Search and Findability, as shown in Fig. 5.3.

With this visual, it is now obvious some tasks need to be adjusted for dependencies, as shown in Fig. 5.4. For instance, the taxonomy, tagging approach, and taxonomy/ontology management tasks need to be completed before a Content Tagging effort can begin.

At this point, your roadmap is beginning to take shape, but the roadmap is more than workstreams and tasks. An effective roadmap also needs to portray user impact and outcomes as part of the visual, as in Fig. 5.5. If your tasks have been defined correctly with measurable success criteria, business outcomes, and ROI in mind, this should be straightforward. Your goal is to mark on the roadmap where key milestones will occur to help your stakeholders and executives quickly and easily see that the KM transformation will incrementally demonstrate value to your users at various key stages, beginning within the first several months of the transformation. Though you do not need to show every point of value or each milestone within, you

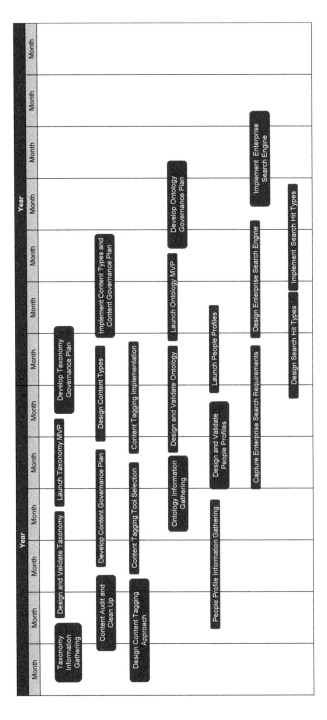

Fig. 5.1 Roadmap graphic showing the placement of foundational, pilot, and extension tasks. © 2021, Enterprise Knowledge, LLC, reused with permission

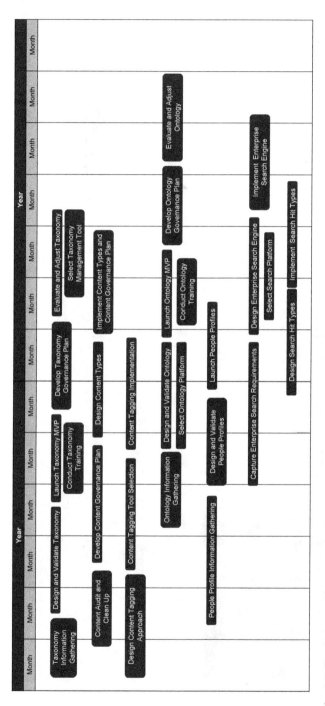

Fig. 5.2 Roadmap graphic amended to include technical tasks including product selection and training. © 2021, Enterprise Knowledge, LLC, reused with permission

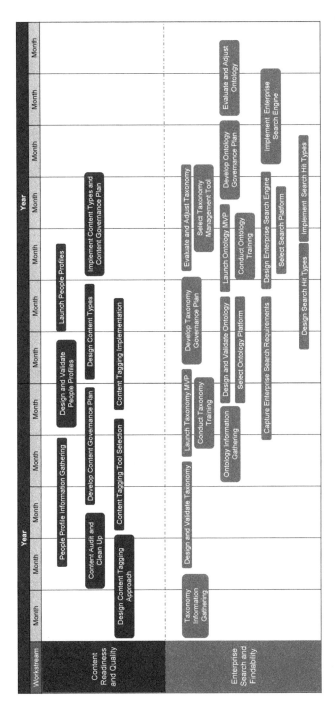

Fig. 5.3 Roadmap graphic further amended to show division into two separate workstreams. © 2021, Enterprise Knowledge, LLC, reused with permission

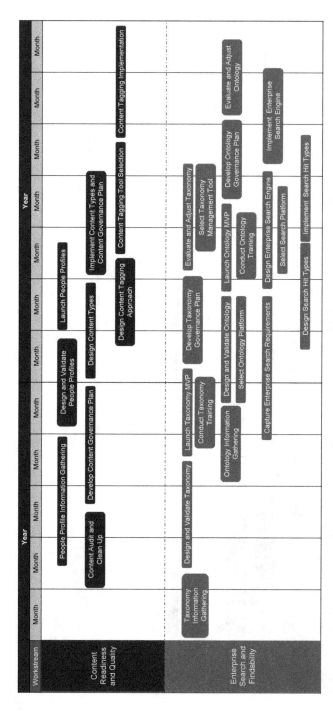

Fig. 5.4 Roadmap graphic further amended to show tasks adjusted for dependencies. © 2021, Enterprise Knowledge, LLC, reused with permission

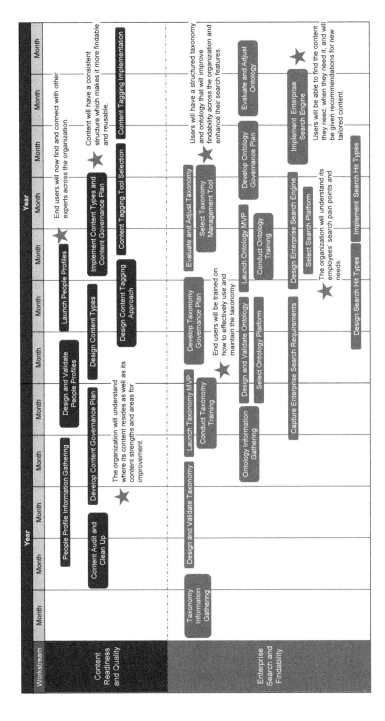

Fig. 5.5 Roadmap graphic further amended to show key milestones. © 2021, Enterprise Knowledge, LLC, reused with permission

will want to convey the many areas where users will directly benefit from the KM efforts and help them visualize the returns they can expect. Adding this to the roadmap is shown below.

This iterative fashion allows for the creation of a roadmap that will work in practice, revealing dependencies and complexities along the way. Expect to go through multiple iterations, and line up a trusted team to critique your iterations to ensure it will be realistic and actionable. Engaging business stakeholders throughout the roadmap development process, while ensuring they find it believable and achievable, will also be important. Both your business stakeholders and internal team should be aligned and support not just the tasks on the roadmap but the overall timeline and order of tasks. You will need their agreement in order to obtain executive support and budget.

5.5   Documenting Tasks

With a series of tasks drawn up for a workstream, you now have your visual roadmap. In most cases, however, that alone will not be sufficient to receive project approval, to adequately estimate cost, or to actually guide the transformation once it is approved. For that, far more detail is typically required. Each task on your roadmap requires backup documentation. We recommend the following for each task:

- Description of activity—A brief (paragraph) description of the purpose of the tasks, what it is intended to accomplish, and what the results of it will be.
- Dependencies (precursor tasks)—A listing of *key* dependencies for the task. Note, we have italicized the word key. One could get carried away with dependencies on a KM roadmap, as virtually everything feeds off of everything else. This documentation of dependencies should be restricted to just those that are complete blockers to conducting the subject task. For instance, you cannot migrate content to a new system if that new system is not in place, and you cannot seed content in new communities of practice if you have not designed and developed the system for those communities.
- Task duration—This should be a rough estimate of the length of the task from start to finish. You will never finish creating a roadmap if you try to get the perfect estimates for each task. Recognize that some flexibility will be required, so estimating in months (or even in ranges of months, i.e., 2–3 months, 6–8 months) is acceptable for these purposes.
- Recommended approach (sub-tasks)—The listing of sub-tasks should not turn into a project plan. The intent of this is not a step-by-step process for the task but a chronological list of major activities in order to ensure any reader has a shared understanding of the task and what it entails. For instance, a listing of sub-tasks might identify engagement with stakeholders to receive design inputs and guidance, but it would not prescribe the specific number of stakeholders or exercise approaches to capture their inputs. These types of details should be left to your project teams, giving them the flexibility to make decisions on what is best at the moment of need.

- Measurable success criteria (measurement of successful completion of task)—As we have asserted throughout this book, KM projects require proof of business value to counter skepticism and maintain executive interest. Each task on your roadmap should include success criteria that define whether the task has been completed successfully. These should follow the SMART (Specific, Measurable, Achievable, Relevant, Time-Bound) format, with a specific emphasis on measurability. For instance, the measurable success criteria for a starter taxonomy is not that the starter taxonomy is created; it would be that it has passed user testing and been instantiated within a taxonomy management tool. As tasks go farther out on the roadmap or are closer to users, the measurable success criteria should be tied to business value as much as possible, including key performance indicators regarding amount of content captured, found, and shared, return system users, overall user activity, and overall user satisfaction.
- Level of effort—Like task duration, level of effort estimates should not be measured down to the hour, but they should offer a rough order of magnitude of the person's time, also known as full-time equivalents (FTEs). Depending on the organization, you may be asked to define this in days, weeks, or even months, but do your best to find a reasonable estimate around which planning can be completed without creating an unruly estimating process that is sure to be wrong. Some organizations wish for slightly more detail, estimating a separate level of effort for business users, IT staff, and external support (i.e., consultants and contractors). This level of detail is relatively easy to estimate and still allows the organization enough visibility to plan for the appropriate time and budget of internal and external resources.
- Business outcome/value of task—Though the measurable success criteria above should hint at the value of the task, you can never be too explicit regarding why a task is important and what the organization will get out of it. Sometimes, especially early on, the business outcome or value may be less tangible. Especially for foundational tasks, the business outcome may be that your organization now has the foundation to do the next task or begin the next phase. Though this is unavoidable, tasks, outcomes, and business value should still be more focused on the actual business of your organization and should be put in terms of the concrete returns on investment we discussed in Chap. 1 wherever possible. Together with the measurable success criteria, business outcomes can be combined to form what we call "Celebratable Moments" on a KM transformation roadmap. The idea behind this is that the KM transformation must constantly be marketed to ensure continued business support and visibility. Celebratable moments are project accomplishments or milestones that are significant in nature, ideally due to new features and/or measurable business value. Each of these celebratable moments should be publicized within the organization to ensure everyone understands the progress that is being made on the KM transformation, and individuals understand the value to the organization and to themselves.

To get a better sense of this, the following are some examples of well-documented tasks.

Table 5.1 shows a foundational task that would be required in many organizations that do not yet have a formalized KM organization or reporting structure.

Table 5.1 An example of a well-documented foundational task to establish KM organization roles and responsibilities

Establish Knowledge Management Organization Roles and Responsibilities
Activity Description
Define the appropriate organizational structure and roles for the <organization> to manage its KM program and associated initiatives.
Task Dependencies
none
Task Duration
3–4 Months
Recommended Approach

4. Inventory KM Capabilities:
    a. Facilitate a series of workshops to design a KM organizational structure to support and drive the KM program. Consider tiers of the structure that take into consideration:
        - Executive sponsors who visibly sponsor the KM strategy, communicate the value of KM, and provide the authority and credibility for KM to be implemented successfully across the organization.
        - Leaders who will be responsible for strategic guidance and resourcing.
        - Individuals who will oversee progress accountability and can support mitigating risks.
        - Individuals who are responsible for tactical execution and proactive involvement in a KM initiative.
    b. Define the primary responsibilities of each identified role.
    c. Define the skills and competencies necessary to carry out each set of responsibilities.
    d. Identify individuals who have the potential to serve on the KM organizational team.
5. Conduct a Gap/Needs Analysis:
    a. Facilitate self-assessments for all identified KM team members.
    b. Compare existing and necessary skill and competency levels across the proposed team.
6. Fill and Train Team Roles:
    a. Develop a training guide that outlines key training goals for each KM role to cover identified responsibilities.
    b. Leverage the training guide to identify specific training courses and materials to prepare team members to serve in their roles and fill any gap/deficiency areas.
    c. Budget allowing, consider filling the deficiency areas by hiring new team members and/or outsourcing to external experts.
7. Conduct 360 Reviews or Team Evaluations:
    a. Capture feedback on how team members are performing in their roles to build a culture of feedback and continual improvement.

(continued)

Table 5.1 (continued)

Measurable Success Criteria
<ul><li>The organization allocates adequate resources and identifies individuals to fill defined roles.</li><li>Each identified role is filled within three months of task completion.</li><li>Training is provided to organizational team members on new processes, systems, and job roles.</li><li>KM organizational team members report having the knowledge and ability to support KM initiatives based on the training they received.</li><li>KM organizational team members fulfill their roles effectively throughout the duration of individual KM initiatives, as reported through 360 surveys or team evaluations.</li></ul>
Estimated Level of Effort
Internal Business—1.5 FTE Internal IT—none External Support—2 FTE
Anticipated Business Outcomes/Value
<ul><li>The <organization> has a KM organizational structure in place that oversees the governance of the KM program. People are held accountable for their commitments, behaviors, and the success of KM initiatives, ensuring that new KM solutions "stick."</li><li>The <organization> communicates with clarity and consistency the meaning, purpose, and value of KM for the organization to align staff around what success looks like long-term and ensure they understand the necessity of their contributing role.</li><li>The <organization> develops individuals who understand the value of KM, are ambassadors within their business areas, and who actively help foster a culture of knowledge sharing, collaboration, and growth across the organization.</li></ul>

Table 5.2 shows an example of a pilot task, which offers immediate business value but also lays the groundwork for a series of more defined extension tasks to follow.

Next, Table 5.3 demonstrates an extension task, where earlier taxonomy and ontology design pilots have already occurred.

This final task example in Table 5.4 represents a longer and more complex technical task. As we stated above, tasks should generally be shorter in length and simpler, but for initial system implementations, there will be circumstances where longer tasks make sense once the KM transformation is under way and buy-in is in place, especially if the task requires software procurement. Note this task is for the selection, acquisition, and installation only, not for design or population, which is addressed through separate pilot and extension tasks.

Table 5.2 An example of a well-documented pilot task to test knowledge transfer techniques

Test Knowledge Transfer Techniques
Activity Description
Leverage a combination of knowledge transfer techniques and tests within \<business unit\> to identify the appropriate knowledge transfer techniques that best suit the organization's needs and to immediately demonstrate the value of a knowledge-sharing culture.
Task Dependencies
• KM Organization Established and Staffed
Task Duration
2–3 Months
Recommended Approach
1. Select up to 5 standard knowledge transfer techniques to test and pilot within \<business unit\>.
2. Conduct a Knowledge Audit—identify key knowledge within the section/division, determine where it is located, and define the nature of different kinds of knowledge (i.e., both explicit and tacit knowledge). Utilize interviews, workshops, and focus groups, and analyze individual documents, key document sets, and major content repositories to conduct the audit.
3. Define Evaluation Criteria for the Knowledge Audit findings (e.g., relevancy, demand, criticality, readability, accessibility/comprehensibility).
4. Create Knowledge Profiles of employees within \<business unit\> that outlines their role, tenure, area of responsibility, areas of knowledge, and specific specialties/skills. Use the Knowledge Profiles to determine those individuals with specific subject matter expertise and those individuals who are frequently asked questions by colleagues.
5. Identify a group of individuals within \<business unit\> to implement the Knowledge Transfer pilot with, and initiate the Knowledge Transfer.
6. Review the outcomes of the Knowledge Transfer using the previously documented Evaluation Criteria, determine corrective measures, and document lessons learned.
7. Survey pilot members to assess the effectiveness of the technique.
8. Collect success stories from pilot participants.
9. Repeat with other techniques.
10. Prioritize lessons learned for techniques with the highest Evaluation Criteria scores for expansion.
Measurable Success Criteria
• The business areas conduct a retrospective to evaluate the effectiveness of each technique, determine lessons and opportunities to improve, and decide whether the techniques are worth institutionalizing.
• Staff feedback surveys demonstrate an increased level of knowledge and ability in the knowledge transfer area.
• Staff feedback surveys demonstrate that staff have a greater awareness of tacit knowledge that exists within their business area, where to locate that knowledge, and who to connect with regarding that knowledge.
• The section or division shares lessons learned beyond the pilot with the larger business area by holding knowledge-sharing events.

(continued)

Table 5.2 (continued)

• The business area implements and improves upon the knowledge transfer techniques for other topics.
• At the end of the task, 80% of participants were satisfied with the outcomes.

Estimated Level of Effort
Internal Business—1.5 FTE Internal IT—1 FTE External Support—1 FTE

Anticipated Business Outcomes/Value
• The <organization> identifies the best knowledge transfer methods for the organization, taking into consideration its culture, size, available technology, knowledge repositories, and level of effort required by employees. • Employees have access to the right information at the right time. • <business unit> improves their knowledge capture, reducing productivity loss by 20% year over year.

Table 5.3 An example of a well-documented extension task to expand taxonomy to an additional business unit

Extend Taxonomy to \<Business Unit\>
Activity Description
Leverage the existing enterprise taxonomy design from \<Pilot Project\> and expand it to cover the needs of \<business unit\>, including the addition of secondary metadata fields, the addition of new taxonomy terms, and synonyms.
Task Dependencies
• Taxonomy Pilots completed. • Taxonomy Governance completed.
Task Duration
2–3 Months
Recommended Approach
1. Collect existing taxonomies or controlled vocabularies presently in use throughout the \<business unit\>. 2. Conduct interviews, focus groups, and workshops to inform the design. 3. Gather sample content from the business area. 4. Complete sample content and text analysis to complement taxonomy design. 5. Extend enterprise taxonomy design to include new metadata fields and taxonomy terms as necessary. 6. Validate resulting taxonomy with \<business unit\> SMEs and representatives from diverse business areas. 7. Conduct knowledge transfer and training with \<business unit\> regarding taxonomy usage and governance.
Measurable Success Criteria
• The enterprise taxonomy is extended to meet the needs of the business unit. • The taxonomy has been validated by a representative sample of \<business unit\> staff as well as enterprise taxonomy owners. • The updated taxonomy design has been instantiated in \<system\>.
Estimated Level of Effort
Internal Business—1 FTE Internal IT—2 FTE External Support—2 FTE
Anticipated Business Outcomes/Value
• Increased findability of content by applying the taxonomy. • The semantic data model lays the foundation for advanced information search and discovery features such as info boxes and recommendation engines. • Stakeholders have a clear understanding of their roles and responsibilities related to the governance and stewardship of the taxonomy and ontology.

Table 5.4 An example of a well-documented, more complex technical task to select and install a knowledge graph database program

Select and Install Knowledge Graph Database Platform
Activity Description
Implement a graph database to host a knowledge graph. The knowledge graph will become a virtual representation of all unstructured content, content sources, repositories and their relationships to each other, allowing the <organization> to make content easier to find and use, break down information silos, facilitate content governance, and enable Artificial Intelligence (AI) and machine learning algorithms to more readily exploit meaningful interrelationships in the metadata. The graph will relate existing metadata repositories and standards in a way to provide additional relevant context to users, so the source metadata is better organized and easier to use and understand, especially for non-experts. Populating the graph database with data will occur as part of the Knowledge Graph pilots.
Task Dependencies
• The <organization> ontology is designed. (Note: This activity can happen in parallel) • The <organization> taxonomy and ontology management system is selected.
Task Duration
8 Months
Recommended Approach
1. Identify requirements for an enterprise graph database platform. The requirements should consider compliance with regulations and integration with the taxonomy/ontology management system, as well as ongoing initiatives that will rely on this technology. 2. Perform an Analysis of Alternatives (AoA). 3. Select the most adequate system based on the AoA. 4. Train administrators and other stakeholders in the use of the tool. 5. Install and configure the graph database system.
Measurable Success Criteria
• Stakeholders across the organization accept and support the process to select the tool. • Stakeholders across the organization accept and support the deployment of the selected tool. • The taxonomy/ontology management system is successfully integrated with the graph database.
Estimated Level of Effort
Internal Business—5 FTE Internal IT—5 FTE External Support—3 FTE

(continued)

Table 5.4 (continued)

Anticipated Business Outcomes/Value
• The <organization> has a graph database platform to unify unstructured content and some structured data, run queries and reports, enable AI use cases, and enable better content governance.
• AI statistical algorithms leverage the knowledge graph to enable advanced cognitive applications and help uncover hidden facts and relationships through inferences in the <organization>'s integrated content.
• Knowledge graphs help the <organization> further identify information it has in disparate data sources throughout the organization on a specific topic, event, initiative, or decision.

Fig. 5.6 Typical audiences in a KM effort. © 2021, Wahl/Hilger, reused with permission

5.6   Presenting the KM Transformation Roadmap

At this stage, likely months of work have gone into gaining a holistic understanding of your organization and defining the target state and current state and then using that understanding to define your transformational roadmap. Ideally, you have been actively engaging your executives, business stakeholders, and IT partners in the effort, and those groups are not only aware but aligned and supportive of the effort. Nevertheless, in most organizations, the official approval and signoff to proceed with the roadmap has not yet occurred.

To ensure your hard work and collective effort comes to fruition with the approval and funding of the KM transformation roadmap, the roadmap itself will need to tell multiple different stories to different audiences, represented in Fig. 5.6. Though the various stakeholders, sponsors, and project participants are likely to have a number of different priorities, the basic priorities tend to be as shown in Table 5.5.

Considering this in practice, the roadmap view for an executive could look like Fig. 5.7.

Table 5.5 Priorities, goals, and roadmap approaches for different personas

Persona	Their priorities	Your goals for them	Roadmap view
Executives	• The cost and potential returns. • Measurable business benefits. • The timeline, specific to when benefits will be realized.	• Approve KM transformation. • Approve and release funding. • Model support by adopting KM practices and participating in project transformation activities where appropriate. • Communicate the value of the KM transformation.	• High-level, executive summary view that focuses on milestones and ROI. • Supporting business case that details costs and anticipated financial benefits.
Business stakeholders	• The value to their business area (and overall impact to their organization). • The impact on their people, including the time it will take for them to participate in the transformation and the new technologies and processes they will be asked to learn.	• Support for the transformation. • Sign up to participate as a pilot group. • Make their people available to support the transformation. • Communicate the value of the KM transformation.	• More detailed roadmap view that shows tasks, timelines, and milestones. • Specific roadmap details for tasks that involve their business area. • Supporting documentation regarding any of their pilots, specifically detailing the time required from their people.
Project participants	• The value they will receive from the transformation. • The amount of time they will need to spend on the transformation. • The impacts to how they work, the changes they will have to absorb (often fear-based, regarding worries of disruption or learning new things and/or changing what works).	• Understanding of the value of the transformation. • Willingness to participate in transformation activities. • Alleviation of fear or worries that could result in lack of adoption or even active opposition.	• More detailed roadmap view that shows tasks, timelines, and milestones. • Specific roadmap details for tasks that involve them, showing specifically what they will get out of the transformation. • Specific "asks" regarding their time and activities.

(continued)

Table 5.5 (continued)

Persona	Their priorities	Your goals for them	Roadmap view
Information technology	• Technical implications regarding current or future technologies to be procured and/or managed. • Avoidance of technology costs or risks that will create undue work or trigger major changes in operations.	• Support for the KM transformation. • Willingness to actively support and participate in technical aspects of the transformation, including software selection and procurement, software implementation and operations, and integration with existing systems. • Potential support for dispositioning obsolete systems and repositories. • Willingness to dedicate technical resources to support the overall transformation (if the goal is to use internal IT resources).	• Technology-focused view of the workstream that details technical tasks. • Supporting details regarding IT costs and timelines for procurement of new KM technologies. • Specific requirements and activities (arrayed over time) detailing IT resource requirements.

Executive View

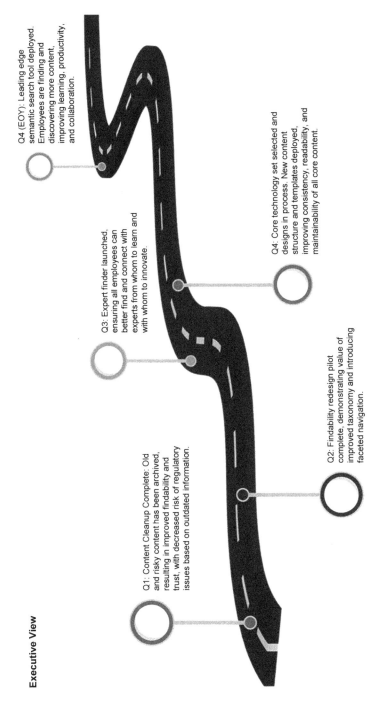

Q1: Content Cleanup Complete: Old and risky content has been archived, resulting in improved findability and trust, with decreased risk of regulatory issues based on outdated information.

Q2: Findability redesign pilot complete, demonstrating value of improved taxonomy and introducing faceted navigation.

Q3: Expert finder launched, ensuring all employees can better find and connect with experts from whom to learn and with whom to innovate.

Q4: Core technology set selected and designs in process. New content structure and templates deployed, improving consistency, readability, and maintainability of all core content.

Q4 (EOY): Leading edge semantic search tool deployed. Employees are finding and discovering more content, improving learning, productivity, and collaboration.

Fig. 5.7 Sample high-level, executive view roadmap. © 2021, Enterprise Knowledge, LLC, reused with permission

A more detailed view for business stakeholders would be similar to Fig. 5.5, whereas an IT-focused view would include much greater detail showing things showing dependencies of software and hardware as well as a more specific set of iterative releases. It would also likely include resource estimates along with required security and testing activities.

Tip:
When considering the visuals for your roadmap, make sure to consider your organization's design standards and style guides. The roadmap should look as familiar as possible to your audiences, so do your best to understand how your organization has visualized similar transformations in the past and leverage those designs. This includes consideration of your organization's color palette, font, and writing style, as well as the manner in which timelines and roadmaps are typically visualized.

The style and tone of KM transformation presentations or pitches will also depend heavily on your audience. C-level and executive presentations may come down to 15 minutes or a half-hour, whereas project participants and IT stakeholders will often want a more in-depth look to understand what they are signing up for and what they will get out of it, likely arrayed over multiple sessions.

With the current state, target state, and KM transformation roadmap completed, you have the clearly understood plan, outcomes, and budget. With the successful presentations and marketing of those materials, you (hopefully) also have the support of executives, stakeholders, and other key players down the line in your organization.

You have done the hard work to understand your organization and envision the KM systems that will be central to the organization's transformation. Now, let us ensure you understand the full set of KM systems options, how they can connect, and what they can do for your organization. The next section of the book will make certain you understand the various KM systems that may appear on your roadmap as part of the transformation. Though few roadmaps encompass all of these KM systems, almost every roadmap will include at least one, if not more. These KM systems are central to making KM clickable, ensuring it offers true business impact to your organization and its people.

Part II

Understanding KM Systems

This part details the many technologies that together make up a KM suite. For each of the technologies below, we explain what it is and how it is used, common vendors and platforms that meet the need, the features and functions available from the type of tool, and the common KM business problems the tool is commonly used to address. These tools are organized in alignment with our logical KM systems diagram shown in Fig. 6.1.

It is important to note that the simple existence of these technologies doesn't make them KM systems. On the contrary, most organizations already have many of these tools in use. It is only with the appropriate design and integration detailed in this book that these tools come together to form a KM system or KM suite of technologies that address the driving KM and business challenges we've identified herein.

It is also important to note that not every organization needs every type of tool listed here to be considered a mature or advanced KM organization. We present the full suite of tools with the recognition that your own KM strategy and assessment will determine which components you need, how they should be integrated, and how they should be designed to best meet your needs and the needs of your end users.

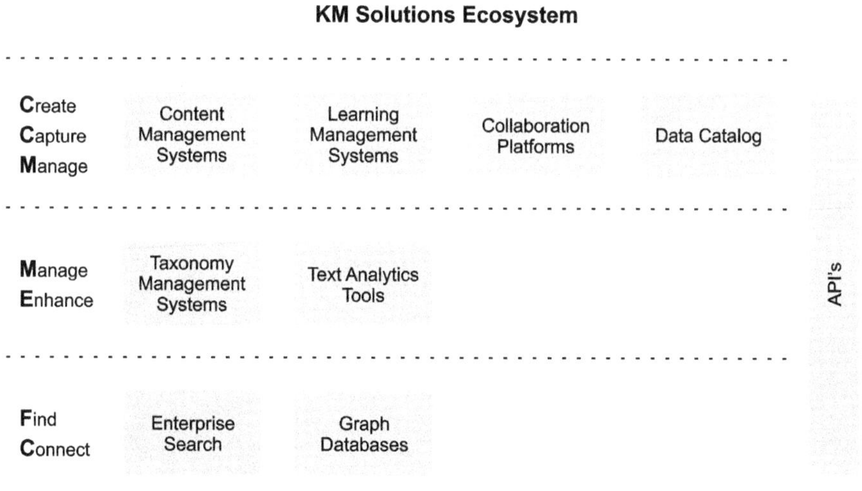

KM Solutions Ecosystem

Create Capture Manage	Content Management Systems	Learning Management Systems	Collaboration Platforms	Data Catalog	
Manage Enhance	Taxonomy Management Systems	Text Analytics Tools			API's
Find Connect	Enterprise Search	Graph Databases			

Fig. 6.1 The KM solutions ecosystem. © 2021, Wahl/Hilger, reused with permission

Content Management Solutions

6

A Content Management System (CMS) is an application or platform that enables business users to create, manage, secure, publish, and share content. It is a critical platform for most KM projects as it gives people a place to safely store and manage their content so that it can be found and reused within an organization.

Content Management Systems cover a broad range of tools. As such, they are often divided into distinct areas:

- Document Management/Records Management
- Web Content Management
- Digital Asset Management
- Business Content Solutions, and
- Headless Content Management

Document Management/Records Management solutions provide a digital repository for documents such as Microsoft Office and PDF files. Enterprise solutions typically include workflow, publishing, and support for metadata and search. Many of the most mature systems also support formal records management for organizations that are looking to implement records management for their electronic documents.

Web Content Management (WCM) solutions allow non-technical users to create and publish content on websites (either internal or public). WCM solutions allow for the democratization of content so that intranets and other information sharing sites can be populated with content from the experts and not just a core set of authors. Any organization developing an intranet or knowledge portal to share information between employees needs to consider the implementation of a WCM system as a way to populate these systems.

Digital Asset Management (DAM) systems are specialized tools used to capture and manage an organization's digital assets, such as images and marketing materials. These tools work like document management systems, but they are specially designed to support the unique challenges of images and marketing materials.

J. Hilger, Z. Wahl, *Making Knowledge Management Clickable*,
https://doi.org/10.1007/978-3-030-92385-3_6

DAMs typically support key imaging features such as publishing images in different resolutions and managing digital rights usage rules.

A Component Content Management System (CCMS) manages content at a granular (component) level rather than at the document level to enable content reuse. These systems enable more structured content, but are also designed to track the specific and relevant metadata about each component—automating live links and relationships between components.

In addition to the more generic solutions defined above, there are a class of purpose-built content management systems that support specific business functions. We call them business content solutions. Examples of these systems include knowledge bases for support or help centers, contract management systems (for legal departments), human resources/recruiting tools, and marketing repositories. These systems are designed to support a single business process and typically do that well. They should not be repurposed for other needs as they often lack key features that other content management platforms deliver. An enterprise KM project will need to find a way to integrate these repositories with the other content management solutions so that the content in these tools is not siloed.

Finally, the newest content management solutions are called headless content management systems. These tools are systems with basic content management capabilities that are designed to be easily integrated with other tools and systems. The vendors behind these systems see the value in sharing features like content authoring, publishing, workflow, and security without tying it to a single system.

Effective knowledge management initiatives need to integrate or improve the capabilities of one or more of the content management solutions described above. You cannot capture, manage, and share information without technology platforms that make it easy to do. Every large KM initiative needs to consider these solutions as part of the overall engagement.

6.1 Common Platforms

The content management space is a very mature space that has commoditized in value over time. Most CMS solutions offer features that meet most of an organization's needs. As a result, there is a robust open-source market and a large number of solutions with very specific features that are used to differentiate their product from the rest of the market. As you select a CMS, it is important to determine which of these features really matters. In the rest of this section, we describe the leading open source and commercial vendors for each of the five types of CMS solutions on the market today.

6.1.1   Document Management

The document management market is old and not always considered exciting. It is however a critical tool for proper management and control over documents across the enterprise. The leading commercial vendors in this space are:

- Documentum,
- OpenText Content Server
- Box, and
- SharePoint (O365)

Documentum has one of the largest install bases but has been bought and sold a few times and is rapidly losing market share. OpenText remains a well-funded leader in the document management space with their Content Server offering. The two most common solutions we have seen lately are Box and SharePoint (A.K.A. O365). Box is a SAAS-based offering that excels in its simplicity and numerous built-in integrations. It is often selected for small and medium-sized companies or departments in larger organizations. O365 is one of the most common solutions we see, and the latest features do a great job of capturing content. When properly implemented, O365 can be a very powerful and user-friendly document management solution.

Document management is the one area within the CMS market where there are not a lot of open-source options. The open-source market is led by Alfresco. Alfresco offers an open-source version as well as a paid version of their software. Alfresco was created by the founder of Documentum and provides a similar but improved framework for managing documents. It is a very powerful tool.

6.1.2   Web Content Management

The web content management market has hundreds of vendors with a wide range of commercial and open-source products. These products are also built on a wide range of technologies and platforms, including:

- Python
- PHP
- .Net (Microsoft)
- Java, and
- React

Organizations looking into WCM solutions have plenty of options and should focus on selecting a platform that they are comfortable supporting with the core features that they need. There are plenty of bells and whistles that look great but are not always useful.

Commercial Options

The commercial market is divided into large and small vendors. The large players in the space include:

- Adobe—Adobe Experience Manager (AEM)
- Tridion—Tridion Sites
- Microsoft—SharePoint
- Sitecore—Experience Platform
- HCL—Digital Experience
- Oracle—WebCenter Content

The commercial market is dominated by AEM and Sitecore. They both take different approaches to marketing their products. AEM provides a full features suite of products that does more than simple web publishing. AEM pushes the idea of a fully integrated solution that supports the entire web experience, managing the way in which users interact with the website through a suite of tools that encompass everything from analytics through personalization on the site. Sitecore provides a Microsoft solution that is often sold as simple and fully integrated. From our experience, the full experience management solutions (like the one provided in AEM) are overkill for the information portals typically required for KM solutions. Having said that, there are a number of features in those tools that can be useful in helping users find the content they need at the point of need.

Open-Source Solutions

There are hundreds of open-source WCM solutions that organizations can choose from. The two leading options are Drupal and WordPress. Depending on the complexity of your needs for publishing web content to your communities and your existing platforms, these open-source tools can be a great option for allowing more decentralized information sharing through an intranet or information portal.

The two most important criteria for selecting your WCM solution are ease of use (you want as many content authors as possible) and ease of support. As you review both open source and commercial WCM options, make sure that you have something that you can implement easily and affordably and that your users are excited to use.

6.1.3 Digital Asset Management

Digital Asset Management (DAM) tools are slightly more specialized content management solutions. They tend to be owned either by IT or marketing organizations, but they have value across the enterprise. Most of today's DAM solutions are available as SaaS solutions which are a great option for this type of solution.

The leading DAM offerings are:

- Aprimo
- Bynder
- Canto, and
- Adobe Experience Manager Assets

All but Adobe Experience Manager Assets are cloud-based solutions. Unless your organization is already heavily invested in AEM, cloud options like Aprimo, Bynder, and Canto are excellent tools for managing and controlling images and other digital assets to be shared across the enterprise.

KM implementation teams should work with Marketing and Corporate communications to integrate with and build upon an existing DAM solution if possible to save money and to get greater value out of the existing technology investments.

6.1.4   Business Content Solutions

Business content solutions are a mix of tools designed to solve specific business problems that also have at least basic content management capabilities. The common purposes for these tools include:

- Knowledge bases for contact centers and help desks
- Customer Relationship Management (CRM)
- Contract Management
- CAD/CAM solutions, and
- Marketing tools (often called Martech)

It is worth dividing these tools into two categories: knowledge bases and all others. Knowledge bases for contact centers and help desks are valuable tools that capture and manage detailed information about how products and services work within an organization. These tools are full-feature knowledge management platforms that specialize in a specific area. Smaller organizations can use them as their primary knowledge management system. Larger organizations will have content in other repositories that require a different enterprise solution for knowledge management. Some of the leading knowledge bases for contact centers and help desks include the following.

- Zendesk
- ServiceNow
- Soho Desk
- Shelf Software

The other set of business content management tools tends to support very specific business functions and processes with little focus on meeting common knowledge management needs. While these tools are not KM focused, they do have important knowledge and information within them. An enterprise-level KM stack needs to account for the content in these systems and make it available through search or other means available to the knowledge workers in the organization. Some of the most common examples of these business-centric repositories of information are as follows.

- Salesforce
- Microsoft Dynamics
- ContentGrow
- HubSpot
- Agiloft (for contract management)
- Slidebank (for presentations)

These tools can be valuable sources of KM content that should be mined and managed as part of any enterprise KM implementation. As part of your larger KM program, evaluate the content management capabilities of these tools against the best practice features seen throughout the rest of this section. They will likely not meet all of these features as content management is not their primary focus, but they will have some key features that are valuable as a source of your overall KM program. These tools, like the other CMS systems in this section, should be considered as repositories of information that are worth mining for your enterprise search and information portals.

6.1.5   Headless Content Management

Headless Content Management is one of the hottest areas in the CMS space. The idea behind headless solutions is that content management solutions offer a number of features that are too tightly integrated or overbearing, such that they lose their value. The benefit of a headless CMS is that organizations can treat the common features found in a CMS (content publishing, workflow, content management, and metadata management) as a service that can be easily integrated with other tools to provide specific features that augment processes or other tools.

The leaders in this space based on our experience are:

- Drupal (can be used as a decoupled headless CMS solution)
- Contentful
- Heretto (better known as an industry-leading componentized content management system)
- Tridion Docs
- Magnolia, and
- GraphCMS

These tools all offer powerful content management capabilities and focus on the content allowing organizations to develop their own methods and tools for rendering and presenting the content. The headless CMS space remains pretty new, so there are no vendors that have separated themselves from others. If you are looking for a Headless CMS solution, spend some time deciding which tool best fits your needs and then try using Agile principles through a targeted MVP) or Proof of Concept (PoC).

6.2 Features and Functions

Content management is far and away the broadest range of systems and capabilities that we explore in this book. They are foundational to nearly any KM implementation and should be considered against the KM spectrum we have discussed above.

Given the large number of capabilities supported by content management systems, I have divided these capabilities across the content management lifecycle:

- Create
- Capture
- Manage
- Enhance
- Find
- Connect

In the rest of this section, we explain each feature in relation to the area of the content management lifecycle in which it best fits.

6.2.1 Create

The create phase of the content management lifecycle is one that is often not considered when thinking about the implementation of a content management system. Frequently the content is created outside of the system and then users are asked to upload or add the content to the CMS. The problem with this approach is that users do not want extra steps in their process. If they create the content in one place and then have to take an additional step to load or capture it in the CMS they will be frustrated and often skip that extra step. Thinking through how to provide features that make it easier to create and edit content within the CMS helps ensure that people store more content within the CMS. The features I highlight in this section are all reasons for people to "create" their content within the CMS. The most interesting features to consider are:

- Collaborative editing
- Componentized content, and
- Collaborative workspaces

Collaborative editing is a newer feature that has grown in importance with the advent of Google documents and Microsoft's O365 offering. Prior to these advancements content management systems relied on workflow and check-in/check-out capabilities to control the way groups of people edited content. Content authors would take turns checking out documents making changes and then checking them back in for others to work on them. While this process worked, it was slow and cumbersome. Collaborative editing allows more than one person to view and edit a document simultaneously. Each person sees the changes the other is making and is aware of where they are in the content. This is not a common feature in most CMS solutions, but critical for organizations who have a need to collaboratively edit and publish documents in a compressed time frame.

Componentized content is another highly specialized feature that is not available in all CMS solutions. Componentized content is the ability to write sections of a document and then merge them together for publication to one or more mediums. It is a critical feature in a number of very specific use cases. The most common is the management of large complex documents like instruction manuals, where text in one document is repeated in other documents. CMS systems that support componentized content management allow authors to create and edit pieces of a document and then merge them into one or more larger documents. The advantage of this approach is that changes can be made in one place and then automatically be propagated to every document that uses that same text. Another advantage is that larger documents can be broken into smaller sections that are searchable. Large documents that have been componentized offer better search results. Search can respond with the appropriate section of a document as an answer rather than a link to a larger document that the user needs to read or search again to find their answer. Componentized content management takes planning and can be tricky to implement. When done well, it is a huge time saver for people maintaining large complex documents and for the users that are able to read only the sections applicable to their needs.

Collaborative workspaces are another great feature for getting people to create content within the CMS. If the CMS offers a place where people can collaborate on a project, task, or topic they are more likely to store their content within the CMS. One of the best examples of a collaborative workspace that encourages people to create and manage content within the CMS is Microsoft's team sites. These sites offer features like security, alerting, chat, and content sharing all in one place. Users spend time on these sites and store their content there because they get value through the interaction with others when they create and share content there. When done well, this approach not only encourages better content management, but it also streamlines and improves processes and the flow of information through an organization. While collaboration workspaces are a great tool, they are often not implemented well and end up unused. If you are planning to implement a CMS with collaborative workspaces, spend a great deal of time up-front testing them out to see if people like them. Also, make sure you find specific use cases where they are helpful and roll those out first.

6.2.2   Capture

While it is always preferable to capture content in the CMS at the point of creation, it is not always possible or practical. As a result, organizations that succeed in content management spend time and effort making sure that there are ways to automate the capture of content wherever possible. This is most commonly needed in Document and Digital Asset Management systems but can be important in other CMS solutions as well. The three most common approaches/features for capturing content are:

- Scanning
- Batch uploading, and
- Integrations

Scanning is a critical feature for organizations with a lot of paper documents either because of their business (banks with paper contracts) or the age of their content. Many enterprise document management systems provide add-on scanning capabilities or integrations with some of the leading scanning solutions on the market. Enterprise-level scanning tools quickly read a document, capture it in PDF form, and use optical character recognition (OCR) to read the text of the document. When looking at CMS solutions that require scanning capabilities, it is important to know the volume, type, and age of content that your system will be working with. Organizations trying to digitize years of content should consider companies that specialize in large-scale digitization efforts. If there is an ongoing need for scanning, you will need to include high-speed scanning hardware into your overall solution. The type of content you will be scanning also matters. If you are scanning diagrams that do not fit on standard paper sizes and that lack text, you will need to consider specialized solutions that are industry specific. In these cases, the scanning solution may impact your choice in CMS. Finally, organizations scanning content that is very old may need to adjust their expectations as to the quality of the scanned content. Old content can be ripped or delicate and will not be sturdy enough to put through a scanner. It can also be faded in such a way that OCR does not work as well. Scanning is a feature that is not needed in every case. When it is needed, it should be a critical part of the decision process around selecting and implementing a CMS.

Batch uploading is another capture feature that is most commonly used in Document Management systems or in DAM systems. Like scanning, this is a capability that simplifies the uploading of content into the CMS. A CMS without content has little value. Investing in capabilities that make this easy is important. The challenge with batch uploading is not loading the content. That is typically easy and something that most systems allow. The challenge is applying metadata to the content as it is loaded into the system. The batch upload process needs to identify which content types each piece of content belongs to and also apply the appropriate metadata along with the content. Small batches make this easier. Larger batches make this a more complex process. Often this is handled through a register (often a spreadsheet of flat file) where the metadata is spelled out and the content to be uploaded is pointed to. This approach solves the problem of specifying metadata but does not address the problem of mistakes. Say one of the pieces of content in the batch has incorrect or invalid metadata. Should the batch upload process stop all together? Should it load everything that worked and then point out the exceptions? All of these are important considerations when investigating batch upload capabilities. If your CMS requires a batch upload process to simplify the ingestion or capture of content, give a great deal of thought into how your tool needs to work and whether the CMS you are investigating really offers what you need. In most cases, I have seen custom uploading capabilities that align with specific business processes used to solve the batch uploading requirement. As such, it is worth planning for some custom development to meet this need.

Integrations with systems that are regularly used to create content are the most common and effective way to simplify the capture process. For example, many document management systems offer a plug-in to Microsoft Word that allows the user to save content directly into the CMS. This approach is of course changing as more and more people are moving to online document creation tools like Microsoft's O365 and Google Docs. Capturing content from productivity documents like the Office or Google Workspace is one of the easiest ways to improve the capture of content and ensure that your CMS is used regularly. However, it is not the only approach for pulling content into the CMS application.

Over our collective decades working in the content management space, we have planned and implemented a number of business-specific integrations to ease the capture of content into the CMS. One client we worked with managed massive numbers of contracts and needed to use the CMS to support their publishing, findability, and archiving processes. They had a contract management system that was widely used to capture all of the contracts being processed. In a few short months, we developed a custom integration between it and the CMS where the contract management system pushed new contracts into the CMS. The CMS captured the contracts and the associated metadata based on information gathered in the contract management system. The CMS became the system of record for the contracts, while the contract management system pointed to the contract and handled the contracting process. In the end, the CMS was capturing as many as 10,000 contracts per week, providing greater visibility through faceted search and better alignment with the organization's records management initiatives. In their book *Knowledge Management,* Gamble and Blackwell emphasize the importance of contextualization while pursuing the capture of high-quality knowledge, both by designing systems that can determine the relevance of content like the features mentioned above and by training employees to understand the type of content that will align with the main business processes in the CMS (Gamble and Blackwell 2001).

As your organization looks at how to create greater adoption of the CMS, consider how these different methods of capturing content into the CMS provide greater ROI for the enterprise and make the CMS the single place to manage and find the content necessary for people to do their jobs.

6.2.3 Manage

Once content has been successfully captured into the CMS, the goal becomes managing the content in a manner that supports the scale of content currently seen in most large organizations. The amount of unstructured content created by organizations doubles every year. Managing this amount of content becomes an incredibly difficult task. The right enterprise CMS solution offers features that make the management of content easier and scalable. As you review the management features of your potential CMS investment, think about the specific business problems they will solve and how these tools will work at a scale that could reach hundreds of thousands, and in some organizations millions, of documents.

While there are hundreds of features we could review, I selected some of the most important features needed to understand how the CMS will function. This list of features includes:

- Content types
- Workflow
- Security
- Records Management
- Manage in place
- Legal holds, and
- Reporting/content analytics

Content types are a foundational element of nearly any CMS. A content type is a reusable collection of metadata for a category of content. Corresponding taxonomies allow you to manage information in a centralized, reusable way. Content types provide structure around the content and information within the CMS that make finding, managing, and securing content easier.

Enterprise-level CMSs should allow for custom content types. A custom content type is one that can be defined and modified within the CMS. Ideally, an administrator with little or no development experience can create a new content type and define the fields (aka metadata) that are included with that content type. Content types are applicable to and should be a feature in any type of CMS. This includes Document Management, Digital Asset Management, Web Content Management, Business Content Management, and Headless Content Management systems.

Workflow is another key foundational element of any CMS. Think of workflow as a predefined series of processes and steps that control the movement of or interaction with content within the CMS. Workflow capabilities vary widely between different CMS tools and should be carefully investigated before making any large investment within a CMS.

When implementing a CMS, it is important to consider where and when you will implement workflow. In our experience, the implementation of CMS workflows is one of the most common mistakes in CMS implementations. Frequently, organizations not experienced in implementing content management solutions will make a number of mistakes that hurt the adoption of the CMS and cause workflows to be seen as a problem rather than a solution. Some best practices around workflow design and implementation are below:

- Keep is simple.
- Identify processes that are good candidates for adding workflow, and.
- Measure and adapt.

The most common mistake is making workflows too rigid and too complicated. Keep your workflows simple and straightforward. "Create, approve, and publish" is one of my favorite workflows. We have seen too many organizations develop complex workflows only to find out that there were exceptions or problems that made the workflow unusable. For example, a workflow that points to a single person for approval breaks when that person is unavailable. A well-designed workflow will allow the author to point to the right person to review a document or allow a group of people to own that step of the workflow.

Workflow can be a great tool for driving adoption of the CMS if done well. Pick a process within your organization that would be greatly enhanced through a simple workflow and implement it. Continually test and tweak the process until it is as close to perfect as possible and make the resulting improvements as visible as possible across the enterprise. A well-designed workflow serving the right process can be one of the highlights of your implementation.

Finally, every workflow should have some form of measurement and reporting. Workflow analytics serve two critical purposes. First, they provide the workflow designer with feedback that allows for continuous improvement of the workflow. Second, they can provide insight into how the process is functioning and the impact the workflow has had on the process. At one client, we implemented a workflow for processing specific paperwork within a CMS. The process identified a key bottle-neck in the process that allowed us to speed up the overall processing of paperwork by over 50%. These types of stories help senior management see the real ROI of the system and encourage continual reinvestment each year.

Security is one of the more complicated design considerations for any CMS implementation. It is also a critical feature to make sure that the content in the CMS is only accessible to the right people. Many organizations select a CMS with the goal of having more control over who can access their content than they would be using shared drives. As such, it is important to identify a plan for security and how it can be managed at scale.

Most CMS tools use a combination of groups and roles to define the security for the content in their system. Roles determine which actions an individual is allowed to take within the CMS. For example, an author might have the ability to create, read, update, and delete content. An editor might only be able to read and update content; a viewer would be limited to reading or viewing content in the system. Groups represent a collection of people with similar needs. They are typically managed within the CMS or as part of an enterprise directory service like active directory. Groups are typically used for two purposes in the CMS. A group can be assigned to a role so that the capabilities/features the user is able to take advantage of are defined.

A group can also be used to determine content entitlements (aka permission to see a piece of content).

Using groups to manage entitlements to content is a complex process that requires a great deal of up-front planning. Organizations with lots of people and lots of content need to find a way to handle security in a simple yet scalable fashion. The easiest security is when access rights are tied to defined organizational concepts. For example, certain content might be visible to people in the HR department only. Another example is limiting access to content based on a person's level within the company, like having content that is available to managers or directors only. As I think through a security strategy for my clients, I always begin with the following:

- Level
- Location, and
- Organization

Defining groups based on these three attributes of a person is always a great way to start and typically gets organizations 80% of the way there. However, the project-centric method of working poses a problem. Often people need limited access to content based on a project or group that they are working with. These projects and groups cannot be identified or managed centrally and need to be changed regularly. In our experience, the best way to handle these ad hoc groups is to provide delegated administration. Delegated administration is the ability to allow others within the organization to have permissions to add or remove people from groups that are relevant to them. Often, we recommend to our customers that each department has delegated administration capabilities so that they can create and manage the groups that are specific to their department.

While most CMS tools offer some delegated administration capabilities, very few have designed their solution to work for an enterprise. When evaluating your CMS, focus on their security model and how they will support delegated administration of security groups. Provide specific use cases to make sure that the tool can really meet your needs.

Records Management is not always used or considered. It is also typically limited to Document Management and Digital Asset Management systems. The purpose of records management is to support an organization's rules around document retention. Historically, the reason for implementing a records management policy was to save money on the cost to file and store documents. As more and more organizations digitize their information and the cost of disk space continues to drop, records management is no longer driven by the need to save money. Records management initiatives are most often driven by industry compliance requirements or the risk of legal exposure due to improperly deleting or saving content.

Records management is difficult to implement. It is a complex subject that many people are not familiar with. Organizations need to develop retention schedules for different types of content, also known as record types. Each type of content or record type may have a different trigger as to when the retention countdown begins. For example, a contract or lease may need to be retained for 10 years after the contract is complete. In this case, the retention schedule does not begin until the contract is complete. In another example, tax information needs to be saved for 3 years. The retention schedule for tax material begins as soon as the tax is submitted. These are two different types of content with very different retention rules and triggers that initiate the retention process.

Most organizations do not need to implement records management schedules across all of their content. If you are not required to implement records management, do not do it. Records management is an expensive undertaking that will slow down other potentially more valuable initiatives. If you need to implement a records management initiative, consider using a big bucket approach to the records schedules. In a big bucket approach, organizations create a smaller number of record types with fewer schedules. This approach limits complexity by giving a smaller number of retention schedules that need to be implemented within the system. There are two other things to consider when implementing records management. First, integrate records management rules as the new content is migrated to the CMS. Second, implement one record schedule at a time to show progress on a regular basis.

Manage in Place is one of our favorite CMS features but it is not very well known. Manage in Place refers to content that is managed in the CMS but not housed there. The metadata and a pointer to the content are stored in the CMS; while the content itself remains in the location where it is already stored. There are a number of reasons for using the Manage in Place capabilities of a CMS.

Manage in Place can be used when content is stored in an appropriate location, but the tool that houses the content lacks metadata or workflows. We used this capability for a large learning and development group whose users were spread out around the country and were unable to find the training options that they needed. Our teams developed a website based on a Web CMS that pointed to the training materials stored in the Learning Management System. The Web CMS had content types that included metadata like a picture, the audience for the course, the method of delivery, and the topics covered by the course. Each individual piece of content also had a link to the course in the LMS. The LMS lacked the ability to add metadata. The Web CMS housed the metadata needed to create a visually appealing and highly findable website that the organization's employees could search to find the courses they needed.

Another case where we implemented Manage in Place functionality was a marketing organization. They wanted to ensure they knew where their content is housed and make sure the claims they made in their marketing material were accurate. They used a number of different systems to store their content. There was a Digital Asset Management system for finished marketing material, a document management system for studies, a collaboration tool for work in progress information, and a workflow management tool to track the progress of new materials. Individually, each of these systems made sense. Taken together, there was no single place to find content or understand where it was. There were also duplicate versions of content in each of the different systems. A CMS with Manage in Place functionality allowed this marketing organization to track all of their content in a single location without having to move content out of the appropriate systems. This implementation provided greater control over their information and streamlined processes that were slowed down by the limitations of having multiple siloed applications.

The Manage in Place capability is one of the most powerful tools in a CMS arsenal. Organizations looking to implement or extend the use of their CMS should consider using this approach as a quick way to gain control over highly distributed content environments.

Legal Holds provide organizations with a way to lock content from being changed or deleted when it is related to a legal case. This is an uncommon feature in a CMS, but one that is critical for organizations that deal with content that is consistent and potentially highly litigious. We bring this up not to encourage it as a decision-making point in a CMS, but to recommend when to use it and when not to. Legal hold functionality is not a cure-all method to track all of the information that people are working on in the event of legal situations. When this is the requirement, an organization is better off looking into an e-discovery platform that manages all parts of the e-discovery process. E-Discovery platforms are products that are specifically designed to support the management of electronic information in the event of a legal concern. These tools allow organizations to quickly gather, share, and lockdown all of their electronic files with regards to a case. They are specifically designed for this purpose and will do a much better job than a CMS. In addition, your users will quickly figure out that keeping content out of the CMS protects them from these hold situations and as a result, the legal hold functionality becomes a deterrent for people using the CMS.

This does not mean that this functionality is not useful. In situations where organizations are processing lots of similar content in a highly automated fashion, a legal hold feature can provide great value. For example, if the CMS is storing highly transactional contracts, leases, or purchase orders that are automatically loaded into the system, the ability to lock some of those documents based on legal situations is both reasonable and a powerful way for an organization to protect itself in the event of a lawsuit. The key to using legal hold functionality is to find the right use case and implement the solution in a way that not only freezes content, but also affects the workflow that the CMS supports.

Reporting/Content Analytics is one of the most important drivers in the long-term success of any CMS implementation. Analytics allow for measurement that helps encourage continuous improvement as well as financial justification to continue to invest in the solution. There are three main areas of reporting that need to be considered when implementing a CMS:

- Content analytics
- Usage analytics, and
- Performance metrics

Content analytics are reports documenting the amount and types of content stored in the CMS. These reports allow administrators to see how much content is stored, where clusters of similar content exist, and where there are gaps in content. Often these reports are segmented based on the groups that own each area of content. These reports allow CMS administrators to understand which organizations are storing the most content and convey that information to management. Content analytics become even more valuable when they are combined with taxonomies and metadata. Topical taxonomies allow organizations to understand how much information they have for each topic. We worked with a large multinational consulting organization that was rolling out a new information portal. They wanted to know when they had created enough information. We developed reports that showed how much information was tagged to each topic in their taxonomy. This allowed leadership to understand where they had holes in content so they could make sure the new information portal answered the questions that people were asking.

Usage analytics fall into two categories: management and viewing of content. Implement analytics around how often people are opening, editing, and removing content to understand engagement with the CMS and when content needs to be refreshed. If the content owned by one group is not being updated often, it may signify a lack of adoption. CMS leaders can use this information to engage and catch problems early before people lose interest in the system. In addition, content that has not been updated for a long period of time may need to be refreshed or archived. Usage analytics on the management of content are a critical part of content governance that people often overlook.

Usage analytics for content viewing offer complimentary value to the content governance process. Analytics that show how often content is viewed allow organizations to understand which content is most impactful and/or most often looked at. If your reporting allows for demographic information about the users, you can gain a real understanding of which content is most important to your constituents. For example, a report that shows counts of content tagged as a particular topic by user type can help organizations understand which types of content are most important to their user communities. If a particular piece of content is more widely viewed by people in one office and not another, it may mean that one office is unaware of the content or that there are differences in needs between the offices. In either case, these usage analytics provide guidance that management might not have access to otherwise.

Performance analytics are most often used to validate the ROI of the CMS. These analytics are the *most* important metrics that an organization can capture, and they are often overlooked. Identify the reason that your organization has invested in the CMS. Develop custom reports that allow the CMS team to regularly update management on the continued performance of the CMS. If the CMS has a workflow that streamlines the way content or paperwork is processed, develop reports that show the speed with which content goes through the workflow, the number of problems that are solved, and the number of times the system is used. These reports serve as a constant reminder to senior leadership of why they originally invested in the CMS and why they should continue their investment. We worked on a large CMS implementation for a major government agency. Early on, we developed reports that showed the amount of content captured and what people were doing with that content. We shared these reports on a quarterly basis and continued to look for other value the CMS could bring to the agency. The project received funding for over 7 consecutive years, and each year the project team identified new things the tool could do. This type of long-term success only happened because leadership could see on a regular basis the value that their CMS was bringing to the organization.

6.2.4 Enhance

The Enhance phase of the content lifecycle is about adding descriptive information to improve the findability and usability of content stored in the CMS. While some CMS systems offer this functionality, it is common to integrate with other tools like a Taxonomy Management System or a text analytics tool to provide these features. Even though these features are often provided through other systems, they need to be considered as part of any enterprise-level CMS deployment. The key features that should be considered as part of the enhance phase of the content management lifecycle are:

*   Metadata
*   Text Analytics
*   Auto-tagging, and
*   Auto-categorization

Metadata is descriptive information used to describe or provide additional information about a piece of content. Metadata typically falls into one of six categories of purpose:

*   Identifying: Metadata used to find or work with the individual pieces of content within the CMS. Examples of identifying metadata include a unique ID or the name of the piece of content.
*   Findability: Metadata used to improve the findability of content, typically in a search engine. Findability metadata is typically used to categorize content so that the enterprise search engine can provide facets to filter search results for users. Examples include things like topic, country, department, or an abstract describing the content.
*   Presentation: Web content management systems and other systems that publish information to a defined location or audience frequently need metadata to identify where the content is supposed to appear or who is supposed to see it. Examples of presentation metadata include location/page, audience, and image sizes.
*   Management/Governance: Information captured about the piece of content that helps with workflows, content reporting, and archiving. Examples of governance metadata include the date of last update, project number, owner, document type, approver, and appropriate workflow.
*   Records Management: Metadata used to apply and control records management policies, typically found in Document Management and Records Management

systems. Examples of records management metadata include trigger date, record type, and disposition schedule.

• Access Control: Often called entitlement information, this metadata is used to determine who has the rights to see or update content in the CMS. Access controls are typically managed through groups but can also be handled by attributes about people and the content they can see. Examples of access control metadata include groups, department, and visibility.

Most content management systems allow for the capture and retention of metadata along with content. This is typically handled through content types. More advanced content management systems allow for the definition of content types so that each organization can define the metadata that works best for them. Some purpose-built solutions have pre-built content types that are not as flexible. This is a consideration when selecting the CMS you will be working with as part of your KM implementation.

Text Analytics or entity extraction involves libraries or tools that read content and identify people, places, and things from the text of the content. It is a common feature that is supported through a wide number of open-source products and libraries, but not often included as part of a CMS. We introduce it in this section because it is frequently part of a CMS implementation. Text Analytics is described in greater detail as a stand-alone capability in later chapters.

Most text analytics tools rely on sentence structure as a way to identify people, places, and things. These libraries parse a sentence into subject, predicate, and object and pull out the subjects and objects as entities. This approach can be very effective but is very language dependent. If you are dealing with a lot of multilingual content, you should expect a great deal of additional complexity in your implementation.

Once the content in the CMS has been read by the text analytics engine, each piece of content will have metadata about the people, places, and things that were described in the content. These entities can then be used as a way to establish relationships between content or important topics. This feature is most often used for use cases where:

• There is lots of unknown, heterogeneous content.
• The content is being used for research purposes.
• People, places, and things can be mapped to existing entities for greater context.

Organizations that have lots of rich content that is not well known and are looking to do research or other analysis are good candidates for text analytics. Organizations with knowledge of what is in their content or how they plan to use it are best served through an auto-tagging solution that can tag content against a preset taxonomy.

Auto-tagging is another feature that automates metadata creation similar to Text Analytics. The main difference is that auto-tagging tools attempt to match content to a predetermined set of tags as opposed to identifying people, places, and things. Auto-tagging is most frequently used alongside taxonomies to associate the taxonomic terms with the content in the CMS. Organizations that have spent time developing a user-centric taxonomy to improve findability and enable faceted search often look for auto-tagging solutions so that they can scale their processes to tag hundreds of thousands of pieces of content in a way that could never be accomplished manually.

Auto-tagging is a powerful tool and something we recommend to nearly every organization that is developing taxonomies to improve the findability of their information. It is important, however, to set proper expectations when implementing an auto-tagging system. Two of the most common mistakes we see are relying on auto-tagging for the wrong types of tags and assuming auto-tagging works flawlessly out of the box.

Auto-tagging can be very successful when the tags that need to be assigned naturally occur within the text of the content. Tags based on topical information or industry information can often be automated through an auto-tagging tool. Tags based on information that does not naturally occur within the content, such as type or department, are less likely to be successfully automated through auto-tagging solutions. For example, the terms policy, procedure, and project document are not likely to exist within content of those types. As a result, the auto-tagging tool will be unable to find the term and tag the content. Those same procedures and policies might be about things like sick leave or travel, with those terms used regularly within the document. These topical tags will be much more easily automated through the auto-tagging tool. Organizations looking to automate the tagging of those other non-topical taxonomies will need to find other ways to automate the process.

The other mistake we often see from organizations new to automated tagging tools is the assumption that they work perfectly immediately. Each use case and each corpus of content is different. The tools cannot anticipate these needs. When implementing an auto-tagging solution, it is good to set aside 2–3 weeks with an expert in the tool to help tune the system so that tagging is accurate. Well-tuned auto-tagging solutions can reach over 95% success rate in many environments.

The tuning process works much like the tuning of a search engine. Content is run through the system and automatically tagged. Subject matter experts then look at subsets of the content to see how accurate the tagging was. When tags are incorrectly applied, an expert can look at the content to see why the tag was incorrectly applied. Frequently the problem can be solved by putting a higher weight to the title of the content or terms found in the beginning as opposed to later on. One other common solution is to create synonyms in your tagging solution when content uses another term that is related to the term that you are trying to tag the document with. The most advanced auto-tagging tools now also offer machine learning algorithms that use concepts like co-occurrence to improve the tagging methodology. Co-occurrence is when two terms frequently appear together. For example, internal documents within a company may include the terms Finance and Accounting together often. Auto-tagging tools will recognize that these terms are related in some fashion because of how often they are found together. When this is the case, the tagging tool begins to understand that these terms are related and can tag content similarly when one or both terms appear.

Auto-tagging is a powerful tool that allows organizations to implement taxonomies and scale to handle hundreds of thousands of pieces of content in a way that could never be done manually. It is worth considering whenever you are planning to manage large amounts of content and make it findable, a common KM requirement.

Auto-categorization is another common method for tagging or classifying content in a CMS. Auto-categorization uses machine learning to categorize content based on the way that other similar content was tagged before. Since auto-categorization is based on machine learning and repetition, it is typically used to sort content into larger buckets of information. This is because it is only useful if the patterns are developed through the categorization of lots of content. If there are too many categories or too little content, accuracy will suffer because there will not be enough content examples for the tool to learn the proper categorizations.

The most common use case we see for auto-categorization is with support departments that receive many requests that need to be acted on in different ways depending on their purpose or topic. In these situations, requests are typically captured in the CMS system using a web page or integration with the product that receives requests. The CMS then runs them through an auto-categorization tool to categorize the request. Depending on the category, different workflows are initiated. Each category may require sending the content to a different person or department and may also require different approval or processing workflows. This is a great use case for auto-categorization because it:

- Shows immediate value to the business.
- Allows for processing a large number of requests across a small number of categories, and.
- Provides a feedback loop for misclassified content.

The nice thing about this approach is that organizations can quickly see its value and can correct things as part of their normal workflow.

Enhancing content is a critical tool in allowing CMS platforms to scale while also showing real value to end users. Very few CMS systems offer these capabilities out of the box, so organizations looking to get full value out of their CMS will need to consider how to add these features either through custom development using established code libraries, third-party tools, or integration of components available in the leading cloud platforms.

6.2.5 Find

An often overlooked area in CMS selection and implementation is findability of content within the CMS. Early on, CMS tools supported very little managed content available to only a small set of administrators. As a result, the original tools were not designed to make it easy for multiple people to manage and find hundreds or thousands of pieces of content. Search and other navigation tools available within the CMS administrative interface are critical features to make the CMS usable for content administrators. The importance of these features is often overlooked when purchasing a CMS because the demos have very little content, which masks the findability problem.

We worked with a large ecommerce site that was managing all of their information in a web CMS. This site grew over time and when we started working with them, they had over 500,000 pieces of content managed within the system. If a person noticed a problem with a page or piece of content on the site, they would report it to the content managers. Because the CMS was not well designed for findability, it could take as long as two days to "find" the content so that an update could be made. This is an extreme case, but one that should be considered when organizations are selecting and implementing an enterprise CMS. There are three methods of findability that each CMS should ideally offer:

- Faceted search
- Navigation (Folders), and
- Metadata

Faceted Search is the quickest and easiest way for content authors to find the content they need. The search experience within your CMS should have many of the same features that your end users see on the intranet or whatever search engine the content in the CMS is published to. At a minimum, the following features should be included in the CMS's administrative search:

- Full-text search
- Faceting
- Synonyms
- Relevancy tuning, and
- Custom result types

Of this list, full-text search and faceting are two of the most critical. Most modern CMS systems use an open-source search engine to power their internal search. The most common solutions are Lucene and Solr. When looking at the CMS, ask how search is implemented. If it is just a database query, you will not have true full-text search capabilities. The problem with this is documents or attachments will not be indexed with search. As a result, your administrators will be able to search for documents by their title but not their contents.

Faceting is another critical component of the search experience. Facets should include the standard ones that are naturally available across all content in the CMS, such as content type, author, and create date. Most CMS solutions will offer this. The best CMS solutions will provide the ability to use metadata fields from your content type as part of the facets as well. These fields are an important way to improve the findability of content because they were specifically selected for that purpose when the content type was configured. Also, they allow for a greater level of granularity when searching across large amounts of content. The best way to make this understandable is through example. We helped implement an enterprise CMS tool that managed hundreds of thousands of contracts. It was common to receive as many as 10,000 contracts during the course of a week. These contracts were fed from another system so for the purpose of the CMS, the author of the contract was the system that sent the contracts over. In this example, every single contract has the same content type and same author. The dates are different, but given the number of contracts received every week, a filter based on the creation date would still bring up thousands of contracts. The content types also had department (the owner of the contract) and location (where the contract was signed). Together, these two fields made it much easier for the content administrators to find the contract they needed.

The other features in this list are described in greater detail in Chap. 9 of this book.

An effective search is critical to allow scalability of any enterprise-level CMS solution. The easiest way for content managers to find what you are looking for is classic search. A well-designed full-text search will simplify and allow content managers and authors to quickly find and manage the content they are working with.

Content managers need a way to find content that is not search based. The most common method for storing and finding content is through folders which provide a method of *navigation* to content within the CMS. Most CMS products provide a user managed folder structure similar to a user's hard drive for storing content. A common mistake I see on most large CMS implementations is that there is not enough thought put into the folder structure and how it is governed going forward.

The folder structure typically also includes security or information access permissions, often called ACLs or access control lists. It is important to understand this as it impacts the way in which the folder structure is designed. A well-designed folder hierarchy restricts access to content for specific groups of people at the highest level. Lower levels within the folder hierarchy will then align with groups of people or processes so that similar content is stored in similar locations to make managing content simpler. One of the most important considerations in creating a folder hierarchy is to make sure that the reason behind the structure is intuitively obvious to a wide group of users so that everyone understands where content exists.

Faceted search only works with a well-designed *taxonomy*. Any full-featured CMS will have a separate place to store managed lists (i.e., taxonomies) and a way to associate these taxonomies with content through the use of standard content types. The best CMS solutions also allow managers to navigate to content through the use of these taxonomies. Rather than store the content in a preset list of folders, the content can be accessed by selecting one or more items from a taxonomy to filter down a list of content items. The advantage of this approach is that content can be accessed in multiple ways and users are not limited to a folder structure that may or may not make sense to the person looking for the content. One of the best examples of this is the way that Microsoft SharePoint allows users to order and access content using metadata in their document libraries. This paradigm is one that we will see more and more as CMS tools offer a way to improve information management at scale.

6.2.6 Connect

Once this information is captured and managed in the CMS, it needs to be shared with others. We categorize the features related to sharing the information into publish (for pushing information out of people) and connecting (for finding ways to connect people to information, information to information, and information to people). The features described in this section all support the publishing and connecting of information. Depending on the type of CMS you are implementing, one or more of these features should be included in your evaluations and implementation plans:

- Content publishing
- Related content
- Content packages

Content publishing is the process of assembling and pushing content from within the CMS to an external location. Multi-channel publishing is the ability to render that content in different formats, so it can be used on multiple devices. Common examples of multi-channel publishing formats include web, mobile, print, and e-mail. Web, enterprise, and headless CMS solutions typically offer publishing capabilities as well as content rendering options. Publishing is generally treated as an automated workflow where a version of the content is copied to a new location and rendered in one or more formats. The publishing and rendering process requires custom development to transform the content from the internal format (typically XML or JSON) to the format that you need for your website, e-mail, or print version. That transformation process is called content rendering and can be very complex. If you are planning to implement any complex rendering logic other than simple web page publishing, it is important to work with an expert who is familiar with the challenges of multi-channel publishing. Standards like DITA (Darwin Information Typing Architecture) make this process easier and should be prioritized for any multi-channel publishing projects.

The best knowledge management solutions relate information assets so that users find the information they are looking for along with any other applicable information. Frequently, users will search for a document to answer their question and find that, while the document answers the question, there are also related documents that are needed as well. For example, the employee handbook might explain the expense policy, but the expense report form and instructions around how to handle travel expenses are found in separate documents. A CMS that allows content authors to define the relationship between content items helps ensure that when a user finds one of these documents, the other documents are referred to, so the user has a more complete guidance on the task he or she is trying to complete.

Relating content can be a complex exercise as there are a number of different ways to implement this in practice. Content can be related based on similar metadata values, directly to one or more other documents, or as a package (described next). In this example, we are talking about a situation where one document is given a direct relationship to one or more additional documents. This is a feature that is not always offered out of the box in many CMS solutions. As such, it is important to ask the vendor to demonstrate how this is handled. When evaluating this functionality in a CMS, find out how easy it is to "find" the related content as well as what happens when one of the related pieces of content is deleted or unpublished so that it is no longer available to users. These two scenarios trip up a lot of CMS solutions that have less mature content relation capabilities.

Another common form of related content is what we call content packages. Content packages are collections of content that are always grouped together as a single package. Two great examples of content packages are:

- Courses built on multiple pieces of content
- Conference or product marketing literature that is shared collectively

With the exception of purpose-built solutions like learning management systems and marketing products, packages are typically something that requires custom development. The most common way we have seen these implemented is to create a "package" content type that points to other content items that are included in the package. This approach creates a parent content item that ties together the individual content items that should be included in the package. When implementing an enterprise CMS, identify use cases where content packages are useful, and build for those. A common mistake that we have seen our clients make is assume everything can be packaged. The result is a very generic content type that is seen as confusing and rarely used. When purpose-built content packages are implemented both in the CMS and in the applications that display them, packages become a critical component of how certain types of information are delivered to users.

6.3   Business Problems Addressed

Content management systems, along with search engines, are typically the core technical component for any knowledge management implementation. At a high level, content management systems:

- Provide a well-defined location to capture, store, and manage unstructured content.
- Provide a purposeful way to share information.
- Enhance content so that it is more usable and findable.
- Assemble/personalize content so that people see the information they need.

Some specific use cases that we often see are spelled out in Table 6.1 by type of CMS.

Table 6.1 Specific use cases for Content Management Systems organized by type

Use Case	Description	Benefit
Web Content Management Systems		
Company Intranet	Allows for decentralized content management by providing a tool for non-technical users to author and publish content about information in which they have expertise.	Employees have a reliable place to get the information they need to do their job. They are more efficient, comply with company requirements, and take advantage of the knowledge of others.
Contact Center Knowledge Base	Contact centers use content management systems to manage and curate content in their knowledge bases, so staff are able to quickly find answers to common questions.	Call time is decreased because employees are able to find the information they need to respond to customer questions quickly. New contact center employees become efficient more quickly because they have a reliable source of real-time information to respond to questions. Product satisfaction increases because customers get quick and accurate answers to their questions.
Information Portal	Large organizations have information portals driven by web content management systems that allow knowledge workers to share relevant information with one another and find answers to questions specific to their job role in the organization.	New employees onboard and add value sooner. Customers receive the wisdom of the organization and not the knowledge of a single person Highly regulated or litigious industries protect against fines and lawsuits by making the right answers and proper processes accessible to their staff.
Document Management Systems		
Contract Management	Many of our clients have used document management systems to store, protect, and manage all of their contracts in a secure and reliable location.	Contract processes are reinforced through formal workflows that ensure compliance with company regulations. Contracts are stored in a location where only the right people can see them, and they can be referred to as needed to properly manage the relationship.

(continued)

Table 6.1 (continued)

Records Management	Federal agencies and organizations have a records management mandate to retain records for a specific period of time and then delete or archive them according to a set schedule (records retention policy). Document management systems allow for the capture, classification, and automation of these retention policies for these organizations.	Organizations remain compliant with federal and industry regulations in order to avoid large fines or lawsuits. The management of this process is automated to save time and money and provide an audit trail in case the organization is required to prove compliance.
Workflows	Formal document creation and management processes can be automated and tracked using the workflow capabilities in enterprise document management systems. The workflow process not only ensures compliance with a process, but it also provides reporting so that steps in the process can be measured so that bottlenecks can be easily identified and addressed.	Workflows ensure compliance with a process to help minimize risk to an organization and to make sure that employees understand how to efficiently complete a task. Workflow dashboards give management insight into the status of key processes and provide insight into where bottlenecks exist that could speed up or lower the cost of the process.
Digital Asset Management Systems		
Image Repository	Marketing and other areas within an organization need a single, reliable place to download and use approved images. Digital asset management (DAM) is a system that is perfect for this purpose. It is designed to handle images, so it is easier to find and manage them. DAM systems also have digital rights management capabilities to ensure the images are approved and legal to use.	DAM systems encourage image re-use and brand compliance to improve the way organizations communicate with their customers and partners. DAM systems also provide digital rights management to make sure that people only use approved images and to minimize the overall cost of image use across the enterprise.
Business Solutions		
Customer Relationship Management (CRM)	Many CRM tools have content stores that include things like product offers, forms signed by customers, and brochures that have been shared with customers. While these tools lack advanced content management capabilities, they offer enough features to capture the interactions with customers to improve the overall customer experience.	Customer information (including agreements and key communications) is stored in a single location so that customers do not feel as if they have to restart a conversation with each new person they speak with. Organizations have a trail of interactions with a customer in case there are legal or other contractual issues that arise.

(continued)

Table 6.1 (continued)

Contract Management Systems	Contract management systems not only capture contracts and interactions with customers, many of them also allow the easy assembly of contracts using approved terms and conditions to ensure contracts follow corporate standards.	Contract management systems allow organizations that produce a high number of similar legal agreements to have greater control over the contracts they produce while delegating the creation of contracts to a wider group of people. These systems also give organizations a way to capture and manage contracts so that they can more reliably handle renewals and contract expiration. This leads to a better customer experience, risk management, and increased revenue.
Marketing Systems	Marketing technology (Martech) companies have invested heavily into products that use AI to capture and manage marketing materials, so the right information can be provided to the right clients. Organizations with a large number of products or a complex set of offerings can get great value from these tools that not only capture and manage marketing literature but also recommend the right information to sales and marketing people.	Marketing systems offer a set of tools that make it easier for marketing and sales professionals to find the latest and most targeted material to share. This can lead to increased uplift on sales and higher revenue overall.
Headless CMS		
Multi-channel Marketing	Headless CMS tools are ideal for publishing content to multiple platforms such as web, e-mail, print, mobile, and other digital platforms (we once did one for hotel billboards). These tools allow organizations to create messaging in a single location that can be pushed out to any number of different products.	Organizations save time and money by producing content once and re-using it on all of the platforms that their employees, partners, and customers use. Organizations ensure consistent messaging by developing a single message and pushing it out to all the tools they use to communicate with their employees.
Chatbots/AI	Organizations are enamored with the AI-based interactions people have with tools like Siri and Amazon Echo. This type of interaction cannot work in a document-centric world that most	Organizations have content that supports quick answers rather than asking employees to read long, complicated documents; this makes the employees more efficient and productive.

(continued)

Table 6.1 (continued)

	internal departments work with. Asking a question about a policy brings back the entire company handbook. It is important to chunk content into smaller parts, so chatbots and other similar tools can provide answers and not links to documents. This type of functionality is called componentized content management and it is found in many headless CMS tools.	Organizations can share information with partners and clients using advanced technology that improves the overall customer experience.
Production of Manuals	Manufacturing organizations often reuse parts across many of their products. Headless CMS tools allow support organizations to create a section of a manual once and reuse it as the final manuals are assembled from those parts and shared with the appropriate parties.	Manuals can be produced with much less work and are more reliable as duplicative content only needs to be updated in one place. Componentized manuals can be shared in search and other cutting-edge tools, so customers can find the answer to their questions as opposed to being pointed to a large, complex document.

Reference

Gamble P, Blackwell J (2001) Knowledge management. Kogan Page, London

Collaboration Suites

7

The purpose of a collaboration system is to improve the way people work together towards a single purpose. This includes everything from improving communication to simplifying/standardizing processes, to improving joint document creation. As expected from this broad definition, there is a wide range of products that proclaim themselves to be "collaboration" tools. The most important thing to understand when looking for technology platforms to enhance collaboration is that there is no single product that will solve all of your collaboration issues. The best way to select the right technology to improve collaboration within your company is to focus on the purpose of what your teams are trying to accomplish. When looking at collaboration tools, start by dividing your collaboration needs into these four areas:

- Breaking down silos (i.e., cross department and team collaboration)
- Improved processes
- Better document creation
- Enhanced teamwork

Once the type of problems that can be addressed are understood, the next step is to identify one or more specific collaboration problems that need to be solved. Examples include the creation of an annual document or processing of legal documents. Another common example is improved project and team collaboration. Collaboration implementations work best when you solve specific problems and then roll the solution out to other departments or business groups within the organization. There are two reasons for taking this approach. First, it is a great way to show demonstrable value up front. Second, it ensures that the collaboration suite fits in with the normal processes that users follow.

J. Hilger, Z. Wahl, *Making Knowledge Management Clickable*,
https://doi.org/10.1007/978-3-030-92385-3_7

7.1   Common Platforms

The most common collaboration platforms in use today are all very different in nature and purpose. The industry leaders include:

- Microsoft O365
- Google Workspace
- Slack

Microsoft and Google both offer a suite of online products to help with all aspects of the digital desktop. They offer tools to collaboratively author, store, and share documents, spreadsheets, and presentations.

Microsoft O365 includes all of the Microsoft productivity applications (Word, Excel, PowerPoint, etc.) as well as an upgraded, online version of SharePoint so that employees can share and work on documents together. It also includes a version of Yammer that allows for threaded discussions across the organization. O365 is a great option for organizations that are already committed and trained on Microsoft products. The interface is familiar, and employees are able to work with the products and file formats that they have already been using. While Microsoft is continuously improving the interface and features of O365, it still often shows its roots as a desktop application. The search in all areas is lacking, and much of the system is very proprietary. If your organization is ready to go all in with Microsoft, then O365 is a fantastic answer. As with early versions of SharePoint, it is critical to develop a good information architecture and proper governance so that the solution does not get out of control. O365, and particularly the more collaborative areas of the tool, can easily get out of hand if they are not well managed.

Google Workspace is similar in purpose to Microsoft O365 (taking over the digital desktop), but the implementation is very different. Like O365, Google offers a suite of productivity applications:

- Docs (similar to Word)
- Spreadsheets (similar to Excel)
- Presentations (similar to PowerPoint)

It also offers Hangouts (chat), Meet (video conferencing), Drive (for sharing documents), and groups for threaded discussions. Based on high-level features, both options allow for very similar functionality for end users. The implementation, however, is very different. Google is very search-centric and typically organizes things by tags instead of folders. Google Drive gives the appearance of folders, but the implementation is more like personalized tags than the more rigid folder implementation that we are used to on our desktops. In fact, folders can be shared, and users are able to create their own hierarchical structure independent of what others are doing for the same folder structure. The productivity applications are also more web-centric as opposed to Microsoft's desktop publishing focus. The focus of these tools is on synchronous collaboration and openness with other documents. Google

Workspace also offers excellent search, which makes it generally easy to find the documents or information your users need. The biggest problems with Google Workspace are the fact that it is different (people are used to desktops and Microsoft products), and it can be a closed ecosystem as well. While Google has made it easy for a lot of third-party add-ons, it is not easy to work with Google outside of the Google workspace. For example, enterprise search engines cannot easily index the content in Google, and the security models offered by Google remain very decentralized and difficult to administer. Having said that, Google is an excellent option for organizations looking for more cutting-edge ways to operate that are not wedded to the Microsoft model.

The other leading collaboration product, Slack, is very different from what Microsoft and Google are offering. At first glance, Slack is a feature-rich threaded discussion tool like Yammer and Google Groups. As you dive deeper into it, however, Slack is much more: it is attempting to change the way organizations work and collaborate. Slack is a very open platform that integrates with almost any modern product. Slack does not replace Google Workspace or Microsoft O365, but it connects with both products to enhance how they work. For example, a Slack channel can link to an O365 document and develop a discussion around that document. In addition, Slack can provide direct access to the document and alert people when changes are made. In this example, Slack offers a new paradigm around working with documents that offers context that would not be available elsewhere. It is very developer friendly and has an open set of APIs that allow for almost any action. One organization we worked with used it as a way to release new versions of software. A simple release command in the right channel of Slack would initiate the release process and create an audit trail of all activities. These features make Slack a new and interesting paradigm that cutting-edge and more technical organizations may find value in.

In addition to these more general collaboration solutions, there are also a number of purpose-built collaboration solutions that solve specific challenges. For example, there are a number of tools for collaborating on project delivery. Four of the most common tools in this space include:

- Trello
- Asana
- Basecamp
- Jira

These tools are very useful for project teams breaking down work into definable tasks and collaborating on the project activities. Trello provides a visual representation of lists and tasks that can have dialogs and attachments within each task. It excels at managing small, agile projects. Asana is a modern project management tool that manages everything from roadmaps to individual projects and the tasks within them. It is a strong option for organizations looking to centralize the management of multiple related projects. Basecamp is a barebones project management environment with a focus on simplicity for organizations looking for simple, easy-to-use solutions. Finally, Jira is a ticketing tool that has been adapted so that it can also be used for large, complex, agile projects. It has become one of the most commonly used project management tools and has strong dashboard and reporting capabilities.

Projects are a key part of any large KM initiative. These project-based collaboration tools should be considered as information repositories that can be used to collect project data while projects are implemented. Creating consistency in the way that projects are structured allows for greater cross-project collaboration and can be a great source of knowledge across the enterprise.

7.2   Features and Functions

While there are many types of collaboration platforms on the market, the features that they offer are often similar. The most common and important features in these products include:

- Document creation
- File sharing/security
- Content organization
- Discussion threads
- Task management
- Search
- Integration

Most organizations remain document-centric in the way that they create, capture, and share information. As such, the ability to create documents quickly and collaboratively is a critical feature to encourage the creation of explicit knowledge across the enterprise. The best collaboration solutions offer collaborative document creation, where one or more people can author a document concurrently. They can make changes at the same time without having to check in or check out documents, and these changes appear immediately for the other authors. This is the new standard for document creation and should be expected from any collaboration solution that your organization is working with.

Once these documents are created, it is important that they can be made visible to others, both internal and external to the organization. Since most leading collaboration suites offer SAAS offerings, they are able to offer sharing that can be extended to employees, partners, and customers as needed. Depending on the use case for collaboration, the ability to share files both internally and externally is a critical feature. When selecting a collaboration platform that allows for file sharing, it is important to understand how the sharing is done and, more importantly, how permissions are managed both centrally and decentrally. The application needs to have strong central controls over sharing to make sure that important documents are not accidentally or maliciously shared where they should not be. At the same time, users need the ability to easily share documents with their peers. If the security controls are too locked up, the system will be seen as problematic, and users will create content outside of the tool so that they can more easily share it. This is one of the most important areas to review when evaluating collaboration platforms. When selecting and implementing a new collaborative platform, work closely with members of IT to make sure that the security model meets the needs of IT and of users.

One key aspect of making content findable is having one or more ways to organize the content so that similar content is together and has context. The most common ways to do this are through folders or metadata. The folder paradigm for organizing information is the oldest and most common method. Folders work well when there is a well-defined and controlled structure in place for how and when folders are created. This typically involves defining a top-level folder structure (that is centrally controlled) and rules for how and where new folders are added by the collaborators. The newer, more modern method of organizing information is through metadata or tags. Each piece of content is tagged with one or more pieces of metadata, and users are able to navigate to content through the metadata fields. The advantage of this approach is that content can have more than one tag on it, and users have greater control over how they get to the content. For example, a document might be about vacation policies and sick leave. In the metadata approach, the document could exist under both tags. In the folder paradigm, the document would have to be placed in one or the other location. Both approaches can work, so review your organization, and determine which one makes the most sense for your users.

Discussion threads have matured greatly over the years. Originally, these threads were for comments on a web page or document. They allowed for text and maybe some images. Now, the threaded discussions drive some of the most cutting-edge collaboration tools on the market. Slack, for example, sees discussions as the basis of all collaboration. Threads, or channels, look more like Facebook and Twitter than comment boards on a web page. Collaborators are able to post links, documents, polls, and regular comments as a way to capture and share information with one another. These newer tools use discussion as a way to turn tacit knowledge into explicit knowledge without stovepiping the information in documents. It also allows organizations to provide contextual information in a semi-structured format that does not limit user interaction. These advanced discussion threads are critical in any collaboration platform or suite that organizations are implementing. It offers one of the best ways to support remote work and is the kind of interaction that the youngest generation of workers is accustomed to.

Effective collaboration involves more than discussions and collaboration around documents. Often collaborators are working on a series of tasks that need to be completed for a common goal. In these cases, tracking and sharing the tasks are as important as the management of documents or files. The best collaboration tools offer a way to create and share tasks with one another. In addition, users can collaborate around tasks in the same way they collaborate around documents. They can attach documents or links. They can have threaded discussions and also organize the tasks in a way that better aligns with the projects. If your organization is using collaboration tools to improve the way people work together, task management capabilities are a critical feature to be considered.

One of the greatest values of collaboration tools from a KM perspective is that these tools provide a natural way to move tacit knowledge to explicit knowledge. Activities like document creation, threaded discussions, and sharing and collaborating on tasks enable the documentation of information so that others within an organization can make use of this information. The key to creating this value is search. Much of this information is created in an unstructured fashion. It exists and is aligned with the task that people are working on. Search allows employees to find this information without having to know the project or document that the person was working on. We talk a lot about search in a later section of this book. The search offered by the collaboration tool should have at a minimum the following features:

- Full text search—So that any text in any element of the collaboration system can be found.
- Faceting—So that users can filter their results based on things like owner, division, and project.
- Result types—Different search results for different types of information.

A strong internal search makes the information that is being gathered usable for others and can really jump start a KM initiative. When selecting the collaboration platform, make sure that it has a high-functioning search so that you can get the best possible value from it.

In addition to the search embedded in the collaboration platform, it is important to look at how the information from the collaboration platform can be indexed for your enterprise search initiative. Many of the leading collaboration platforms do a wonderful job of searching for the information in the platform. Very few of them make the information available to other search engines so that organizations can create a single search that indexes content from multiple applications. As you are selecting a search engine for your enterprise search initiative, find out if there are any connectors that will index content from your collaboration platform. A collaboration platform that can support both its own search and external search engines provides the greatest value to the organization.

Collaboration typically involves working with more than one application. Ideally, a collaboration platform should have a number of different integration points that make it easy for the collaboration platform to receive tasks and information from other systems or send tasks and information to those systems. For example, a professional services firm would have a project platform that automatically creates a working space for the team once the project begins. This workspace is then where the project team collaborates and creates deliverables. This type of integration helps ensure that new project workspaces are spun up quickly and easily. It also creates a level of consistency with the way project workspaces are set up and how people work within them. This consistency makes it easier to mine information across projects so that employees can learn from the work of other project teams working on similar projects.

7.3   Business Problems Addressed

Collaboration systems provide a great way to capture information that allows organizations to learn from prior work experience and to work more efficiently. In addition, these systems can help standardize processes so that everyone in the organization is able to quickly deliver on their tasks at all levels of experience. Table 7.1 lists some common examples of how organizations are using collaboration platforms to improve business outcomes.

Table 7.1 Common use cases for collaboration platforms

Use Case	Description	Benefit
Collaborative Process Automation	Complex collaborative processes, such as the development of an agreement or creation of a proposal, can be streamlined through the use of a collaboration workspace. This is where all of the people involved can interact and share information digitally so that the work is better tracked, controlled, and completed in less time.	• These workspaces lead to faster turnaround time on complex collaborative projects with more user interaction. • Content created as part of the process is managed in a single location so that it is better secured. • Activities from the processes are captured and can be shared with others doing similar tasks to help streamline future initiatives. • Information is captured about why things were done so that questions about the decisions in the process can be answered after the fact in order to improve customer management and ensure compliance with the spirit of the output from the activity.
Organization-Wide Collaboration	Large organizations are typically divided into divisions and project teams. While this structure allows people to focus on what they are good at, it creates silos of information that can be difficult to break down. Collaboration platforms support sharing of information through things like online communities of practice. These tools allow people to more easily share information from their organizational units or project teams with others in the organization.	• Organizations with strong communities of practice are better able to innovate because new ideas can be shared and expanded upon more easily. • Organizations that offer better ways to collaborate create a sense of belonging that improves employee happiness and leads to better employee retention. • Organizations with strong cross-functional collaboration are more easily able to identify and resolve problems that could affect customer satisfaction.

(continued)

Table 7.1 (continued)

Project Management	One of the most common uses for collaboration platforms is classic project management. There is now a suite of collaboration tools whose sole purpose is to support project team planning, collaboration, and delivery.	• Project workspaces help improve the quality and speed of project delivery by ensuring a common understanding of project goals so that the products better meet everyone's expectations. • Projects that use collaboration workspaces are more compliant with company standards because the rules and processes are integrated into the project workflow. • Projects are more visible so that business leaders have a better understanding of when these projects will be delivered so that they can make better decisions around resources to evangelize or support the new products.

While collaboration systems seem general in nature, they offer great value when the implementation is tied to specific business use cases such as the ones described above. When this is done correctly, organizations can quickly gauge the value of the tool and get greater adoption.

Learning Management Systems

8

Most people think of content management systems, collaboration suites, knowledge bases, portals, and enterprise search tools when thinking about the systems that make up a KM initiative. Learning management systems (LMS) is another equally important tool in the creation and dissemination of information so that the people in the organization have the knowledge to contribute to the mission more effectively. Knowledge is not always passed from person to person. Structured and semi-structured training are important ways to share knowledge with people across the organization. The importance of self-paced learning and learning at the point of need has grown as technology has improved and employees' expectations for access to information have changed. Employees now expect short, interactive learning similar to what they can get on YouTube at the point of need.

In many ways, learning management systems are similar to content management systems. They capture, store, and manage content. LMSs manage course content as opposed to documents or web pages, but the features for capturing and managing content are very much the same. The biggest difference has to do with the way the LMS tracks and manages the use of these courses. A full-featured LMS will track the courses users take, the courses they need to take, and the results (assessments) from what they learned from these courses. These LMS platforms identify the capabilities required to be effective in a role, assign people to roles, and map courses to those capabilities. The result is a performance management solution that allows organizations to create individual learning plans based on the capabilities required for a role and the courses needed to develop those capabilities. When properly implemented, these LMS tools allow organizations to measure the knowledge that employees have against what is needed to do their job. They also provide a visible roadmap for employees of what they need to know in order to move to a new position within the organization.

8.1   Common Platforms

Learning management systems can be grouped into three general categories:

- Open source
- Learning management only
- Full-featured performance management solutions

With the rise of massive open online courses (MOOCs), a number of open-source learning management platforms were created. These tools are free and open source so that they can be customized, but they often lack some of the advanced corporate features of the paid tools. Moodle is the leading open-source LMS and brands itself as "the world's most popular learning management system" (Moodle 2021). Moodle allows for courses to be created and managed within the tool, and it uses themes so that employees can have a customized and branded experience within the tool. Users can take courses and be assessed on what they learn from the course. The standard Moodle experience is very much like that of a university course that employees can enroll in. Features like certification or performance management need to be handled through plug-ins or integrations with other systems.

There are also a number of reasonably priced commercial options available that allow for the creation, management, and delivery of courses. Two of the leading solutions in this space are Docebo and Adobe Captivate.

8.2   Features and Functions

The common features in these learning management systems can be divided into three areas:

- Learning material authoring and management
- Course usage
- Performance management

The LMS is a highly custom content management system designed to support the authoring, management, and tracking of learning materials. Some of the most important features for the creation and management of these important assets include:

- SCORM compliance
- Mobile support
- Metadata management
- Integrated content development tools
- Support for video

Sharable Content Object Reference Model (SCORM) is a set of technical standards in the e-learning community that makes learning content portable to other systems. SCORM has three primary purposes. First, it describes the way that content is structured so that it can be packaged and easily moved from system to system. Second, it offers a structure that explains how the content should be run and how it will communicate with the LMS. This means that any SCORM-compliant content can be run on any SCORM-compliant LMS. Finally, it supports the navigation between content within a course. The course sections are divided in a consistent fashion so that users can move from one section of the course to another in a simple, repeatable fashion across any compatible LMS platform. SCORM enables the componentized course management that leading learning organizations use. Courses can be developed in chunks and then automatically assembled using the SCORM framework to allow for greater reuse of course content and more personalized courses that match learners' specific needs.

We are all accustomed to looking up information on our mobile phones. In KM, we frequently talk about information at the point of need. That point of need may not be while your learners are sitting at their desks. As a result, mobile course support has become critical in every learning initiative. As your organization evaluates LMS tools, make sure that they truly support mobile courses. That includes the creation of courses that work on mobile as well as the availability of courses in a mobile environment that can easily be accessed through the phone.

One area that many LMS tools frequently fall short in is metadata management. Like any content management system, the content is best managed when it has a custom set of metadata attached to it. Metadata management is more than the ability to add tags to a piece of content; a true metadata solution will allow administrators to define one or more fields (metadata elements) that are associated with different types of learning content. For example, one type of content could be a web-based course. The second type of content would be a video or PowerPoint presentation. The metadata to describe these different types of content is likely very different. The video would include the length of the video along with the size of the video. The online course would have metadata describing the length of time it takes to complete and the platforms that are supported. This metadata can then be used to group related content into courses or learning journeys. It can also be used to find duplicate content or simply find all of the content of a specific type or topic. As you evaluate LMS tools, ask them to show you the metadata on different types of learning content. Ask the vendor to show how to add a new metadata element or a new metadata structure for a brand-new type of learning content. If the solution cannot do this, your ability to manage learning content as your needs scale will be severely limited.

Another key area for a LMS is the integrated content development capabilities. An LMS that allows learning content authors to develop content within the system makes it easier to decentralize the creation of learning assets. With some basic training more of your subject matter experts and learning content authors will be able to create courses in a repeatable way that they might not have been able to do before. Most of these authoring tools offer WYSIWYG editing and a set of components like navigation buttons, videos, questions, text, and images that make it so people with limited web knowledge are able to create courses. In addition, these courses typically have central styling so that all of the courses have a similar look and feel and branding that matches the company's branding. Developing courses through an integrated content development tool creates a level of consistency and professionalism that makes learning initiatives more successful and allows for more content to be created by a larger group of experts.

YouTube has changed the way people expect to learn. We all expect to learn new information by looking it up and watching a three-to-five-minute video that gives the appropriate answer. Employees have come to expect that same experience from their employers. It is important that your LMS offers support for managing and making videos available as training tools. There are two ways that this can be done. The tool can offer video management capabilities within it. While this approach meets the need, it is not the best way to support video learning. There are a lot of tools that are very good at managing videos from public sites like YouTube and Vimeo to enterprise tools like Brightcove and Kaltura. Rather than capture and store videos in your LMS, it makes more sense for the LMS to point to videos in other systems. The metadata and activity on the video can be managed within the LMS, but the videos can sit with the tools that best host and serve up videos. Videos will become a cornerstone of your training program. Make sure that any solution you select offers the best possible video management capabilities.

LMS platforms are not limited to support for the creation and management of course materials. These solutions also provide a way to manage and deliver these tools. Serving up courses, tracking the progress of courses and learning journeys, and reporting on the status of these activities are features that really make LMS systems unique and different from the content management systems described earlier in this chapter. Some of the most important features include:

- Personalized dashboards
- xAPI
- Social learning

LMS systems give individuals a way to manage their own learning while also providing metrics to management to understand where learning takes place and where there are learning gaps. Personalized dashboards should be designed to help both parties. Individual learners should have a dashboard that shows what courses they have taken, what still needs to be taken, and where they are on their own personal learning journey. Managers and leaders should be able to see that information for themselves as well as summary information allowing them to better understand what courses their people have taken, what courses have not been completed, and where there are learning or information gaps within their teams and organizations. Dashboards can be custom built, but a good LMS will offer enough features out of the box so that the organization can focus development efforts on other more important activities.

xAPI is a hot new technology in the learning field. xAPI is a standard that allows learning managers and learning systems to track course progress in a highly granular fashion. Organizations that use xAPI can find out not only which courses people take, but where they stopped and where they spent the most time in the course. In addition, xAPI is a standard that works across systems, so if another system supports xAPI then the results from the activities had with the other system can be captured in the LMS to provide a more complete picture of the activities that the learner undertook.

Finally, social learning is another hot and important capability in the learning field. Experts understand that people retain only a small amount of the information they learn from courses. As such, it is important to find ways to reinforce the learning from each course. Social sites that allow the course attendees to share their experiences and to continue to collaborate with one another offer a great way to reinforce learning concepts and to allow course participants to continue to grow and collaborate with one another on a topic of interest. When selecting an LMS find out what social learning they support. In most cases the social learning capabilities are pretty rudimentary. There are great open source or collaboration options that offer discussion threads and other strong social capabilities. These tools can be integrated with the LMS so that course attendees have a collaborative area for each course or topic that they are involved in.

Performance management is the next phase for LMS tools. These LMS tools integrate with HR systems and can quickly become one of the most important ways in which employee growth and development is managed across the organization. Performance management features include:

- Learning paths: responsive personalization
- Assessments
- Badging
- Integration with HR systems

Employees need more than just access to courses. Each employee should have a customized learning path that ensures they know what they are supposed to know for their current job as well as offering a path to plan for their future role in the organization. Personalized learning paths allow each employee to identify a series of courses that help them understand how to do their current job and allow them to plan for growth within the organization. Organizations that prioritize this type of learning have employees who know how to do their jobs and have a vision for where they are headed. These employees are more fulfilled in their jobs because they are successful and because they have a vision for where the company can take them. LMS tools that allow for more personalized learning paths offer a great deal more than just a tool for learning. They are a retention tool and a tool to make sure that organizations operate as efficiently as possible.

Performance management requires measurement to help understand what the employee learned from the course. Most often the measurement as to what a person has learned is handled through assessments. These assessments should be associated with one or more courses, and they should provide scores/feedback that is captured and associated with the learner's account. The assessment is a way to know what has been learned and then tie it back to the overall performance of the employee. If there is a pattern of employees passing assessments for courses associated with their jobs that are still not performing, there may be an issue with the course. If employees have passed an assessment for learning with regards to a new job, then this is an additional data point as to their readiness for the new position. Assessments are key to understanding if the LMS is making a true difference and they should be incorporated into any learning management plan.

Badging is another important way to measure employee progress around a learning topic. A badge should be thought of as demonstrated expertise in a specific topic area or capability. Badges typically require proficiency in more than one course, and they provide a way to measure improvement at a higher level. The awarding of badges should not be limited to course completion. Often badging includes things like participation in events or conferences. Many organizations also include management feedback in the awarding of badges. Because badges can be tied to proficiency in a topic or specific skill, badges can be used as a way to determine overall proficiency for a position. Badges differ from assessments because they measure capability and not just the learnings from a single course. A badge likely requires proven proficiency or learning from many related courses. Our clients have used badging to determine staffing for projects or shifts. They also use badging as a way to increase employee satisfaction as there is a sense of accomplishment for people who have achieved badges. As we measure knowledge of specific areas, badges can be a key driver in solutions like expert finders or planning for knowledge transfer as people leave the organization.

Finally, these performance management features work best when the LMS is integrated with the HR system that the organization uses. The HR system is typically the system of record for information about an employee. An LMS providing performance management services needs two-way communication with the HR system about the employee. The LMS needs to be aware of all employees as well as their role in the organization. The HR system needs to be made aware when an employee has completed a course and when they have earned badges. When these two systems are tightly integrated, leadership can have a full picture of what people know, what they should know, and the work they are ready to do. Linking badging with specific positions gives employees and managers a clear roadmap of what it takes to do each job and how to get there.

LMS platforms provide a way of sharing knowledge that is intentional. When employees' interactions with these systems are tracked and aligned with their roles and the organization is able to proactively manage employee growth and knowledge.

8.3 Business Problems Addressed

LMS systems were once thought of as a tool for capturing and sharing courses. These important tools now do much more than course management and sharing. Table 8.1 identifies examples of how LMS tools can solve key business problems.

Table 8.1 Examples of key business problems that can be solved by learning management system tools

Use Case	Description	Benefit
Employee/Partner Product Training Videos	The LMS provides quick videos to train employees and partners on your products and solutions so that they are enabled to sell them more quickly	• Salespeople and your partners are better able to communicate the value of your products to increase sales. • New salespeople and partners are brought up to speed much faster so that they are able to sell solutions much faster.
Performance Management	The LMS provides an established pathway for employees to learn and grow in their careers. This includes classes, assessments, and badges that align with specific job functions within the organization.	• Employee turnover is decreasing because employees have a visible pathway for how they can grow in their career. • Employees have the training to do their job properly because it is documented and measured through the LMS.
Employee Onboarding	New employees have a set of training videos and classes to help them better understand the mission of the organization and the requirements of their position.	• New employees get up to speed much faster so that they can contribute to the organization sooner. • Employees understand the policies and processes of the organization so that they are compliant with the requirements of their position.

Learning is a key part of knowledge management. Organizations that understand this relationship and build the implementation of or integration with an LMS into their KM plan will see great benefits.

Reference

Moodle (2021) The world's most customizable and trusted online learning solution. https://moodle.com. Accessed 28 Apr 2021

Enterprise Search

9

Search engines are one of the most critical tools in any Knowledge Management (KM) platform. A well-implemented enterprise search engine enables easy access to information and breaks down information silos. The premise behind a search engine is quite simple. It is a tool that reads content (text) from multiple sources, compiles it into a set of words and phrases, and allows people to search for those phrases in a very fast manner.

While this sounds simple, there is a lot of complexity behind search engines. First, they need to be able to read or index information from a wide variety of document types and applications. Second, they have to automatically read new and changed information so that the search engine remains current. Third, they need to provide advanced methods for matching search terms with results. Finally, they have to be able to respond to these complicated search requests across millions of pieces of information in less than a second. The complexity is even more difficult if the search engine needs to secure information that not everyone is allowed to see. Figure 9.1 is an example of what a mature search engine implementation looks like.

The Enterprise Search market has moved beyond traditional keyword search to more advanced cognitive technologies with a focus on artificial intelligence and machine learning. Gartner has renamed their evaluation to Insight Engines, while Forrester uses the term Cognitive Search. In each case, the goal is to advance search across the three main areas shown in Table 9.1: improved cognitive understanding, natural language processing, and increased automation.

It is easy to get caught up in all of this new technology. Search engines continue to add more features and capabilities that are very impressive. While these new features make great demos, they are not the most important aspect of building a successful search. The best enterprise search projects:

- Prioritize the user experience
- Use taxonomies to provide faceting or filtering of results
- Treat information as things and not strings

J. Hilger, Z. Wahl, *Making Knowledge Management Clickable*,
https://doi.org/10.1007/978-3-030-92385-3_9

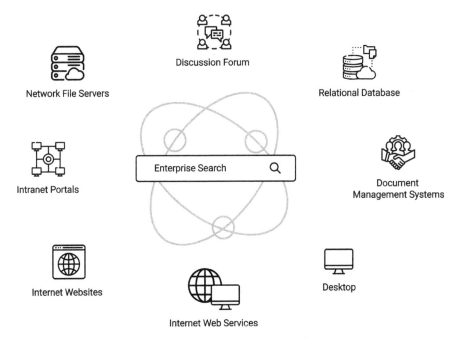

Fig. 9.1 Representation of an enterprise search engine. © 2021, Wahl/Hilger, reused with permission

User Experience

People use search because they have a job to do, and they do not have the information needed to do their job. A well-designed search experience understands this and provides search results that answer the question they are looking for and not just a list of documents that match the search query. At EK, we call this action-oriented search. With each new type of information being searched, we ask why searchers are looking for this type of information and what will they do with it when they find it. A great action-oriented search experience provides results that offer immediate answers to questions or allow the search to take an action that simplifies the work they are trying to do. We have found that a well-designed search experience leads to as much as a 50% increase in search satisfaction scores.

Taxonomies

Amazon has spent millions of dollars creating a search experience that makes it easy for their shoppers to find exactly what they are looking for across millions of products in seconds. Amazon is able to provide this because of the left-hand facets or filters that they include in search. These facets allow shoppers to filter results based on categories that make sense to them. Amazon has categorized their products in an intuitive way that makes it easy to take a search term and quickly filter to a small number of results.

Table 9.1 Definitions and uses of cognitive understanding, natural language processing, and increased automation

Cognitive Understanding	Natural Language Processing	Increased Automation
The focus of search is transitioning from strings to things. Vendors are developing ways to associate information assets through techniques like entity extraction and integration with knowledge graphs to provide contextual information as opposed to a list of links to documents or web pages.	Search engines are using natural language processing to enhance the value of content as it is ingested and indexed to support cognitive understanding. In addition, vendors are providing more and more support for natural language queries in the hopes of supporting interactive voice queries similar to Siri or Alexa.	Search engines are adding increased machine learning capabilities to improve the quality of the indexed content and to improve the accuracy/relevance of search results. Leading vendors are implementing auto-tagging and entity extraction capabilities based on machine learning principles. They are also using machine learning to track user searches and interactions to automatically improve relevancy over time.
Supports: Richer search experiences highlighting people, places, and things rather than documents.	**Supports:** Chat bots, question and answer tools, and improved identification of related search results.	**Supports:** Automated faceting of content without metadata, improved search relevancy.

KM search solutions need to offer the same experience. A well-designed, user-centered taxonomy is the perfect way to implement a faceted search experience that is simple and easy to use. The best faceted search taxonomies mirror the way people ask for information. For example, you may be looking for the accounting department's policy on expense reporting. A great faceted search experience would allow you to filter results based on department (Accounting), type of information (policy), and topic (expense reporting). Faceted search solutions based on well-thought-out taxonomies make it easy for searchers to get to the information they want faster and easier.

Things Not Strings

The most recent enhancements in search are around machine learning and AI. Google and other leading search products word or phrase matching does not deliver a good enough search experience. Modern search experiences understand the people, places, and things that exist in the corpus of content that people are searching. These tools pull out the people, places, and things in each document they read. They connect this information based on these things and how they relate to one another. We call this a **Connected Search** experience. The best way to understand the power of connected search is to see examples of it in action. As an example, consultant Johnny Smith may work on a project for a company that is in the insurance industry. The project was a large web content management project. If we were searching for people that know content management or are familiar with the insurance industry, a connected search experience would bring back Johnny Smith. It would also allow us to see all of the projects that Johnny Smith worked on and which clients he worked with.

Google demonstrates this capability with their knowledge panels. When I search for people, places, or things of importance the right-hand side of the search result screen shows specific information about what was searched for. For example, if you do a Google search for "Intel." The results page shows information about the company, its products, and its competitors. This gives the searcher a great way to discover more about the topic they are searching on and provides context for the results that appear in the main search screen.

Great search is possible as long as the focus is on design and not just adding a bunch of interesting features to a long list of documents.

9.1   Common Platforms

The good news is that the search engine market is now quite mature. Nearly every search engine has all of the most common search features that you need for your enterprise search project. As a result, we typically divide the search engine market into two categories: open-source and commercial search engines.

Open-source search engines have some of the widest usages of any search engine. This is because the open-source search engines have as much as 90% of the same features as those found in the most popular commercial search engines. Organizations with strong IT capabilities and more common search needs can get all the value they need from search at a fraction of the license cost. The two leading open-source search engines on the market are Solr and Elasticsearch.

Solr search is forked from the original open-source search engine, Lucene. It is feature rich and used by people and organizations around the world. It is proven to scale, and the list of search features it supports is pages long. There is very little that it cannot do. The biggest issue with Solr is that it requires knowledgeable developers to implement it well. The long list of features and flexibility means that you need someone who truly understands what they are doing in order to make Solr successful. With the right technical people, Solr is a great answer for most organizations.

Elasticsearch is another large, well-known open-source search engine. It is not as mature as Solr, but it has been around long enough (officially since 2010) to have proven itself as a stable solution for any enterprise search implementation. The biggest difference is around their visions. Solr search is primarily designed for text search. Elasticsearch supports text search, but also supports log analytics and visualization. In our experience it is a little easier to implement.

While the list of commercial search engine vendors has shrunk, there are still some leading vendors worth looking at when selecting an enterprise search engine.

The biggest players in the market today are Lucidworks Fusion, Coveo, and Sinequa. Each of these vendors has their own strengths and weaknesses.

Fusion is a solution that was originally built as an add-on to Solr by a group of Solr contributors who were offering search consulting services. The add-on became more and more powerful and is now a full-featured enterprise search tool. Fusion has added a number of features that promote it as one of the most advanced machine learning and artificial intelligence-based search solutions. Fusion has had most of its success with e-commerce search. In our experience, it is a powerful tool that is trying to do everything. Should you choose Fusion, make sure that you are working with an independent integrator that can advise on how to integrate Fusion with the rest of your suite.

Coveo is another common search engine that a number of our customers use. Coveo has several intuitive features built in for companies that lack development capabilities but are looking to implement enterprise search. The dashboard is powerful and easy to understand, there are a number of prepackaged integrations, and the search screen makes it easy to tweak your search weighting for improved results. It does not have some of the cutting-edge features of Fusion but is a good safe selection for organizations that want to keep things simple.

Sinequa is the other search engine that we see a number of customers use. Sinequa, like Fusion, uses machine learning and AI technologies to automatically enhance content and the order in which search results are presented. We see it as more advanced (also complicated) than Coveo but not quite as cutting edge as the Fusion product. With over 200 connectors, it is definitely an option for organizations looking to buy, not build, their enterprise search solution.

One newcomer in the market is Squirro search. Squirro is built on Elasticsearch and offers a very strong pipeline/indexing functionality that allows for a much more robust and controlled indexing experience. Squirro is worth looking into because it is built on one of the most robust search products on the market (Elasticsearch) and it has a number of preexisting connectors for tools like SharePoint and Salesforce.

The search market changes regularly. In our experience, if your organization has development capabilities open source is a great way to go. If you are looking for a canned solution that requires less development, commercial search engines can be a good option.

9.2   Features and Functions

Enterprise Search engines sound simple. They index content and then help users quickly find the information they are looking for. A well-designed solution will make the search look and feel simple. The solutions themselves are highly complex and contain a number of different features that should be considered when putting together any search solution.

When thinking about features and functions for enterprise search solutions, we typically divide those features into three categories:

- Indexing/Machine Learning
- Visual Features
- Non-Visual Features

9.2.1 Indexing

Indexing is the process of reading/parsing content from a source system and capturing it in a format that allows the search engine to quickly search for terms that exist within the source content. There are a number of things to consider when evaluating the indexing capabilities of an Enterprise Search engine. Some of the most important questions/features with regard to indexing include:

- File parsers
- Connectors
- Machine Learning

File parsers are a critical component of any search engine. In order for a search to make information readable, it needs to be able to read the text within a file of nearly any format. Just about every search engine handles standard formats like Microsoft Office files, PDF files, and web pages. File parsing capabilities become more important when you consider more complicated file formats like videos, images (with text or of people/things), and audio files. If your goal is to make these more complex file formats searchable, there are two options to handle this. First, speak with the search engine vendors to understand if they offer indexing solutions out of the box. Second, your technical team can develop readers as part of indexing that will extract text from these files and then feed them to the search engine. File parsers are a critical and often overlooked feature when evaluating search engines and planning out your enterprise search implementation.

Indexing files from common applications like Microsoft O365, Adobe Experience Manager, or Salesforce is a problem that has been solved numerous times. Commercial search engine vendors and even some of the open-source vendors have developed connectors that index information from more common repositories. Less complex search projects can use connectors as a way to speed up the search implementation and have a supported solution for indexing. More complex search projects (those that are supporting file security or applications where there is lots of content or it is changing frequently) need connectors. Security information (A.K.A. Access Control Libraries or ACLs) needs to be indexed along with the content of the application. This is a very difficult and complicated process. Vendors that provide connectors to products that have ACLs will typically include logic for indexing the security information along with the content. This is critical and one of the things that we look for when selecting a search engine vendor for the larger, more complex projects. If you are looking to select a search engine and solve your enterprise search project, the most important question to ask is do I need to respect the security of the content I am indexing and if so, does the search engine vendor have a connector that will do this for me.

Machine learning and AI are hot buzzwords that are frequently misused or misunderstood. Machine learning has always played a critical role in the way search engines work. Machine learning helps search engines make content more searchable during the indexing process. It also helps improve search queries, which we will discuss later on in this chapter. On the indexing side, search engines use statistical analysis for:

- The generation of topics.
- The development of a dynamic taxonomy for content.

Topic generation is a common feature found in most mature search engines. This is a powerful concept that is very useful for research-based searches where the organization has lots of content (often both internal and external) that needs to be sorted through. Search engines derive topics using statistical analysis techniques that have been around for ages. The search engine identifies terms or phrases that are common in the document being indexed, but not common through the corpus of documents that have already been indexed. The theory behind this practice is that these terms better identify the document as they are important to the document, but unique to the set of documents that the search engine has already indexed. Given a large enough corpus of documents, this can be a great way to mine information out of documents that helps quickly identify their importance. The problem with this approach is that it can lead to some odd results. In our experience, researchers are often comfortable with unusual results. Everyday business users searching for documents to help them do their job, often find the anomalies troubling and may lose confidence in the search if they see non-sensical answers among the topics. For this reason, we typically encourage organizations to use auto-generated topics (often called clustering) only on research sites and not on more targeted search sites.

Today's more advanced search engines also use machine learning to auto-tag content to enable faceting of untagged/unmanaged content. Some of these tools are quite good at this process and it can be a real differentiating factor for organizations that either have too much content to tag or are unable to associate metadata with the content they are managing. In these cases, it is a great solution that allows organizations to provide a faceted search experience even if they do not have the metadata to support it. There are, however, problems with this approach. The facets created by these search engines are based on the content they are indexing. Organizations develop user-centric taxonomies to ensure that the terms used to classify content are intuitive and meaningful to the organization. These taxonomies are user focused and not limited to the terms in the content. In cases where the content uses terms that are out of date or confusing, the search engine would not be able to map the older or confusing term to a preferred term that has passed user testing. As such, we recommend that organizations develop a user-centric taxonomy first and then use taxonomy management and auto-tagging tools to tag content for search whenever possible. These tools can use things like synonyms or training to ensure that the tags used to drive faceting are the ones that the searchers understand and not just the terms that existed in the content being indexed.

9.2.2   Visual Features

As search has grown in importance and visibility, a number of cutting-edge and creative search features have been tried and are now available across a wide range of platforms. Some of the most common and impactful visual search features include:

- Type-ahead search
- Faceting
- Custom result types
- Geospatial search
- Best bets
- Recommended search terms
- Saved searches/briefcases
- Previews
- Related search results
- Hit highlighting

Each of these features solves a specific search-related problem. While they all add value, implementing every possible search feature on the same search screen will create a complex and unusual search experience. Before implementing an enterprise search, it is important to understand the problem that each of these features solves and when to use them.

Type-ahead search provides a list of recommended search terms in the search bar as the user types in their search. To the user, this feels like the search solution is helping speed up the entry of their search terms. For the search administrator, type-ahead search helps guide users to the preferred terms that will help them best find the answers that they are looking for. It offers a simple looking, but very powerful way to guide searchers to more successful terms without making the searchers feel as if they are being controlled or limited. The key to effective type-ahead search is making sure that the typeahead values direct your users to the right search terms. Often our customers use the taxonomy for these values since they are terms that bring back logical search results. One other option is to add key terms that you want people searching on as part of the type-ahead values to encourage specific searches.

Faceting has been called the most important search enhancement since the advent of full-text search. People think of faceted search as the Amazon search experience. Faceting, or the ability to filter search results based on additional criteria about the results, is most common in e-commerce sites, but has great value for any knowledge management search. Faceted search improves relevancy and helps solve the challenge of single word searches. Search engines are not omnipotent, as such they do not understand the meaning behind your search term. A single word may have more than one meaning and the search engine has no way to discern what you are looking for. As an example, if you search for the word eagle are you searching for the band, the bird, or the (terrible) professional football team? Facets allow people to provide additional context around their request in a way that does not feel burdensome so that they get better search results.

The best faceted searches mimic the way people speak. For example, a searcher could be looking for a Human Resources policy about sick leave. In this case, a great faceted search would allow searchers to filter by department (Human Resources), type of content (Policies), and topic (sick leave). Facets that align with the way people speak feel natural and are used more often. These facets are best developed based on a user-centric taxonomy that is specifically designed for search. User-centric taxonomies are tested to make sure that the terms are intuitive such that people know what to expect within each taxonomy term. This removes the guess-work and makes the search experience for the user efficient and predictable.

Custom result types (something we often call information assets or action-oriented search results) are search result types that differ from the standard linked title, teaser text, and date information seen in most old-fashioned search results. You can see these custom result types when looking at most Google searches. Examples include restaurants where the searcher sees a map and pushpins; news where people see an image and information about the news article; and shoes that show up as pictures with pricing information. These unique search results typically appear at the top of the Google search because they provide the most value. Most search engines provide the ability to develop custom result types based on the type of information indexed. These result types create a more visually appealing search and bring important information to the search results screen so that people using the search are more efficient. While this feature is available in nearly every search engine, it is something that needs to be planned for as part of every search implementation.

Geospatial search is a common solution that organizations either need or do not need. If you have ever searched for a hotel on Google maps, or looked for a house on Zillow, you are familiar with geospatial search. Geospatial search is a search that filters results based on location/distance from a fixed point. In order to implement geospatial search, organizations need a way to record the location of the assets being indexed so the location can be compared to the center point for the geospatial search. In our experience, many organizations get excited to implement geospatial search, but frequently do not find the right use case as to where it can be applied. As such, they spend time and money on a feature that is rarely used.

Best bets or promoted search results are search results that are automatically raised to the top of the search results screen for specific search terms. Implemented properly, best bets allow search business owners increased control over the order of search results for important search terms. We have found best bets useful for two purposes. First, best bets can be used to prioritize specific pieces of information for a period of time as a way for management to push important information to the team. This is similar to management putting an article or piece of information on the front page of the intranet, but this is much more targeted. The best bet will only appear when people are searching for a particular topic, and it is important that this information is shared. An example of this would be changes to a policy that you want to highlight whenever people search for that policy. Without best bets, this could not be done. The second use for best bets is to allow the business to quickly solve relevancy issues. We had one client who looked at their top 20 search terms. They identified the most likely answer for each search term and set it as a best bet. The percentage of times that the searcher selected one of the first three results. Before using best bets users selected one of the first three search results on 12.5% of the searches. After setting the best bets of just the top 20 search terms, users selected one of the first three search results just over 33% of the time. That is nearly a 300% improvement that was made without the need for IT. Best bets give search administrators greater control over their search results without having to ask IT to make technical changes.

Recommended search terms help guide users to using the right search term when the results are not showing the information or piece of information that the searcher was looking for. This feature is often called "Did you mean. . ." Search engines will use the most common topics for the search results to generate a list of related terms that might also be applicable to the search that the user ran. This feature should be used when the content being searched uses a lot of jargon or has complex terms that could cause people to not find what they are looking for. We include this feature in less than 50% of the searches we design because it can add complexity to the search screen and the dynamically generated results can at times suggest unexpected terms which could cause some searchers to question the search engine.

Saved searches and briefcases are similar search features that allow searchers to quickly come back to important search results. A saved search saves the search query so that the search can be returned to at a later date. This is helpful for more complex search results typically seen with research search sites. Briefcases are a feature in search where individual search results can be saved in a briefcase to be returned to later. Each searcher has one or more of their own briefcases that can hold a set or related documents that can be returned to at a later time. This feature is quite popular in research searches or in situations where users need to return to or pull from a collection of documents often.

Previews are images or information that lets the searcher see the details of the search results without having to click on the search result and leave the search screen. User experience research warns that searchers are most often frustrated when they reach a dead end. Previews give searchers additional insight into what they are about to select in their search results. This feature typically shows well in a demo, but in our experience, it is rarely used. The most common place where we have seen it used successfully is with digital assets like brochures or PowerPoint decks. These highly visual documents can be easily distinguished in a preview window and make the selection of documents much more accurate.

Related searches are results that are identified as statistically similar to the results from the search screen. Search engines can do this automatically, without the need for tagging or manual interaction. These recommended results will typically not have the term or terms searched for in their content so they provide the searcher with content that is relevant but would not be found in the search based on the users' search term. This approach is a good way to support discovery of new and important content for searchers. The one risk with this automated search-based approach is that the related content may be unimportant or something the organization does not want people using. In our experience, this feature should be delivered using a recommendation powered by a knowledge graph first. If that is not available, then the feature can be driven by tags or manual links between content. If these first two options are not available or not feasible, the feature can be driven by the search engine.

Hit highlighting is a simple feature available in nearly every search engine, but it plays an important role in making sure that searchers trust the search application they are working with. Hit highlighting shows the first instance of the term searched for in the context of where it exists in the document. This highlighting in context lets the searcher see more context around where the term was found so that they can confirm that they have found the right document and it provides an explanation as to why the document engenders greater trust in the search results.

9.2.3   Non-visual Features

In addition to all of the visual features that search engines offer, there is an equally long list of non-visual features that are often more important than the visual features explained prior. A brief list of some of the most important features is listed below:

- Security
- Relevancy
- Multiple schema support
- Query parsing
- Stemming
- Synonyms
- SQL Support
- Numeric or Date fields

Security is the most complex problem in search, and it is one that occurs most often in KM searches. The challenge is that content stored in different systems has different security models as to how access to the content is controlled. The search engine needs to replicate the security model of each system that it is serving search results from. It also needs to provide search results in seconds or sub-second response times. In order to understand how difficult this is, we have provided an example of the security logic in the paragraph below.

> I am a user in SharePoint, and I have access to content based on the groups that I belong to. The file and the folder that it resides in identify the groups that have access to this file. The search engine needs to know which groups have access to each file (this includes the folder that the file resides in) and then determine if the user executing the search is in a group that has access to that file. This logic needs to be applied to every single search result (which could number in the tens of thousands) in order to provide a list of relevant and accessible search results.

The logic described above shows the problem in terms of one user and one application (SharePoint). What if the search engine is indexing content from eight to 10 different applications and each application has its own security model that needs to be replicated in search? This is where the problem gets hard, and search gets expensive.

There are ways to mitigate this problem and make it more manageable. Many search engine vendors have developed solutions for this very issue. Their connectors (the packaged indexing solution) index content, metadata, and the security logic. In addition, they develop connectors to collect information about user groups so that the groups are readily accessible during the search. Finally, these same tools have a security module that applies this complex security logic as part of the search query so that organizations do not have to build this themselves.

When looking at developing a KM search that requires document-level security, it is important to do the following things:

- Triple the estimate for implementation services as search is that complex.
- Select a commercial search vendor (the open-source vendors do not have good answers for security) that has connectors and solutions for as many of your secure repositories as possible.
- Prioritize insecure content first so that search can deliver some values early while the secure content framework is put in place.
- Simplify the security model as much as possible by using consistent logic across applications and securing content only as necessary.
- Work with an expert in secure search who understands the complexities of this effort.

Search with document-level security is possible and can be handled successfully with the right preparation and a proper understanding of the actual challenge.

Relevancy is the way in which a search engine orders search results. Search engine relevancy is typically based on a formula that looks at the number of times the search term appears in a document, where it appears in the document (including metadata) and for phrases the proximity of the terms to one another. This information is used to create a relevancy score that drives the order of search results. Results with a higher score appear before those with a lower score. With this understanding, it is easy to see why out-of-the-box search engine relevancy is actually quite dumb and lacks the content to provide a proper order to search results. This is the reason that faceting (which allows for greater context and filtering of unwanted results) and tuning is so important to creating a good search experience.

There is no reason to do any tuning work until the search application and the initial content is fully indexed. Once this is in place, there are a number of ways to tune the order in which search results are displayed including:

- Weighting
- Boosting
- Personalization
- Contextualization

Weighting is the factor that is applied to the relevancy score for any field within the search results. For example, a match of terms in the title of the document might need to be weighted higher than a match in the body of the document. Weighting is typically tuned with the combination of a search administrator and a subject matter expert who knows the content. A set of searches is executed, and the weighting of the search fields is adjusted until the search results provide the best possible order according to the subject matter expert. This is usually the first step in improving search relevancy.

Once weighting has been adjusted, certain items can be boosted so that they always score high whenever there is a match. Boosting is the process of raising the score of certain types of search results so that they appear higher up in the search. A great example of when this can be used is with people's results. Expert search is a key part of identifying people who have tacit information that can help solve problems. We regularly create a person search type that includes information about an individual such as their contact information as well as any areas of expertise or places that they have worked so that these people can be found to answer complex questions. The person search type will not score high in relevancy because they do not have much text with which to improve their relevancy score. The person result can be boosted so that people who match a search criteria always end up near the top of search scores. In our experience, boosting is one of the best ways to move the most important information types to the top of the search results screen.

Personalization and contextualization are more complex ways to improve the order of search results. Personalization involves influencing the ordering of search results based on information about the searcher. For example, if a searcher is a member of a specific department, they might want to see content from their department higher up in search results than content from other departments. Personalization is a complex feature that not every search engine offers. It can be a powerful method for ordering search results in specific situations. Contextualization is another method of influencing the search result order. In this case, the results are influenced based on the location of the site when the search is executed. A great example of contextualized search results is a healthcare site that we worked on. The healthcare organization had a number of local hospitals. If a person was on the website of a specific hospital, we assumed that the searcher was most likely looking for something specific to that local hospital. As such, the results from the local hospital were prioritized over results from other hospitals. In both cases, search results are being influenced based on information about the searcher or what they are doing that could potentially suggest additional intent over the search term or phrase that was entered into the search engine. The better understanding the system has with regard to the intent of the search, the more likely the search engine will provide properly sorted results. While these two approaches can be powerful methods for improving search relevancy, we would not recommend beginning with these changes. A best practice for tuning search results begins with classic weighting and boosting of results. If those practices do not provide enough value, then more complex approaches like personalization and contextualization should be considered.

Most search engines store search information in a flat format. The text of the content is stored with the search engine as a single record per search result. This design is purposeful as it allows for the fastest and most efficient querying of content so that the engine can provide sub-second response time. Unfortunately, a flat format does not always make sense for many types of search results that people work with.

Two common formats that can be useful for search are hierarchical formats and relational or graph formats. Hierarchical formats are most common when dealing with componentized content. For example, when a large document is divided into multiple sections, it is nice to see search results that show the individual sections as well as the larger document to which they belong. These parent–child relationships are not easily shown in the flat file format of the common search engine. Another structure that has become more common is the graph. Graph databases store relationships between elements. This can be very handy when providing a search experience where one search result is shown with relationships to other knowledge assets for each search result. In both cases, these unique structures can cause an organization to select purpose-built databases (either JSON, XML, or graph based) that offer search as a capability on top of the database. These solutions are often more complicated and may lack some key search features, but they solve an important problem when dealing with complicated search structures in atypical search implementations. It is worth considering these tools if you are working with a complicated and unique search requirement.

Query parsing is the act of processing queries before they are sent over to the search engine. While this is not a feature of a search engine, it is a capability that is often used in more advanced search applications. The best example of this is with natural language search. When developing a natural language search tool, the phrases need to be broken apart so that they may be properly processed by the search engine. This involves breaking down the query phrase into its component parts and then deriving intent so that the search engine can receive the proper request and that request can be responded to based on more than just keyword matching as happens with normal queries. If you are considering offering more advanced query capabilities, find an experienced developer or firm who understands search and how natural language queries are implemented and then set aside time for query parsing as part of your search plan. This is a complex capability that requires training and maintenance for it to work properly.

Stemming is a basic feature available in every modern search engine. Stemming is the process of reducing words to their base form for search purposes so that a query about "running" finds all documents that contain all forms of the work such as run, ran, or running. Stemming should always be turned on as a feature and is one way to separate a search engine from database queries.

Synonyms are another basic search feature available in every modern search engine. Synonyms are exactly what you would expect. They are words that have the same meaning as other words. Search engines typically have a file, API, and interface that stores synonyms that the search engine needs to be aware of. Synonyms are important tools in making search perform properly. Synonyms are often used to handle acronyms so that users are not required to know both the long and short forms of the word or phrase that they are looking for. Another reason in which synonyms should be used is when there is a word that is common in the industry, but the organization uses a different word. Synonyms help searchers find what they are looking for even when they are not using the "right" word or the one that resides in the document that is being searched. Synonyms need to be determined up front as part of the search design work. The reason for this is that many search engines process synonyms as part of the indexing process. What this means is that any time a new synonym is added, the content needs to be reindexed. In large search tools, the reindexing process can take hours or worst case, days to complete. As a result, synonyms add great value to the search experience, but they require careful planning in order to implement them properly.

As the distinction between structured and unstructured information continues to dissolve, some search engines are now offering support for SQL queries. The concept is that a single tool can allow people to search for content or data using whichever approach works best for the searcher. While this is an interesting option, there are a number of newer ways to handle the integration of structured and unstructured content. The current trend is to use knowledge graphs which can formally link reports and the data sets used to generate that information. These knowledge graphs can be integrated into the search experience so that content and data are both returned in search. As for querying data, knowledge graphs are now able to dynamically generate SQL queries based on mappings between the business model in the graph and the data tables where the data resides. This is called data virtualization and it is the more modern approach to solving the data querying problem. Given these new more modern tools, we see little reason for organizations to prioritize search engines with SQL capabilities.

Search results are stored in fields that are part of each record. In most cases, these fields are filled with full text (the content) and metadata values that describe the search record. Numeric and date values can be stored in these records as well. The ability to store and manage numeric and date values in search engines allows for very interesting faceting and sorting capabilities. Search engines that understand and can work with numeric or date fields allow for more interactive faceting experiences. For example, the searcher may select the start and end date for a range of search results in the facets. As another example, the searcher may be searching articles with high user ratings. These articles are shown as stars, but the value stored is typically numeric. It is helpful to be able to limit search results to only those items with four to five stars. In either case, the ability to work with numeric and/or date fields and apply calculations against them is a critical requirement for delivering the search experience.

9.3   Business Problems Addressed

Enterprise search is the #1 feature requested in nearly every KM engagement that we have worked on. Large organizations have a number of different systems to store content and information. It is not easy to find and reuse that information if the employee needs to access and search for content across a large number of systems. Enterprise search provides searchers with a single place to find the information they need without having to move the content to a consolidated platform or asking employees to enter and search within a large number of systems.

Table 9.2 shows some common business problems addressed by enterprise search implementations.

Table 9.2 Common business problems addressed by enterprise search implementations

Use Case	Description	Benefit
Contact center search	Enterprise search that is implemented within a call center to create faster access to multiple systems that the call center uses in order to respond to customer questions. This is most common in complex fields like insurance, financial services, etc.	Call times are reduced as employees have faster access to information across multiple platforms. New contact center employees are onboarded and become efficient sooner because they have a tool to help answer key questions.
Enterprise Search	A company wide search that provides access to at least three critical repositories of information for employees.	Improved employee satisfaction and retention as employees feel well equipped to do their jobs. Faster employee onboarding as employees have access to the information they need to be effective in their jobs. There is less rework because projects and tasks completed before can be found and reused. Employees are able to easily find important information around policies and procedures so that they are compliant with the organization or industries required actions.
Research Portal Search	Research portals for research departments and professional services organizations provide access to content that allows information professionals to research information in their field so that they can develop better solutions for their customers.	Customers receive better solutions in a timely manner because the research portal search provides quick access to curated and valuable information about the products or services the researchers are supporting/providing. Customer retention is higher because the solutions the organization produces are all based on similar information which leads to more consistent service and better results.

(continued)

Table 9.2 (continued)

| Sales and Marketing Portal Search | Sales and Marketing organizations have information portals that provide access to any material needed to answer questions for prospective buyers and to provide on brand, reliable brochures and information that customers use to decide on a purchase. The search within this portal is critical as a quick way for sales and marketing professionals to sort through all of this information. | Salespeople get up to speed quicker because they have a fast and reliable way to find information about the product or services they are selling.

Sales win rates increase because the sales and marketing professionals are quickly able to develop brand compliant and on target responses to customer questions/needs.

Staff are able to conduct holistic customer conversations across products and services, facilitating cross-sales and an enhanced capacity for revenue generation. . |

Taxonomy Management

10

Taxonomies allow organizations to categorize information in a consistent fashion so that it is universally accessible, even across application silos or repositories. As all types of information continue to grow at an enormous pace, it is more critical than ever to have tools that simplify the way that information is classified. Taxonomy management tools allow organizations to build, manage, and maintain taxonomies that can be replicated across all of the organization's different content silos. The leading taxonomy management platforms also support more advanced features such as auto-tagging and ontology management.

Many of our clients ask if they really need a taxonomy management tool since each individual content repository has a way to manage taxonomies (e.g., SharePoint offers this through their managed metadata capability). In our experience, taxonomies can be kept in sync manually across up to three content management platforms, as long as they are owned by the same administrators. If your organization has more than three tools where content is stored and managed, or if different groups manage different content management systems, you will need to invest in a taxonomy management tool to keep your taxonomy in sync across all of your content management applications.

10.1 Common Platforms

Taxonomy management is an important KM tool, but it is also a very niche product. There are a small number of vendors in this space with three leading vendors:

- Semantic Web Company's PoolParty
- Synaptica's Taxonomy Suite
- SmartLogic's Semaphore

All three of these products provide many of the core features that organizations need for taxonomy management, such as:

© The Author(s), under exclusive license to Springer Nature Switzerland AG 2022
J. Hilger, Z. Wahl, *Making Knowledge Management Clickable*,
https://doi.org/10.1007/978-3-030-92385-3_10

- Support for multiple hierarchical taxonomies
- Roles and permissions to delegate taxonomy management
- Auto-tagging
- APIs for synchronizing taxonomies across systems
- Analytics around the use and effectiveness of taxonomies

Any of these tools can provide the glue that allows taxonomies to be managed and implemented across multiple divisions and siloed applications in a large enterprise. While there are other tools in the space, they neither have a large market share nor the features and capabilities to offer this same level of enterprise taxonomy support.

Most taxonomy management tools are moving to support knowledge graphs. Knowledge graphs power many common AI functions and require a more complex set of features. As you evaluate taxonomy management tools, it is important to consider how they will enable your future knowledge graph plans.

10.2   Features and Functions

Taxonomy Management Systems (TMS) have historically served two primary purposes: managing taxonomies and auto-tagging content based on the taxonomies managed in the TMS.

In a true enterprise implementation (one that supports taxonomies for multiple groups across the organization), there are a number of key features that are critical to a successful implementation, including:

- Delegated administration
- Support for SKOS and other standards
- Synonyms and hierarchies
- Multilingual support
- APIs for integration

An enterprise taxonomy includes elements that are best managed by different divisions or groups across the organization. Enterprise TMSs can be configured so that these different groups are able to manage the taxonomies they own without being able to edit or change the taxonomies of other organizations. This is typically called delegated administration. The separately managed taxonomies can then be merged back together into a single structure that is usable by systems across the organization. As an example, the manufacturing division may have a list of products and materials that they own and manage separately from the rest of the taxonomies owned and managed by the library or information management services of the organization. All of these taxonomies are managed and made available to systems across the organization through the TMS.

Over time, a number of standards have been developed for the information management space. In the case of taxonomy management tools, there are two standards that any TMS should support. The first is called Simple Knowledge

Organization System (SKOS), which is a format for the way individual taxonomy elements are captured. SKOS is defined and agreed upon by the W3C, so it is a widely recognized standard that all taxonomies should follow. SKOS compliance will ensure your taxonomy can be portable in case you need to move it to a new system. In addition to SKOS, the TMS needs to support the Resource Description Framework (RDF). RDF is another W3C standard that was created to simplify the exchange of information across the web. TMS tools that work with RDF can pull in data from external sources, often called linked lists. This is an important feature that allows organizations to take advantage of curated, public lists of information to extend their taxonomies.

In addition to delegated administration and standards compliance, it is important that TMS support the management of synonyms and polyhierarchies to best capture the way information is stored and managed. Synonyms are terms that have the same meaning as other terms. These are most commonly used to support acronyms or terms specific to an organization that may differ from the industry standard terms. Synonyms can be used to enhance search and are a critical component for tuning the auto-tagging capabilities that these systems offer. Polyhierarchy is a situation where one term has two parent locations. For example, if we had a taxonomy of countries and continents, there are a number of countries that span two continents. One example of this is Egypt, which sits in both Asia and Africa. Polyhierarchies support this type of cross-association that is often needed when categorizing information.

As more and more organizations become global, the TMS needs to support both the maintenance of taxonomy terms in multiple languages and the auto-tagging of content that is written in those varying languages. When selecting a TMS, confirm that the TMS vendors provide support for multilingual taxonomies in two ways: (1) they allow for the creation of a taxonomy that includes related terms from multiple different languages and (2) the tool provides support for auto-tagging content written in different languages.

TMS should be thought of as middleware organizing the information of an organization. In order to meet this need, these tools need a strong set of APIs that make integration with other systems simple and robust. Later in this book, we will document the way in which these TMS tools are integrated with content management systems and search. These APIs should, at a minimum, provide the following:

- Access to a list of taxonomy terms at any level of the taxonomy.
- The parent of any taxonomy term.
- The synonyms in the system.
- Capability to add, edit, or delete taxonomy terms.
- Auto-tagging recommendations for a piece of text or a document.

These APIs will allow other systems to read and replicate taxonomies so that the TMS can serve as a central repository of all taxonomies. The auto-tagging API allows other systems to auto-tag documents by sending content to the TMS and receiving back recommended taxonomic terms.

As described above, auto-tagging is an automated capability offered by most TMS systems (and some search engines) where content from a document or web page is sent according to the defined security policy to the TMS to be evaluated. The TMS reads the content and recommends tags based on the text within the content. These auto-tagging capabilities reduce the need for staff to manually enter required metadata, either by suggesting metadata tags and enabling users to accept or improve suggestions or by entering metadata tags automatically without user intervention.

Not all taxonomy vendors offer auto-tagging capabilities from the outset. Given the large amount of content most organizations have and the inconsistency in the way it is tagged, auto-tagging support is a critical component of most KM initiatives and any digital transformation. Under the auto-tagging heading, we have grouped some other similar automation features that should be considered with each vendor. These include:

- Machine learning (to enhance the auto-tagging)
- Entity extraction
- Auto-classification

Vendors with more advanced implementations will support all of these features from within their tool. Support for these capabilities is typically handled through representational state transfer (REST) APIs that application developers can use to augment the way their solution manages content and metadata.

Finally, most TMS solutions are now touting integration with graph databases so that they can provide a platform for enterprise knowledge graphs. Any organization looking to implement a knowledge graph should prioritize the TMS tools that offer SPARQL and integration with a leading RDF graph database platform. While this is not a core capability of a TMS, it is key to moving to more advanced knowledge management capabilities like knowledge graphs.

10.3   Business Problems Addressed

TMS should be thought of as middleware solutions to improve the way organizations arrange and manage their information assets. As such, the solutions they drive are typically more about supporting other systems, rather than providing end solutions. Table 10.1 shows some examples of common business solutions enabled by TMS.

Table 10.1 Business solutions enabled by taxonomy management systems

Use Case	Description	Benefit
Enterprise Search	Enterprise search is a search that includes content from no less than three systems across the enterprise. The best enterprise search applications have faceted search so that users can filter search results based on a common set of intuitive terms. TMS makes sure all of the applications that feed search have the same set of terms so that the facets are aligned.	Searchers are able to find the information they need to do their jobs quickly. As a result, there is more time saved (often as much as three to five hours per week) and greater compliance with organizational practices.
Content Migrations	Frequently, when content is moved from one system to another, there is a need to enhance the metadata used to describe that content. TMS auto-tagging solutions can automate the tagging of content as it is moved from the old system to the new system.	Content migration is automated, so it is much less expensive for organizations. Content in the new system is organized in a way that is intuitive, so employees find the information they need quickly and efficiently.
Discovery of Phantom Content	Organizations often have content that is available to people who should not have access to it. This content may reside on shared drives with no security or in content management applications that also lack the proper security. Senior management often does not find it until it is too late. A TMS can be configured to automatically tag content based on a series of terms that suggest a need for security. The documents that map those terms can be reviewed to see if there are security issues.	Potential compliance, legal, or HR risks can be spotted before problems arise.
Standardized Reporting	Data warehouses collect data and information from multiple sources. Often the fields that would be used to aggregate and report on that information have inconsistent values in them. A TMS and the associated synonyms can be used to standardize the values in these fields so that aggregate reporting can be handled easily.	Organizations are able to provide critical information to all appropriate parties quickly and without complicated data mappings. This saves money in the production of reports and delivers critical information to the appropriate people faster.

Data Catalogs and Governance Tools

11

Historically, organizations limited the scope of knowledge management initiatives to content management, while ignoring data warehouses and business intelligence platforms. The problem with that approach is that data is as much a source of knowledge as the content that describes it. The combination of data and content together is quite powerful. For example, a complex report or analysis paper may be the result of one or more data sets. Having access to both allows the reader to see the report and its findings as well as the data that was used to determine those findings. This same benefit can work in the other direction as well. A person trying to understand the purpose of a data set can see the reports people develop based on that data to get a better understanding as to what others are doing with it. Clearly, the association of both content and data greatly improves the value of both of them in providing knowledge.

Data Catalogs capture and manage the metadata that describes data sets and data elements. They are analogous to document management systems that use metadata to describe documents, only their purpose is strictly for structured data. Large business intelligence initiatives rely on this metadata to make the meaning and purpose of different data sets available to all. These tools describe the purpose of each data set, categorize them so that related data sets are findable, and provide definitions around data elements so that people working with this data know what they are looking at.

Data Catalogs also allow organizations to define things like:

- Data access rules
- Data lineage (how data is put together and where it comes from)
- Data quality

This information allows organizations to better govern the use of data. Organizations with mature data governance programs rely on these tools to help them understand which data people are allowed to work with as well as how the data was derived in case problems arose during the creation of the data. In addition, these tools can identify inconsistencies in the data that could suggest data quality issues that make the data less reliable for people doing analysis against the data.

11.1   Common Platforms

While there are a host of platforms available in the data catalog space; three modern tools currently stand out:

- Alation
- Collibra
- data.world

Alation is a modern, SAAS solution for data catalogs. Its focus is on the democratization of data by creating a collaborative platform for organizations to collaborate together to manage their data sets. It is a modern looking application with a focus on machine learning, search, and collaborative features like their Wiki pages where data analysts across the organization can share thoughts and ideas with one another as they try to better understand the data that they have access to. Alation is a fast-growing platform with a lot of buzz in the industry. Its cloud-first and user-centric approach to data management has met the mark for a lot of organizations looking to modernize the way that they work with data. Alation works best in organizations that value data and have a large number of people who actively work with and collaborate around that data. Organizations that stovepipe their data scientists or have a small number of people accessing data will find it more difficult to get the full value out of their Alation implementation.

Collibra is the most mature of the platforms that we regularly see on the market. Collibra offers an on-premise license model that is of interest to organizations that are not comfortable mapping, storing, or working with their data in the cloud. It is a powerful data catalog with a strong search and a number of detailed and configurable features for examining and maintaining data quality across the enterprise. Collibra is the most mature of the data catalog platforms that we have brought up. While the maturity is helpful in some ways, it also means that Collibra has a less modern approach to data management that is not up to speed with the other two products we have mentioned.

data.world is the newest entrant into this space and also the most aggressive. data.world is not just trying to create a data catalog for the enterprise. It is trying to create a data catalog for the world. data.world envisions creating an eBay for data across the world. Imagine a platform where your data and most public data are managed and available on a single highly collaborative platform. Should data.world succeed in this endeavor, they will change the way that data is shared around the world. For now, they offer access to a wide range of public data sets that are fully managed as well as a platform that allows organizations to manage their own data in a secure fashion. The platform itself has an emphasis on collaboration similar to Alation, but also offers an integrated graph to help support the modern graph approach to data management. data.world is the right choice for organizations that work with a wide range of external and internal data sets. They are a new and hungry vendor so they are creative in working with organizations to help them manage external data sets, particularly those that can be shared with other, future customers.

11.2   Features and Functions

Data catalogs have features similar to the features found in document management systems. Some of the most important features of these tools include:

- Search
- Glossaries
- Metadata management
- Collaboration
- Security
- Data lineage
- Support for graphs

Products that implement these features well offer an environment that ensures that data is accessible, offers high quality, and is secure.

Data Catalogs capture a great deal of information about the data that each organization possesses. This information needs to be easily findable so that analysts and data scientists can find what they are looking for and understand how the data fits together. Search is the capability that makes this happen. The data catalog search should provide users with a single place to see all of the information about their data, including the data sets, the data elements, and how this information fits together. The best data catalogs offer a best-in-class search experience that includes things like faceted search based on metadata, search across all types of information, and discovery features like suggested search terms and related items. Search makes the information in the data catalog accessible so that your users can take full advantage of it.

Glossaries are the heart of any data catalog. The glossary should have the ability to define every single field and data set for the data that your users work with. This includes internal data in a data lake along with external data sets that your users subscribe to or work with. The ability to integrate with external data sets has become more and more important with the growth and standardization of open data sets. The data catalog you work with should have a way to automatically ingest data fields through integration with your internal databases and using standards like RDF for the external data sources on the internet. This automated approach captures the fields, but not the definitions. Challenge your data catalog vendors to show how the management of this glossary can be automated so that it can scale to meet your needs. There are a number of possible approaches that these vendors can take. It is important that their approach will work with your needs. The combination of a comprehensive glossary and a best-in-class search will make the data in your organization accessible to a wider range of data analysts.

Once you have collected information about the data sets and data elements that your users will be working within the glossary, it is important to be able to capture metadata that catalogs and describes this information. This metadata serves a number of purposes including improving findability, identifying security requirements, and defining the audience of data so that the data catalog can provide a more personalized experience to its users. If you are selecting a data catalog, make sure that the catalog allows for your organization to define its own metadata elements so that you can use metadata that supports your specific needs. If you own a data catalog and are implementing it across the enterprise, make sure that you define your metadata structures and use taxonomies to ensure that these data elements are described in a consistent and meaningful way. Metadata creates consistency and structure that further breaks down the silos inherent in a broad set of independent data sets.

The best tools in this space understand the value of social and collaborative features as a way to capture information about the data sets and data elements that might not be captured through definitions or metadata. For example, some data catalogs provide Wikis that allow data owners to provide real context around how they use data and what they have learned from it. This context offers much more value than a simple definition or list of fields. It can describe inconsistencies in data or interesting relationships between data sets that can be useful to others. Another example of the power of social features comes with discussion threads. Discussion threads aligned with data sets encourage users to collaborate with one another and answer questions that arise. These discussions and the wiki pages, when associated with data sets and exposed in search, can provide a great deal of context and valuable information about the data sets that can jump start analysis activities in large research organizations.

Most organizations struggle with properly managing permissions to their data sets. Some data sets are purchased with specific usage limitations. Other data sets have information that needs to remain highly confidential and should not be seen by all members of the organization. Data Catalogs can serve as the central repository of information as to who has access to the various data sets that the organization owns or licenses. In a best-case scenario, the catalog is able to automatically update these permissions with the data sets. If that cannot be handled out of the box, then an integration and plan should be implemented to make sure that the security permissions defined in the Data Catalog are replicated across the data repositories throughout the organization.

Data lineage is the documentation as to what happens to data as it flows from the original source through to consumption and use by data analysts and scientists. Data lineage is a key tool in ensuring data integrity. Data originates in a specific state with data quality that met the needs of the system for which the data was being used. That does not mean that it meets the reporting or analysis needs of people downstream. As such, this data is frequently manipulated through various processes to summarize, consolidate, or cleanse the data so that it can be better used by the downstream users. Data catalogs when properly set up, allow their users to see how and why the data was manipulated. This helps people understand what to expect with the data they are working with. It can also help identify issues that occur early in the process that can affect data quality further down the line. Data lineage looks easy, but it requires a great deal of planning and integration. It is important to budget for this work up front and then include requirements for the capture of data lineage with each new data set that an organization works with.

Finally, knowledge graphs have become one of the most important tools for managing data across an enterprise. Gartner calls the use of graph databases for this purpose, data mesh. Graphs identify how information elements are related to one another. Organizations use these graphs to define a business model and map their initial data structures to the more business-centric model without requiring expensive extract, transform, and load (ETL) processes to make the data usable. Data catalogs should support this new method of data modeling either by being developed on a graph or providing a tight integration with graph solutions. This is an immature, but important space, so not all data catalog providers offer this capability. Take time to find out if it is currently available or planned soon. This new graph-based approach is one that most organizations will be moving to in the coming years.

11.3   Business Problems Addressed

Data Catalogs are known for their strong ROI and business cases. This is driven by the way that they control and create accessibility to data across the enterprise. Table 11.1 shows the business cases for implementing Data Catalogs.

Table 11.1 Business cases for implementing Data Catalogs

Use Case	Description	Benefit
Data Accessibility	Data catalogs provide greater access to data by a wider range of people because they allow their users to understand what data is available and how it fits with other data sets.	Access to data and information is made much easier so a wider range of people can work with and use data to improve their decision making. Data reporting is decentralized so that the business is able to access data directly without as much need for IT, which provides greater speed to information and lower IT costs.
Data Security	Data catalogs provide a single source of truth for access to information.	Users are not able to see or access information they should not have access to protecting the company from fines or potential public embarrassment that could impact future business plans.
Data Quality	Data rules and data lineage automate and create visibility into how data is manipulated to ensure that data scientists and analysts are not relying on data that is inaccurate to make important business decisions.	Data quality rules are in place and the way in which data is developed is tracked to ensure that decisions are made against data that is accurate. Automated methods for tracking and validating that data quality exists lower costs on fixing data quality issues.

Text Analytics Tools

12

Text analytics tools specialize in mining information from unstructured content. We like to think of text analytics tools as products that provide meaning and increased control over large, unwieldy corpuses of information.

It is important to understand how these tools work before deciding when and where you need text analytics solutions. Text analytics products use a basic understanding of common sentence structure to identify people, places, and things within a document. Unlike the auto-tagging capability in taxonomy management tools, they are not trying to force alignment with a pre-existing term set. Text analytic tools are ideal in situations where organizations are trying to identify unknown patterns in a large corpus of information or to better associate people, places, and things with the documents they are mentioned in. These tools are most often used in research functions.

Some of the most modern text analytics tools have added knowledge graphs as a way to better understand who and what the people, places, and things are. They identify these entities and then match them with a knowledge graph to understand what the entity is and how it relates to others. Text analytics tools are frequently used with knowledge graphs to help tie together information from a wide variety of sources.

12.1 Common Platforms

Like the search space, most text analytics tools are based on open-source libraries like General Architecture for Text Engineering (GATE), Stanford NLP, and many of the Python libraries. As a result, there are three common approaches to solving text analytics challenges:

- Open-source libraries
- Cloud-based solutions
- Packaged offerings

© The Author(s), under exclusive license to Springer Nature Switzerland AG 2022
J. Hilger, Z. Wahl, *Making Knowledge Management Clickable*,
https://doi.org/10.1007/978-3-030-92385-3_12

Which approach to take depends on the problem you are trying to solve and the skills of the people in your organization.

If you have a highly technical organization and are integrating with a larger product suite or need very fine-grained control over the way text analytics works, the open-source libraries can be a great solution. They are inexpensive and can be used quickly by developers to understand the technology.

Organizations that have invested in cloud computing can get a quick gain on text analytics without a lot of work by turning on products like Amazon's Comprehend or Microsoft's Cognitive Services. These tools still require integration with your content repositories and some training, but they are packaged offerings that are automatically kept current, and they have administrative consoles that allow for training and configuration. The only downside of this approach is that your content has to be on the cloud, and there is a cost per transaction that can add up quickly.

Finally, there are a number of out-of-the-box products that provide text analytics either as a service or as a product. Expert System's Cogito product is one of the best text analytics tools that we have worked with. Not only does Cogito identify entities and phrases, but it is also able to understand what they are because of the knowledge graph behind their system. For example, it can understand the differences between bearing arms (weapons) and bare arms (appendages). Another similar product is Thomson Reuters' content APIs. Thomson Reuters offers domain-specific APIs for identifying relevant entities within the unstructured text. These products require less training and are very powerful. They do, however, tend to be the most expensive upfront solutions.

12.2 Features and Functions

These text analytics tools are quite targeted in the features that they offer. As organizations look to invest in text analytics, it is critical to understand which features are available and what can be done with them. The primary features that can be found in text analytics tools include:

- Entity extraction
- Phrase identification
- Co-occurrence
- Sentiment analysis

While this is a small list of features, each feature enables a number of cutting-edge, AI-type solutions that solve difficult business problems.

Entity extraction is the identification of people, places, and things from a large, unstructured piece of text. In this new world of knowledge graphs and artificial intelligence solutions, it is one of the most important capabilities for breaking down the silos created by documents and delivering information through new and cutting-edge methods. Entity extraction tools use sentence structure to identify subject and object nouns and pull those out as candidate entities. An entity extraction tool will read a piece of text and provide a list of entities with a confidence score as to how important those entities are in relation to the text that it just analyzed. Applications can use this information to associate these people, places, and things across documents and automatically relate the strength of that relationship based on the importance of the entity to each document.

Entity extraction can be even more powerful when implemented in association with Named Entity Recognition (NER). NER is entity extraction that uses a predetermined list of entity names to drive entity recognition. The power of NER is that the predetermined list of entities is known and understood even before they are pulled from content. This allows organizations to do more with the analytics gathered from the NER. For example, the named entities could be products, and the content being analyzed could be social media posts. The topics of the posts could then be aggregated by-product to better understand what is being said about the products. NER would make this easier and ensure that more product entities are captured as part of the entity recognition process.

Phrase identification is similar to entity recognition, only instead of identifying entities, the analytics tool is identifying phrases within the text. Analyzing patterns of significant phrases across large corpuses of text can provide valuable insights that would often not be seen otherwise. For example, medical organizations can analyze patient notes for a large group of patients to find patterns of symptoms (described as phrases) that might allow the organization to find trends they would not have seen otherwise.

Co-occurrence is when one entity or phrase appears with another entity or phrase. When this occurs frequently, good text analytics tools will recommend that these two entities or phrases are related based on how often they appear together in the documents being analyzed. Co-occurrence is a great way to identify cause and effect situations or words/phrases that are similar. Co-occurrence is a form of machine learning where the system gets smarter as it sees more content/data. The most common place where KM experts will see co-occurrence in action is when taxonomy management tools use machine learning to improve their auto-tagging. One of the ways in which they do this is by calculating how often a term not in the taxonomy occurs with a term in the taxonomy. Once the co-occurrence is frequent enough, the taxonomy management tool will tag any document with either term with the term in the taxonomy. This is a form of learning that makes taxonomy tools more effective.

The final function for text analytics tools is sentiment analysis. Sentiment analysis reads text and identifies whether the text is positive or negative. Sentiment analysis can be very hard to do with a great deal of accuracy and often requires lots of tuning. Two challenges for sentiment analysis are sarcasm and word ambiguity. Computers do not understand sarcasm. When someone says that the meeting was just great, a human will understand that the statement is sarcasm. A computer will read the word great and assume a positive score for the sentence. Another challenging aspect is when words are ambiguous in their meaning. For example, we could describe clay as being very malleable, and that is a good thing. If we say that a leader is malleable, that is likely not a positive statement. Sentiment analysis can be implemented successfully, but it takes time and effort to get it right. These tools demo well, so

Table 12.1 Solutions supported by text analytics tools

Use Case	Description	Benefit
Social Media Mining	Organizations can learn a great deal about their reputation or the reputation of their product through comments on social media. It is not possible to wade through this information without the use of text analytics tools. These tools can use NER to identify tweets about their products and then use sentiment analysis to understand if there are any positive or negative trends that customers are talking about.	Market analysis from social media mining allows organizations to make product adjustments proactively, thereby maximizing revenue.
Call Center Analysis	Call center activity, including phone calls, chats, and e-mails, can be analyzed using text analytics tools. These tools will use NER and things like co-occurrence to identify patterns of problems or issues that might not be caught through product testing or anecdotal stories from support staff.	Call center analysis allows organizations to proactively identify problems or issues that affect their products. Quick resolution improves customer satisfaction and will help grow sales.
Knowledge Graph Creation	Knowledge graphs enable key AI features like chatbots and natural language search. These solutions work best when they respond with answers and not documents. Knowledge graphs do this by gathering information around entities so that answers can be centered on the entity or topic that was requested. Text analytics use entity extraction to help populate the information in these graphs. Entities are identified, and the information in the content is then associated with the entity within the graph.	Knowledge graphs support cutting-edge search and chatbot solutions that can be used to: • Lower support costs through automated question answering • Increase employee productivity through quick access to answers and not just long documents • Improve employee satisfaction because employees have the information they need to do their jobs successfully

it is important to account for the time needed to tune the solution when planning to add sentiment analysis to your KM portfolio of products.

Each of these features has value when implemented independently. As they are combined, organizations can gain powerful insights across large amounts of unstructured information internal to the organization or external through social media or other content repositories.

12.3   Business Problems Addressed

Text analytics solutions are typically used for processing large amounts of unstructured information. While they are not an end solution for organizations, they add structure to content (typically in the form of metadata) that enables a number of powerful solutions to help organizations gain value from both internal and external sources of information. Table 12.1 explains some of these solutions and how text analytics tools contribute to the solution.

Graph Databases

13

Graph databases are the storage tools behind knowledge graphs which drive many of the common knowledge AI capabilities that we see today. If you are wondering what a knowledge graph is and why people are interested in these tools, look no further than your phone. Knowledge graphs power those ask and answer engines like Siri and Ask Google on both Androids and iPhones. They also power products like Amazon Alexa and Google Home. The difference between knowledge graphs and search engines has to do with three key capabilities: context, connections, and interface.

Context is about an improved understanding as to what things are. Initially, search engines helped people find information through text matching and statistical analysis. The searcher would enter a term, and the search engine would find web pages, chats, and documents that had that term or a variant of the term within it. The search engine would then prioritize the order in which these results are returned (a.k.a. relevance) through statistical algorithms based on the frequency and location of these matching terms within each search result. While this approach works to support simple text-based search, it cannot properly support the knowledge and understanding that is required for AI solutions like Google Home and Siri. These tools work because they capture information assets and not just documents. They look for people, places, and things and use the documents and web pages to further inform those "things" and provide context about what they are and what attributes are relevant to each item.

An easier way to understand the importance of context is to compare the important attributes of three very different but related things. A painting like the Mona Lisa has attributes like size, painting style, painter, subject, and coloring of the painting. A person like Leonardo Davinci has attributes that explain when he lived, where he was from, what he looked like, and what he accomplished. Finally, the Louvre is a museum that has attributes like where it is located, how much it costs to visit, and what is on display there. These things are all related and may frequently appear in the same documents or web pages. Knowledge graphs allow for these things to be understood in the context of what they are. When a person asks a

© The Author(s), under exclusive license to Springer Nature Switzerland AG 2022
J. Hilger, Z. Wahl, *Making Knowledge Management Clickable*,
https://doi.org/10.1007/978-3-030-92385-3_13

question about the Louvre, a knowledge graph returns answers about the Louvre, as opposed to web pages or documents describing the Louvre. This approach allows these AI systems to provide answers to questions rather than links or documents that a person can read to determine the "answer" to each question.

Connections are another important capability that separate knowledge graphs as an ideal answer generation machine. Graph databases, based on graph theory, store information objects based on how they relate to one another. This approach better aligns with the way people think. When you consider a person you know, it is typical to describe them in relation to other things. For example, that person you know might work at a company or is married to or friends with another person you know. Even famous people are described in relation to other pieces of information. For example, Brad Pitt starred in the movie *A River Runs Through It*. He was married to Jennifer Aniston and later Angelina Jolie. This is how our brains naturally work. We think of Brad Pitt by describing the people or movies he is connected to. Graph databases store information in that same fashion.

This power of connections offers other advantages as well. Not only can it help with AI solutions, but it is also a valuable tool to enhance the search and discovery experience. As people look for information, those relationships/connections can be very helpful in the discovery process. An employee searching for information about the company travel policy would likely find the policy (assuming the search is well designed). The graph will allow the employee to see other information that is relevant to the policy. For example, he or she might see the form that needs to be filled out for the travel policy or additional information about the city by city per diems for travel. This additional information turns the search from something that relies on people using the "correct" term to find what they want to an interface that allows people to find the information they need by traversing the graph, seeing all of the related information along the way.

The final benefit of connections has to do with integrating different types of information. One of the goals of cutting-edge KM platforms has always been to integrate structured and unstructured information. Imagine if you could search for a report and quickly see the data sets that provided the proof behind the statements in the report. Also, imagine if you could ask your chatbot a question, and it would automatically respond with a chart or graph calculated across multiple disconnected data sets. Graphs are being used as a way to connect data sets to content and to one another. Organizations are using this to develop research portals that connect reports, data, and other analytical tools into a single search-based portal for finding and researching information. Organizations are also using this same approach to develop graphs that model business functions and connect disparate data sets automatically so that they better align with the information needs of business leaders. As one business leader we worked with said, one cannot democratize data/information if it requires an IT person to generate the report. Graphs are the solution that allows data and content to integrate and better align with normal business models.

Inference is the other key AI capability enabled through graph technology. The easiest way to think of inference is to identify attributes about an information object by looking at attributes of other related objects. For example, two countries might have a similar climate or GDP. Analysis, information, or reports relevant to one country might also be relevant to the other country because of their similar attributes. This type of analysis allows for discovery that might not have been possible just a few years ago. A researcher can look for information about building bridges in places like Venezuela and find guidance from bridge building in Columbia, a country with a similar climate. Inference is the reason these new knowledge graph systems appear to be learning or providing insights beyond the old way computers delivered information.

Graph databases and knowledge graphs are truly the next steps in knowledge management. Organizations looking to improve the way they mine and manage information, aggregate information from a number of highly disparate and bespoke systems, map disparate data sources to align with business needs, and provide answers rather than links to documents need to plan out a path using knowledge graphs as part of their knowledge management roadmap.

13.1 Common Platforms

The graph database space is like most new, up-and-coming technology spaces. There are a large number of product vendors in the space, none of which, with the exception of Neo4j, have a significant market share. Organizations looking to select knowledge graphs in this early phase need to be aware and plan for the fact that many of these tools will be purchased, bought, or merged. As such, it is critical to focus on standards as opposed to picking and siding with a particular vendor who may not be there in the long run. Graph databases are divided into three types of systems:

- RDF graphs
- Property graphs
- Multi-modal graphs

RDF is a W3C standard that is widely acknowledged as the graph standard and used by most graph databases. Having said that, Neo4j, the most active graph database in the world, is a property graph. As such, the determination as to which type of graph will win out in the graph wars is not yet decided. RDF databases are designed to handle everything as a relationship. Each entity is related to another entity. It truly is what we call a triple store. What we used to consider properties, like the height of a person, is seen as a relationship in an RDF graph. RDF graphs focus on standards using SPARQL as the query language. The upside of this approach is that moving from one RDF graph to another is much easier. The downside of RDF graphs has always been scalability. Each of the vendors is working on ways to improve scalability, but this will continue to be the main concern with RDF databases. Having said that, in our experience, there are a number of ways to work around the performance limitations. For example, some of the implementations we have been involved with use a search engine for high-frequency queries to minimize the performance limitations of queries against some RDF databases. Also, by focusing on use cases, the graph can store less data/information while pointing to the original data stores. This approach has allowed for incredibly complex solutions that still perform in a reasonable fashion.

Some of the most common RDF databases on the market include GraphDB by Ontotext, Anzograph by Cambridge Semantics, Allegrograph, Stardog, and Virtuoso. There are many others, but these are the most common ones that we have seen.

Property graphs are the other major type of graph databases on the market. Property graphs, like RDF graphs, track the relationships between entities or nodes. The difference is that each node or entity can have a set of properties associated with it. Interestingly enough, the relationships can also have properties further defining the purpose and reasoning behind each relationship, hence the name property graphs. This model makes a great deal of sense and is very useful for specific modeling scenarios where entities need to be described with properties that better define them. One great example of an excellent use for a property graph is with content management solutions. We worked on a project where we were trying to track content across as many as eight different content management tools. We needed to manage the content and attributes of each piece of content, and we also needed to relate content items to one another even though they existed in different systems. This was a perfect reason to use a property graph, and we selected Neo4J as our solution because not only did the model fit what we were looking for, Neo4J's market presence assured us that it will be around for a long time.

While property graphs make a lot of sense and definitely fit many problems, they should be selected carefully. Property graphs do not align with the industry standards created by the World Wide Web Consortium (W3C). As such, selection of a property graph typically requires a commitment to the product you select. It is harder to transition from one property graph to another if the vendor you are working with is bought or goes out of business. As stated above, the biggest name in property graph databases is Neo4j, as it is by far the most downloaded and used graph database and worth considering for specified graph projects. As a result, Neo4j will likely be around for the long run given its massive user base.

The final type of graph database option is called a multi-modal graph database. These solutions are exactly what the name suggests. They are databases that support graph technologies, but they are not limited to classic graph design. There are typically two reasons that multi-modal graph databases exist. Either the vendor started offering a different capability (Marklogic with their XML database model) and have gone back and added graphs as a part of their solution, or they are building a different model that allows for greater performance or targets a specific type of solution. Given the immaturity and excitement of the graph database market, it makes sense that these vendors would exist. Frankly, we see it as a good thing. It is common that more established vendors move into hot, new technology spaces. These investments by more established vendors help validate the technology as real and worth investing in; that is good for the entire market. It is also beneficial that vendors continue to innovate around graph technology. Many of these multi-modal vendors have come up with new and interesting ways to serve the market or support scalability and performance. This type of innovation can become part of the standard, and this pushing of the envelope will lead to improved performance and capabilities for cutting-edge technologies.

The most common vendors in the multi-modal space include Marklogic, OrientDB, ArangoDB, and TigerGraph. Depending on your need or use case, it is worth looking at these vendors for your knowledge graph implementation.

13.2   Features and Functions

In many ways, graph databases should be thought of in the same way that regular databases are. As such, most of the features of these tools are similar to the features you would seek out in a relational database. When evaluating graph databases, there are four primary categories of features to evaluate:

- Standards compliance
- Availability and scalability
- Integration
- Administration and security

Standards Compliance
Graph databases are new, and as a result, there are a number of competing standards, and it is likely that there will be consolidation over time. As such, it is important to select tools that are standards compliant to ensure that your organization can move to a new database if necessary or integrate with multiple sources. Some of the most important standards to consider are SPARQL, graph query language (GQL), and RDF.

SPARQL Protocol and RDF Query Language (SPARQL) is a W3C standard for semantically querying databases. It was initially released in 2008 and was upgraded in 2013 with version SPARQL 1.1. SPARQL is specifically designed for RDF databases and nearly all major RDF graph databases support SPARQL, while many of the other graph database solutions now support SPARQL to some extent. SPARQL looks a lot like SQL, and having a standard for querying graph databases helps ensure that you are not caught in vendor lock in. In addition, SPARQL is used by many third-party, front-end tools for accessing graph data. Selecting a database that is SPARQL 1.1 compliant gives the organization more options for adding packaged solutions to its database, simplifies integration, and simplifies migration to a new graph database if necessary.

Graph Query Language (GQL) is the latest new query standard on the market. It is designed for property graph databases and is meant as a response to SPARQL for the property graph database market. This standard is newer, and at the time this book is being published is not yet in place. A proposal was submitted and approved in 2019. Once complete, GQL will give property graphs a standard similar to that of RDF databases.

Resource Description Framework (RDF) is an XML-based standard originally created for describing information on the web. It is a W3C standard with very high adoption across the Internet. RDF is the most used relational framework on the web. If you are developing a solution that is web centric or that will use content across the web, RDF is a good standard to support and use.

The graph database market remains immature. There are lots of players, and standards are continuing to evolve. Selecting standards compliant solutions protects the buyer from the eventual change that is likely to happen in the industry. As database companies are bought and merged into other solutions, standards compliant solutions help ensure a smooth and efficient transition that allows for continued growth.

Scalability and Availability

As with any database, scalability and availability are critical topics when evaluating vendors. Most graph databases are designed for the querying of information and do not support transactional systems. Relational databases are better suited for transactional systems, and as a result, they are designed to handle high-speed transactional applications where adding new transactions has to happen quickly and safely. Graph databases are more like data warehouses or search systems. They need to support the querying of information at scale and high availability so that the solutions built on them are always accessible. As such, it is important that any production-level graph database has the ability to cluster so that the graph can continue to respond to queries even if one or more servers have issues. In addition, clustering should allow for a higher volume of queries when the graph is supporting products like search engines or chatbots.

Scalability and performance are about more than just clustering though. Graph databases are notoriously slow for certain types of queries. As you evaluate graph options, the type of structure of your data and the type of solution that you are implementing will help define which type of graph (RDF vs. property) and which graph engine provides the best overall performance for your needs. Graph performance tuning has a great deal of complexity to it. Even the way in which queries are written and the information is stored has a drastic impact on query performance. As such, it is critical to work with an experienced graph subject matter expert who knows how to structure information and queries to lead to optimal performance. It is also critical to define the use cases you are trying to solve in advance so that the graph expert can structure things in a way that will perform as the solution grows.

Integration

Graph databases are typically used as tools to integrate information silos. They connect information from multiple content repositories or data sets and organize them in a way that better aligns with the way people think. As such, integration is a key aspect of the effectiveness of any graph database solution. Compliance with common standards like RDF and SPARQL help simplify some integrations, but that is not the only thing buyers of a graph database should be looking for. Some important features that should be considered include data virtualization, search integration, and connectors to common repositories.

If the purpose of your graph is to better organize data so that it is more accessible to a wider audience, then integration with relational databases is critical. Many modern graph databases now offer data virtualization capabilities. Data virtualization transforms SPARQL queries into SQL queries so that information can be modeled in a graph and pulled from a SQL compliant database automatically. Organizations using data virtualization define the graph ontology (generalized semantic data models) and then map the entities and properties to fields in a database through standard SQL queries. Once the mapping is complete, end users can query the graph as they normally would, and it automatically pulls back data from the relational database.

Another common integration point with graph databases is enterprise search. There are two reasons organizations would want to integrate their graph database with search. First, search engines typically offer faster query performance. Graph databases can be used to aggregate information from multiple data sources and then feed the search engine so that users can quickly search for entities defined within the graph. The second reason to integrate with a search engine is to allow for knowledge panels, like the ones Google creates. An organization can create knowledge panels based on things like customers, employees, or important topics and display those next to the search results in the same way that Google does. These integrations enhance the search experience and make the information in a graph database more accessible.

Finally, graph databases are typically used to pull information from complex content management/collaboration systems. Graph vendors that specialize in working with unstructured information frequently offer connectors that automatically pull information from common content sources like SharePoint. These connectors can make it much easier to pull information into the graph, since the original integration work is already complete.

Administration and Security

Another key area of any graph database is the ease with which the database is administered and the security embedded within the tool. All of the graph databases offer some sort of administrative console. While a technologist will likely need to manage the graph database, it is important that it is as accessible as possible. Since the graph database space is still relatively new, the administrative consoles vary widely. As you evaluate graph databases, make sure that the administrative console is well organized, easy to use, and offers more than command line controls to manage and work with the database. A mature and easy-to-use console makes it easier for more people to work with the database.

One key area of the console to focus on is security. It is quite common that the information in the graph should not be visible to certain users. As such, it is important to have a security model that can secure information by entity, entity type, property, and relationship. Ideally, the console should have an easy way to define these security rules and manage the users, their groups, and the roles that allow them access to specific information within the graph. Embedding the security model in the graph ensures that graphs are able to aggregate both public information

Table 13.1 Common use cases for graph databases

Use Case	Description	Benefit
Enhanced Search	Internal search at most organizations was document or web page centric. The search engine would index a large number of documents and return them in a search interface. Graphs allow for information to be aggregated based on topic, person, place, customer, or product. As a result, search interfaces can provide immediate answers to questions as opposed to a list of documents that the searcher needs to read through in order to get the answer they are looking for.	An organization's enterprise search provides direct access and not just documents so that searchers find the information they need quickly and are more efficient in their jobs. This leads to better service and more job satisfaction for employees.
Democratization of Data	Data stored in a data lake is modeled and mapped in a graph so that the organization of the data better aligns with the way people think. Typically, the original sources of the data capture data in a transactional format that aligns with the activities the tool is tracking. While this helps with performance, it makes reporting a difficult process that requires a great deal of data transformation by experienced IT personnel. The graph database sits on top of the data lake, defining relationships between data tables and data elements that make the information more accessible to corporate management.	Managers and senior leadership at organizations have faster and more flexible access to information so that they can make smarter decisions that increase revenue or decrease costs. IT departments are not required to develop custom reports or data transformations as often, so they can focus on other forward-thinking initiatives. As a result, IT costs are reduced.
Data Quality	It is critical that organizations are able to trust the data that they are reporting on. Unfortunately, it is quite often that the data is missing values or the information associated with it is not what is expected. Graph databases are now being used as data catalogs because they not only allow for definition of data files and data elements, they also can be used to define the relationships	Improved data quality helps ensure that organizations can trust the metrics and reports that they received from their reporting systems. This proactive approach to data quality allows for smarter decisions based on higher confidence in the data and lowered costs in evaluating and ensuring that data remains accurate.

(continued)

Table 13.1 (continued)

	between information and any properties about how the information should appear. This more flexible model for defining data allows for the definition of data values so that data can be monitored for quality more easily.	
AI and Chatbots	Interactive conversations with systems are quickly becoming the norm. We all use tools like Siri, Alexa, and Google Home to ask questions and get back quick and informative answers. Employees within organizations are expecting the same level of service when they look for information within their company. Customers and partners also expect this type of interaction and quick access to answers. Graph databases enable these more modern interfaces by aggregating and storing information in a way that aligns with the way people think and speak.	Employees can use their chatbots or AI interfaces to quickly ask questions and receive reliable answers. This leads to more efficient and compliant employees. It also creates greater employee satisfaction. Customers and partners that are able to access company support systems through cutting-edge AI and chatbot applications are more likely to remain with that company and purchase more services.
Recommendation Engines	Graph databases provide a number of different features that allow for much more powerful recommendation engines. The items that need to be recommended, along with metadata that describes them, are stored in the graph database. Recommendations can be generated based on the properties of each of these items, their explicitly defined relationships, inference between relationships, and a tool called vector scoring that identifies the similarity of two items based on the closeness of two items within a graph. These recommendation engines can be used to proactively push information to user-based activities like scheduling a meeting or searching for information on a website. The recommendation engine can also be applied to product catalogs on e-commerce sites or support sites to provide customers with access to information they might not have searched for on their own.	Employees receive the information they need so that they can make smarter decisions. They are not required to know to search for something, as the engine knows based on their activities what they should be seeing. Customers looking for support or purchasing products are proactively shown information that they may find valuable based on where they are on the website, which question they asked, or what they are purchasing.

and information that should only be visible to certain users. For example, I might be creating a graph that shows information about a customer. Some of the information needs to be kept private to the people that work with that customer, while other information can be seen by anyone in the company. Graph security at the entity and relationship level will enable this level of information security.

13.3 Business Problems Addressed

Graph databases are the storage tools for knowledge graph projects. They provide a way of aggregating and modeling information that better aligns with the way people naturally think. As such, much of their value comes from their ability to map information, both content and data, from across multiple silos and provide it in a way that makes sense to the users. Table 13.1 explains some common use cases that are built on graph databases.

KM as a Foundation for Enterprise Artificial Intelligence

14

Artificial intelligence is one of the hottest areas in IT investment. Gartner's 2019 CIO Survey indicated that 92% of respondents had begun AI-related projects or at least had been thinking about it. In contrast, the survey revealed that only 19% of those respondents had a currently functioning AI initiative underway (Brethenoux 2020). As Gartner notes, uncontrolled publicity about the wonders of AI techniques as business problem solvers and generators for ROI have led organizations to begin projects without a sense of realistic business outcomes, and therefore, those projects are highly unlikely to succeed. KM technologies are key enablers to making information-based AI initiatives work. They provide the knowledge and information that is behind the intelligence that these systems purport to have. Organizations that do not invest properly in building a KM infrastructure that cleans, organizes, and provides structure to this information will be unable to successfully deliver on their AI plans. Knowledge management is foundational to achieve some of the more advanced information management, findability, and semantic web capabilities organizations refer to as AI.

In our experience working with AI solutions, we regularly run into organizations that have been promised AI capabilities but have not realized them. Big companies with "AI" software that promises the capability to win at game shows or provide the "out-of-the-box" ability to have natural conversations has been procured and prototyped. The message we consistently hear, however, is that these tools have not lived up to the promise. Though the demos are impressive, the reality is deflating.

There are many routes to AI, but the most likely and cost-effective path for many organizations is to leverage their existing knowledge. This knowledge needs to be harnessed in a more structured manner through a combination of taxonomies, ontologies, and graph databases and then surfaced through well-designed digital web interfaces, enterprise search tools, chatbots, and push mechanisms.

Though many organizations fully understand and are eager for the potential business value that AI offers, they recognize they are not prepared to realize it. This is where the foundational value of KM systems implementation comes in. A well-designed KM program offers a vast array of benefits, including:

- **Content Quality**—An awareness of the necessity for clean content, as well as the appropriate content governance, analytics, and cleanup processes/programs to ensure the long-term quality and enhancement of data and information. Our experience shows us that only one in five documents belongs within an enterprise index, as the rest are old, obsolete, incorrect, or duplicate.
- **Information Integration**—Enterprise-level programs need to relate content (through system consolidation but more importantly via an enterprise taxonomy and ontology design) focused on relating content based on what it is about, who it is for, and what it does.
- **Content Standardization**—Designing, developing, and implementing content types and templates that standardize content capture, management, and presentation. This often results in smaller, more manageable "chunks" of content that can be combined in a more flexible manner.
- **Content Variability**—An understanding that information does not all look the same and that, though structured information is easier for a "machine" to understand, an individual end user needs an array of information types, including videos and graphics, "easy" answers, and extensive details.
- **Culture of Knowledge Sharing**—An appreciation for, recognition for, and trust in knowledge being shared from and to multiple sources throughout the organization. So often, good KM is driven by the right people being rewarded and encouraged for sharing knowledge within the organization.

What is remarkable about these benefits of KM, in particular, is that each of them is foundational to achieving real AI. Content quality ensures that any extraction of content via AI is "reading" only the right information and not duplicating inconsistent or conflicting data points.

Information integration allows for content discovery and the generation of knowledge panels and graphs by relating multiple sources and types of content. The associated taxonomies and ontologies build structures for the AI system to leverage different vocabulary and provide more "human" responses to questions. Ultimately, this has become commonly known as search engines or cognitive search.

Content standardization enables the AI to "read" answers more effectively. It surfaces the right answers, displays the easy responses, and points to the more detailed and complex answers.

Content variability ensures that the AI is drawing from a comprehensive set of answers, relating different content types, and creating a real web of information from which the end user can choose. Different situations call for different types of content, and a true AI interaction allows for that to occur.

Finally, all of this is powered and enabled by a culture of knowledge sharing. Any organization's true vision for AI rests on the concept that good information will result in even better information over time. We refer to this as the self-feeding beast of KM. AI will not be perfect immediately (and may never be). It will require a true culture of effective KM for people to train the AI and the content that powers it, ensuring system improvement over time.

The other key to each of the elements above is that they will offer meaningful business value long before AI is enabled within the organization. Each of these KM foundations is a building block on the path to AI. We are currently working along the range of these efforts. For some organizations, we are building their basic KM foundations and plotting a roadmap to achieve AI. For other organizations, we are implementing the full suite of AI capabilities in earnest, having already established their foundations.

14.1   KM Tasks to Prepare for AI

As mentioned earlier, KM needs to be in place before knowledge-centric AI solutions can be successfully implemented. Organizations preparing for this work should plan to undertake the following tasks:

- Content cleanup
- Content modeling
- Taxonomy design
- Ontology design
- Content chunking

Content Cleanup
Over 80% of the content within an organization is old, duplicative, or simply inaccurate. The content cleanup exercise is needed to ensure that your content quality is ready for AI. It is important that organizations complete a content inventory and associated content cleanup before attempting to implement an AI solution for their employees, partners, or customers.

Content Modeling
Many of today's AI tools purport to read and manage content without structure and provide meaningful answers. While that is partially true, content that has been modeled with additional metadata that further describes its use and purpose will be easier for the AI system to read and understand its intent. Intent drives much of what these AI systems do to understand both the user's request and the purpose of the information that is received. Content modeling creates the content standardization that allows AI systems to perform their best. Structured content with metadata that describes intent is easier to process for the AI systems and will be prioritized over content without descriptive metadata.

Taxonomy
A taxonomy is a formal and structured method for categorizing information across systems. Developing a taxonomy can help AI solutions be more effective in two ways. First, the taxonomy typically includes a list of important topics for the enterprise. These topics can be used to train the AI tools toward common forms of

intent that the system should expect. Second, the taxonomy provides a consistent way of describing content so that disparate types of content can be integrated across applications.

Ontology Design
Ontologies offer a way to create information models that align with the way people think. Ontologies identify a structure for people, places, and things along with the relationships and characteristics that define them. This structure allows for advanced content integration and content variability. Ontologies support this by converting individual pieces of content into fully described information assets about employees, customers, products, and topics. Once an ontology is defined, organizations can pull information into knowledge graphs that will power things like chatbots, advanced search, and other AI tools.

Content Chunking
AI solutions work best if content is removed from a large document and grouped topically. For example, if we ask for information about a specific HR policy like sick leave, it is not useful if we are sent the entire employee handbook. Users expect AI solutions to provide immediate answers to people's questions and not links to other information sources that may contain the answer. Content chunking is a process where larger documents are divided into topic-specific content that can be assembled into a larger document but also returned in search or other systems as answers to specific questions. Without this up-front content chunking, the AI systems either need to respond to questions with links to documents, or they need to pull information out of a document automatically. While many tools promote the ability to do automatic chunking of content, the process is not perfect. If the information is pulled incorrectly, users will lose faith in the AI solution. Chunking and organizing content before it goes into the AI tool goes a long way to make sure that the tool performs effectively.

These five tasks are critical to having the right KM infrastructure to enable successful AI solutions at an enterprise level.

14.2   Five Levels of Artificial Intelligence

Once the KM infrastructure is in place, organizations can reliably build out their artificial intelligence platforms and solutions. Over time, we have discovered that there is a maturity curve for organizations building out their AI capabilities. AI has a number of exciting applications that will drastically transform our reality, from driving cars to performing medical operations. In terms of an organization's knowledge, the future of AI is much closer but potentially just as impactful.

To this point, the vast majority of work in the knowledge and information space has come down to findability. Though search has progressed greatly, a number of organizations still struggle with the ability to design, implement, and maintain an effective search engine that surfaces the right content for the right people in a way that feels intuitive and natural. For some, search has progressed beyond simply returning a conglomeration of links. Through advanced design features like faceting and action-oriented search, we can now deliver a great deal of value. However, many other organizations are still struggling with more basic searches, including the simple challenge of having the relevant materials returned and weighted correctly so they may be found.

As we approach AI, we can go beyond find in order to deliver even more value to organizations. At EK, we talk about these elements as a set of capability levels of AI for knowledge and information management, ranging from the easiest to the hardest to achieve as shown in Fig. 14.1.

Answer

The closest to what advanced searches offer, answer not only returns a link to an answer but provides a specific block of information that directly responds to a natural language question. The most common example of this today is asking Siri or Alexa for an answer. Organizations are now beginning to put this into place for their own purposes via advanced action-oriented search, chatbots, and voice assistants. An example of this is a customer support knowledge base that surfaces a succinct answer to questions asked via search, extracted from larger and more difficult to navigate documents.

Recommend

With Recommend, indexes of different types of information (ranging from unstructured knowledge, to structured data, to directories of experts) have been linked and related via ontologies. Recommend identifies connections between different types and sources of information and provides relevant recommendations so that the end user can discover new material and make new connections. Basic recommendation engines have been wired into e-commerce experiences for years, but more mature recommendation capabilities are now being put into place for other organizational purposes. For instance, we helped a client with a recommendation tool that recognizes the background, education, and functions of individuals, as well as the title and topics of meetings to which they are invited in order to recommend meaningful pre-meeting reading information for them.

Combine

Up to this point, the capability levels of answer and recommend related content, but each piece of information remains separate. With Combine, knowledge AI takes a big step to begin automatically integrating different types and sources of content into more cohesive and contextualized blocks of knowledge. Like Recommend, this feature is powered via an ontology, often with a graph database behind it. A common example of this is Google's knowledge panels, which integrate information from multiple sources into a view that is easy to absorb and explore. Gartner calls this Enterprise 360, and it can be used to show a complete view of information about employees, customers, products, or topics within an organization (Foo Kune 2021). For example, one client we worked with had a large list of complex products.

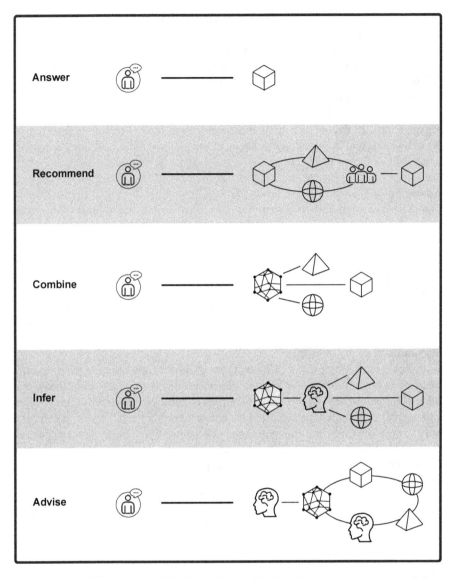

Fig. 14.1 Capability levels of AI for knowledge and information management, arranged from easiest to hardest to achieve. © 2021, Wahl/Hilger, reused with permission

Customers were looking for all of the information about any product, including sales literature, product specifications, and technical documentation. The knowledge graph used taxonomies and ontologies to automatically associate all of the documentation together through a process called proximity analysis. Once this new graph was in place, customers were able to dynamically show product information pages on their websites that combined information from as many as 10 different repositories.

Infer

Infer goes a step beyond Combine and introduces programmed decision-making logic into the mix. One client we worked with created a tool called Sales Brain, which, based on data including client demographics, behaviors, and logged needs, would automatically build a sales pitch with supporting material including sales training and ongoing coaching. One of the most powerful capabilities here is that, with the combination of tracking, analytics, and feedback measuring outcomes, the Sales Brain will effectively learn how to make better pitches over time. The potential ROI on an investment like this quickly becomes meaningful, with higher conversion rates, less time needed to close deals, and more time focused on client interactions instead of creating and recreating material. With Infer, an organization's content of all types and all locations will not just be better leveraged, it will actually be automatically combined and enhanced to create richer and more effective knowledge over time.

Advise

Beyond Infer, the primary target for many organizations regarding knowledge AI is for their systems to spot trends, identify potential risks and opportunities, and provide actionable guidance leveraging a complete view and understanding of the knowledge and information that exists. Though the potential and even much of the necessary technology is there, for most organizations, the structure of information and the documented decision-making logic will be the limiting factors to achieving this level of knowledge AI. Each step along this range of capability levels, if designed correctly, will help organizations get closer to their end goals for knowledge AI as long as the overall business drivers of the organization and goals of the individual end users are kept at the center of the process.

Moving along each step of the knowledge AI capability levels offers a significant potential for business value and hard returns on investment. With the right design process and forward-looking approaches to software, governance, and iteration, knowledge AI can begin to become real for your organization in a matter of months, with increasing value and capabilities clearly visible on your roadmap.

References

Brethenoux E (2020) What is artificial intelligence? Seeing through the hype and focusing on business value. Gartner. https://emtemp.gcom.cloud. Accessed 17 Jul 2021

Foo Kune L (2021) A 360-degree view of the customer is a destination, not a journey. Gartner. https://blogs.gartner.com. Accessed 17 Aug 2021

Integration Patterns for KM Systems

15

A true KM platform encompasses a wide range of systems that need to be properly integrated in order to meet the overall objective of making content and information more widely accessible across the enterprise. This section details how these tools are implemented in order to meet common KM needs.

15.1 Centralized Taxonomy Management

A Taxonomy Management System (TMS) is designed to be the sole location where taxonomies are managed while also maintaining the single source of truth regarding all taxonomies as they exist across the enterprise. Figure 15.1 illustrates how we would recommend a TMS be related to a variety of entities within the organization's technical landscape.

Process

Taxonomies are entered and managed from within the TMS by approved taxonomy managers/owners. Periodically (typically nightly), the updated taxonomies are pushed to all of the repositories that use those taxonomies to classify information. The taxonomies are also pushed to metadata stores for content management systems and pushed to look up tables for lines of business applications and key source tables for data warehouses.

Requirements

In order for this to work, the TMS needs to provide an API that allows for the retrieval of taxonomy terms from within any section of the taxonomy's hierarchy. Custom code is then developed so that a specific section of the taxonomy is pushed to the appropriate list in the repository system. There should be a frequent review process in place to confirm that the proper APIs exist to avoid sync failure.

© The Author(s), under exclusive license to Springer Nature Switzerland AG 2022
J. Hilger, Z. Wahl, *Making Knowledge Management Clickable*,
https://doi.org/10.1007/978-3-030-92385-3_15

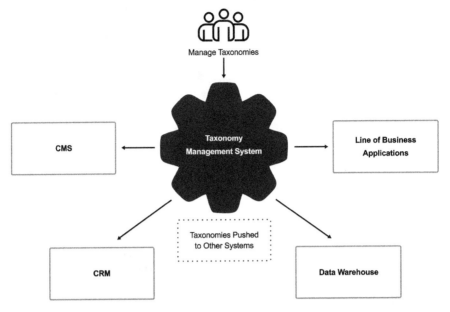

Fig. 15.1 Relationship of taxonomy management system to other entities. © 2021, Wahl/Hilger, reused with permission

Outcomes

When this is implemented properly, the organization will have a single place to add and edit taxonomy terms, and all integrated systems will use a common vocabulary.

15.2   Auto-Tagging for Search

The best search experiences provide faceted search interfaces similar to what we see on Amazon. The facets in this interface come from metadata attached to content in the source systems. While some of this metadata may be tagged manually, most enterprise implementations have too much content for manual tagging to be reasonable. As such, Taxonomy Management Systems provide a method to read the text of a piece of content and automatically recommend tags to describe that content. These tags are limited to terms in the taxonomy so that the tags are consistent with the enterprise taxonomy.

Note, many search engines offer a similar tagging feature. We recommend tagging content in the source repository for the following reasons:

- Tags are stored in a persistent storage location.
- Tags can be reviewed and edited if needed.
- Tags are selected from a carefully crafted taxonomy.

- Source systems can take advantage of this metadata for findability within the source system.

Figure 15.2 shows how we recommend auto-tagging be implemented in a CMS that feeds content to a search engine.

Process
Content is entered or loaded into the CMS. The CMS immediately sends the text of the content to the TMS to be tagged. The TMS analyzes the content and returns recommended tags along with a confidence score to the CMS. The tags that meet the proper confidence threshold are applied to the content in the CMS. Note that the application of tags can happen while the content manager is working with the content, so it can be reviewed automatically behind the scenes if a review is not required.

Once the tags are added as metadata to the content, the content is now ready for indexing by the search engine. The text of the content, its metadata, and any security-related information are sent to the search engine as part of the regular indexing process. Once the indexing is complete, the content and its metadata are now available for search. End users are now able to query content and receive an Amazon-like faceted search experience to help find content.

Requirements
The TMS must have built-in, auto-tagging capabilities that provide tags from a predefined taxonomy and can be tuned to improve the reliability of the tagging. It must provide a series of APIs that allow for content to be sent to the TMS and return a series of taxonomic tags with a confidence score. The tags must also allow the source system to see where in the taxonomy the tag/term exists to make sure that the proper metadata is updated.

The CMS solution needs to allow for scripts to run either during or after content entry that can call the TMS APIs, so the tags can be applied. It must also allow for structured content types with predefined metadata fields. Finally, the CMS must allow for the content and metadata to be accessed by the search engine, so it can be indexed and exposed in search.

The search engine needs to be able to index the content and metadata stored in the CMS and provide a faceted search experience that takes advantage of both the content and the metadata to provide an enhanced search experience.

Outcomes
Organizations that implement this approach improve the findability and usability of content across the organization. Their content is created and tagged in a consistent fashion according to a predefined, user-centric taxonomy. This content can be found and managed by content managers more efficiently because it has metadata that can be used to filter and organize content within the CMS. In addition, the organization is able to provide a cutting-edge, faceted search experience that provides a consistent

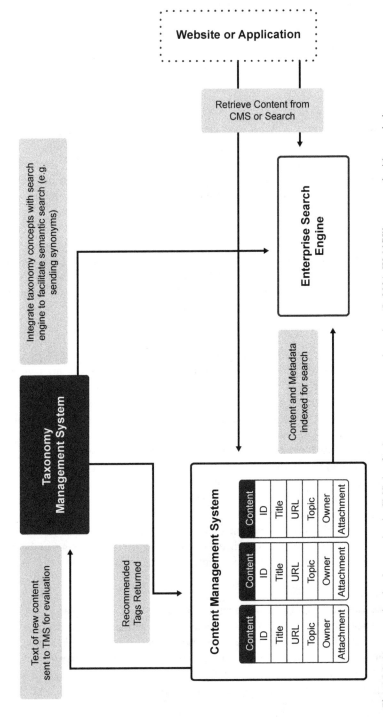

Fig. 15.2 Auto-tagging implementation in CMS that feeds content to a search engine. © 2021, Wahl/Hilger, reused with permission

and reliable way for people across the organization to access the content that they have permission to see.

15.3   TMS and Search Integration

The TMS is the central source of terms, synonyms, and vocabulary across the enterprise. As such, this information should be shared with the search engine to break down silos and encourage a consistent way to describe and access information across the organization. The TMS needs to be integrated with the search engine in order to achieve this consistency. There are two ways in which this integration can happen:

- Synonyms are sent to the search engine, so synonyms are managed in a central location.
- Taxonomies are sent to the search engine, so they can be used for type-ahead functionality.

Both of these integrations are optional, but we recommend that organizations implement them in most cases because they help ensure a consistent way of talking about and accessing information across the enterprise. Figure 15.3 shows how this integration works.

Process
On a predetermined schedule, the TMS sends a file of synonyms for the search engine to ingest. The next step depends on how the synonyms are implemented in the search. If synonyms are implemented at query time, no additional action needs to be taken. If synonyms are implemented during indexing, content will need to be re-indexed in order for the synonyms to take hold.

If the search engine is going to use the taxonomic terms for type-ahead functionality, these terms can be sent to the search engine to be indexed nightly, so any new or changed terms appear in the typeahead.

Requirements
The TMS needs to support the use and management of synonyms by multiple people from within the administrative console of the application. It also needs to have APIs that can be used to call these synonyms, so they can be sent to the search engine. Finally, the system needs APIs that allow access to any group of terms within the hierarchy of the taxonomy.

Outcomes
Leading KM organizations improve the way they find and share information by using a consistent set of terms to describe that information. When these changes are implemented, the TMS will provide a single place to define synonyms across the

Fig. 15.3 Integration of
taxonomy management
system and enterprise search
engine. © 2021, Wahl/Hilger,
reused with permission

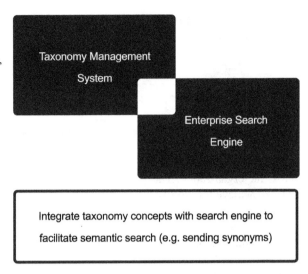

Integrate taxonomy concepts with search engine to
facilitate semantic search (e.g. sending synonyms)

organization. It will also encourage use of these terms through type-ahead functionality exposed in search.

15.4 Search Security

One of the most complex and poorly understood areas of search is with document-
level security. Not every piece of information should be available to everyone in an
organization. Typically, source repositories have their own security model to properly secure information for the users of the application. Enterprise search exposes
content from a large number of systems. As a result, the search engine needs to
support the security models in each of these repositories. This is a very complex
process that involves understanding who is executing the search, what groups they
belong to, and what attributes define their information access credentials. It also
requires that the search engine indexes these access permissions for each repository,
so they can be applied based on the user's credentials. A depiction of this process is
shown in Fig. 15.4.

Process
The process of applying security is divided into two sections. The first is the capture
of security information of both the content and the users. The second process occurs
during a query when the search engine applies the user's credentials against the
content security information to determine which search results to display. The rest of
this section explains both processes.

In order to replicate the security of each application, the search engine needs to
capture both the user credentials and the security rules for the content (also known as
ACLs). The search engine regularly queries the identity management system to

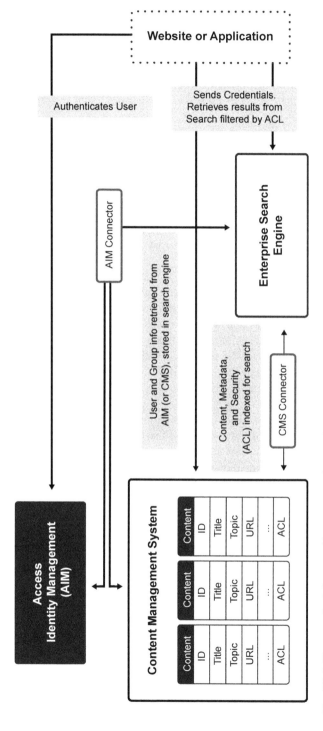

Fig. 15.4 How security is integrated into an enterprise search. © 2021, Wahl/Hilger, reused with permission

group the users appropriately, as well as any other specific attributes that are relevant to user permissioning. This is done in advance to increase query performance, so the search application does not have to rely on access to the identity management system each time a person runs a query.

The indexing process is a separate process that runs on its own schedule. This process indexes the content, relevant metadata, and any security-related groups or attributes that will be used to filter out search results that a user does not have access to.

When the user executes a search query, the security logic is applied to the query to filter or trim results. This process is called security trimming. The search application should know the user's credentials and pass both the credentials and the search query, so the search engine knows who the searcher is. The search engine uses the credentials to identify the individual groups and attributes. This information is then used by the search engine to trim the search results where the ACLs associated with the content do not align with the searcher's credentials. The search engine then returns only the search results that the user has access to.

Requirements

Search security is one of the most difficult processes related to enterprise search. This process gets even more complicated when there is more than one repository with different search rules and when there is a multiuser repository defining what people can have access to. In order to validate that the search engine truly supports security, it is important that the tool has a connector for capturing user credentials and connectors for each repository that indexes ACLs as well as the content. While it is possible to develop this functionality, it is quite complex and could extend a project by years.

In addition to the connectors for users and content, the solution needs to have a fully developed security trimming process that can apply different logic to different repositories and has been proven to work at scale.

Security trimming is the number one differentiating requirement for selecting a search engine in any organization looking to implement an enterprise search with complicated security logic.

Outcomes

Enterprise search applications that cannot offer security trimming capabilities are severely limited as to what content they can display. An enterprise search with robust security trimming capabilities can safely allow users to query content from a large number of repositories in a single location. Compliance and security requirements are held in place, and users are able to access their content in a single location without worrying about which application it resides in.

One other unanticipated outcome from implementing a search like this is the identification of rogue or unsecured content. It is quite common for content to be put in applications without proper security measures. Implementing secure search will often identify those problems and allow organizations to properly secure content that was accidentally left open.

Part III

Running a KM Systems Project

This part details how to take the strategy from Part I and the technologies from Part II and integrate them with the appropriate design and implementation to put your KM systems successfully in place. In this section, we detail the standard project approach and methodology, identify common challenges with KM systems initiatives, discuss foundational design elements critical to success, and cover the nature of content in all its forms as they relate to your KM systems and KM transformations.

KM systems projects are uniquely challenging tasks because of the problems that these systems are trying to solve. First, we are building a solution that breaks down information silos across the enterprise. As such, the clients of this system typically span the entire organization. This means that the user base of the solution being built is almost always everyone in the company, and these users have different tasks and responsibilities. In larger organizations, they frequently work in different manners. As a result, it is hard to define a single way in which the knowledge workers will interact with each new KM solution or to identify a single business owner for each new system.

The second problem with KM systems projects has to do with the complexity of the information being shared. Most KM systems projects work with information stored in more than one application. As a result, each application has its own way of storing and managing that information. Finding a way to standardize these information assets in a way that makes them shareable across the enterprise is a challenging modeling problem and one that needs to be planned for in every KM project.

The third problem is integration. KM systems are built to break down information silos by making it easy to share information across systems. This means that nearly every enterprise-level KM system project requires integration with one or more systems. This level of integration can be very complex. It requires communication between multiple development teams and assurance that the integration does not materially affect the performance of the existing systems that the KM system is being integrated with.

While this sounds challenging, the benefit of breaking down these silos across the enterprise is significant. Organizations that go through this process tend to have better information management and security, as well as more robust systems and greater access to information.

The key to successfully delivering on these complex projects is to take an agile, iterative approach that allows each system to gain traction within one business function or department and then slowly grow across the enterprise. We have implemented literally hundreds of enterprise-level KM projects. Our most successful implementations follow the core tenets of the Agile Manifesto [Agile Manifesto (n.d.)]:

INDIVIDUALS AND INTERACTIONS over processes and tools

WORKING SOFTWARE over comprehensive documentation

CUSTOMER COLLABORATION over contract negotiation

RESPONDING TO CHANGE over following a plan

In practice, this means that each of our projects begins with a pilot project in a chosen business unit where we can prove the value of the tool and adjust to what we learn from the business unit we work with. We learn how the knowledge workers interact with the solution and adjust policies, procedures, and system processes to align the system and users as effectively as possible (INDIVIDUALS AND INTERACTIONS over processes and tools). We quickly develop and release a MVP version of the software so that the pilot teams can interact with the tool and provide feedback as to what works and what does not work. Our teams then add new features iteratively based on feedback from the client, making sure that they always have a working version of the software that is usable and not too documentation heavy (WORKING SOFTWARE over comprehensive documentation). This process allows the users of the system to provide more detailed feedback because they are using the application in production and making requests based on how they are using the system and not a long list of paper-based requirements (CUSTOMER COLLAB-ORATION over contract negotiation). Once the pilot is complete, we have a strong understanding as to how the application is best rolled out to the pilot group. We also have a champion to help ensure that others are excited about what is coming. At that point, we can make a plan to roll out to the next group knowing that we will learn new things with that group (RESPONDING TO CHANGE over following a plan). As we roll out the KM solution to more and more groups, the process becomes more routine and predictable, and an enterprise rollout becomes not only possible but highly successful and smooth.

Throughout this process, it is important that each system has measurable success criteria so that the core KM team can regularly update senior management on the progress and positive impact of the new KM solution. Our most successful KM implementation leaders divide their time equally across the following tasks:

- Supporting the development and implementation process.
- Sharing measurable success stories with business leaders and building interest in the solution.
- Negotiating agreements on standards and features across business units.

In the rest of this section, we are going to show what running one of these projects looks like. It is important to remember that a KM implementation is often a series of workstreams, each of which is a different project that can be run independently. For example, a KM initiative might need the following workstreams:

- Implementation of a document management solution.
- Implementation of a web-content management solution.
- Implementation of an enterprise search tool.
- Development of a KM governance structure.

Each of these projects needs to be managed individually, and the process described below explains the best way to manage each project.

16.1 Project Planning and Scoping

At the end of a KM strategy engagement, your organization should have a list of projects that need to be implemented as part of the KM program. It is important to note that many of these projects are pilots that will be rolled out to a small, targeted group before being implemented across the enterprise. The project leaders should review each project to understand answers to the following critical questions:

- How do I measure success for this project?
- What foundational work needs to be completed first before any projects can begin?
- How does the implementation of this project affect the other projects in the KM program?
- Which is the best group to begin with?
- Who will be the hardest group to convince?

Answering these questions will allow the team to make the proper decisions as to the order in which projects are undertaken, who to begin working with, how to roll out to larger groups, and how to know when each phase of the project is complete.

As these complex KM migrations begin, it is important to have an overall plan that can be shared with leadership and with the team members that will be working on the project. In our experience, it is best to have a detailed project document describing the goals of the KM initiative along with each of the projects to be undertaken. This should be accompanied by an executive overview presentation that explains what is being done to senior leadership.

When preparing these documents, the questions listed above need to be answered for each of the projects in the project document. Each project should include a description of the project and how it fits into the overall KM initiative. It should also include a series of SMART success measures that can be used to focus the team and regularly provide updates to senior management about the progress of the implementation. SMART measures of success are specific, measurable, achievable, relevant, and timebound. These success measures will be used throughout the project to ensure continued focus on the measures behind the KM initiative and to give the team a way to regularly communicate successes to management over time.

In addition to SMART success measures, it is also important to understand the order in which each project should be completed. Every KM initiative has foundational activities that need to be completed before other projects begin. For example, a faceted search will not be successful without a taxonomy and properly tagged content to generate the facets. These project plans should include information about which projects occur first and which ones are dependent on things like content cleanup or the completion of other projects first. Once that is well understood, the KM project team can properly order the way in which projects are implemented.

Lastly, most of these projects are implemented by one group or business unit at a time. This approach simplifies the implementation and allows people to see value from their KM projects sooner since they are not having to wait until all development is complete and the solution can be launched to the entire organization. The project team needs to identify which groups are best suited to be the first users of the tool. These are typically groups that meet the following criteria:

- They have shown an active interest in the KM initiative and the solution being rolled out.
- They are willing to invest in the system and work with the KM team to make sure it is successful.
- They offer the strongest use case or the greatest ROI.
- They have a less complex implementation.

The information in this project plan will provide senior leadership and the project team with a solid understanding of each project, its value, and the order in which it should be implemented.

16.2   Software Selection

Selecting the right KM solution can be tricky. These tools tend to serve niche markets; they have very specific features and need to serve a wide variety of users. We have helped with a lot of these selections and have identified the key considerations when selecting these tools, as well as an Agile approach for making the selection as quickly as possible. To begin, it is important to understand the key criteria for selecting your KM solution.

- Community/support
- Past performance
- Features
- Integration
- Proofs of concept

Community/Support
KM implementations continue to grow and adjust over time. This means that the tool you select will need regular support beyond the initial design and build. You want to select a tool that has a strong support community and many affordable support options.

As you evaluate KM products (both open source and commercial), investigate the online support communities. How active are they? Can you easily get answers to your questions online, or do you need to work with the software vendor? A strong support community makes it easy to get help when something does not work as expected.

Online forums are helpful, but sometimes you need an expert. Software vendor professional services can be expensive. You want to ensure that you have options for external support. Check out job sites like Dice and Indeed to understand the market for independent contractors. Also, find out what boutique firms are out there and what their rates are. This information will help you understand how many support options you have with your chosen technology set.

Features

Throughout this book, we have shared many of the most common and important features for each type of KM tool. These features are critical in evaluating different software vendors and deciding what you need. We like to divide these features into two categories: differentiating and non-differentiating. Differentiating features are those features that are critical to your organization but not available through every vendor. Features that are important to your organization that are available through nearly every vendor will not help narrow the field of vendors to select from. Use the differentiating features as one of the key criteria to identify a short list of vendors that can meet your needs. You can then use a proof of concept (identified later on) to ensure that the features really work as you expect them to.

Integration

The ultimate goal of any KM program is to break down silos of information. These can exist between people, organizations, or systems. Given the importance of breaking down silos, it is critical that all new KM systems are properly integrated with other systems so that information is easily available. For example, an enterprise search system needs to index content from each of the main repositories of the organization. It needs to be set up to index (read) that information from each repository. Another integration example is a collaboration solution that supports project communication. The time and billing or CRM system needs to alert the collaboration tool that a new project is beginning so that the collaboration space can be created. The content in this new space would need to be integrated with the document management system on record as well. As you are looking to select a new system for your organization, spend time understanding how easy it is to integrate with other systems. Ask the following questions:

- What existing systems does this new application need to integrate with?
- Does the system have modern APIs or methods to share information with these existing applications?
- Does the system have hooks that allow for the pushing or pulling of information between the new system and the existing applications?

- Are there canned integrations that can be used between the new application and the existing systems that you are integrating with?
- Can the vendor share the name of other companies that have integrated with the application that you plan to integrate with?

Integration is a critical part of the overall success of any KM system implementation, but it is almost always overlooked when selecting a vendor. Spending some time up front helps ensure that the tool you select will play well with others and be successful at solving the content silo dilemma.

Past Performance
KM system implementations are all different. Having said that, there are always environments that are similar to your environment. If you are looking for a search engine, find organizations indexing similar applications. If you are implementing a CMS, find organizations that are solving similar business problems. As you evaluate vendors, ask them to provide references of other organizations that have similar situations. Interview the references to understand how well the tool has been adopted and what were the greatest challenges they faced in the implementation. This is a great way to understand how well the KM solution will work in your environment. It provides insight into some of the problems you may face, and it also gives you a potential resource to call upon when you have issues or surprises. There is no better resource for help than organizations that have dealt with similar problems. They will be able to give you honest, real-life answers.

Proofs of Concept
Once your organization has selected a short list of vendors who are likely to meet your specific needs, it is time to definitively confirm which product is the best solution for your organization. POCs are the fastest and most reliable way to make a proper selection. You may have to pay for the Proofs of Concept (POC), but it is a wise investment. You will be stuck with the tool you select for quite a while. A little money up front is worth it to make sure that you select the right tool and get it started quickly.

These POCs are most successful if they are run in the right manner. We recommend an Agile approach to POCs. This approach is divided into three sprints (including a sprint 0 for setup) that allow for planning, implementation, and evaluation of the POC. Each of these sprints is explained below.

Sprint 0: Planning and Organizing (Typically Two to Three Weeks) Software vendors develop their applications with many features so that they can check the box of meeting most feature requirements. While the system you are evaluating may have a certain feature, that feature may not truly solve your business need, or it may be difficult to work with. We have found the best way to understand if a product truly meets a business need is to define a set of multistep scenarios that your users would encounter. During Sprint 0, work with key stakeholders to identify business problems the solution will address. Select three to five scenarios for the vendors to implement as part of the POC. At least two of these scenarios should represent common problems that need to be handled often. One of the scenarios should represent a more challenging need that will really test out the vendor's product. Once these scenarios are together, you can develop a POC RFP and send it to your short list of vendors, asking them to work with you to develop a POC. Depending on the complexity of the solutions, the vendors may ask to be paid. It is okay to pay, but be aggressive about the amount. The software vendor wants your business and will likely invest for a chance to win it.

Sprint 1: Engaging (Typically Two Weeks)   Once the RFP is out and the vendors have either agreed to participate or not, it is time to start engaging. Typically, this includes identifying where the software will be installed/used and making sure that personnel on both sides have proper systems access so that the system can be implemented and properly tested on both sides. In addition, there should be an agreed-upon list of tasks (a backlog) for implementing the POC and showing how it meets the business scenarios identified in Sprint 0.

As part of the engaging process, it is important to make sure that a member of your IT team is working on the implementation of the POC. They will have to get introduced to the tool and the people from the software vendor. Having input from IT on the complexity of building out these solutions is important to properly understand how difficult it is to manage and maintain each product being evaluated.

Sprint 2: POC Build Out (Typically One to Two Weeks)   The goal for this sprint is to build out the initial POC. The vendor's professional services team should work in partnership with your IT team to install and customize the software so that your organization can test that it works. The vendor will want to include some of their more compelling features, which is fine. At a minimum though, it needs to be able to support the business scenarios agreed upon as part of the POC.

Once the sprint is complete, a demo should be shown to the primary users and stakeholders that displays its best features along with examples of how each business scenario is met within the POC. The vendor can show this themselves, but it is better if a member of your team is able to figure out how to do it themselves.

Sprint 3: POC Modifications (Typically One Week)   At the end of Sprint 2, it is likely that some of the proposed approaches do not meet your specific needs. This is common with any project and not necessarily a condemnation of the software. It is possible that the professional services team did not understand the need properly. In the end, you are evaluating the capabilities of the software and not the vendor's ability to understand your business needs. This final sprint is an opportunity for vendors to adjust their software based on feedback from the demo. This sprint will end with another demo showing what changed and how the changes were made.

This same process will need to be repeated for each vendor that is a finalist. At the end of the selection process, your organization should have:

- Hands-on experience with the product and a good understanding of its capabilities.
- A detailed understanding of how difficult this was to implement technically and what it will take to support the tool.
- A working implementation of the software and a backlog of requirements that can be used as the basis of the software implementation going forward.

While this selection process seems involved, it can happen pretty quickly if everything is organized. This approach allows both the business and the IT to be actively engaged in the selection process and make a choice that meets the business needs and is also supportable by IT. Given the cost of selecting the wrong software and/or replatforming to a new solution, this selection process more than pays for itself.

16.3 Design

When planning systems design activities, people often think of user interfaces or technical architectures. While that is a key part of the design process, there are other equally important activities that are specific to KM systems implementations. Much of the design work will be done as part of the iterative implementation process, but there are some tasks that need to be prioritized as they affect all other activities. This includes the following tasks:

- User experience research
- Architectural design
- Content modeling
- Taxonomy design
- Security design
- Hit type analysis
- Ontology design

The user's experience with any KM system is critical to adoption of that tool, and adoption is critical to making KM systems matter. If people are not using the tool, there is no way to capture, manage, and find the information because it will not exist. User experience research is the best way to understand how people work, what they need, and how to design a system that best aligns with those needs. At the end of the design phase, the KM implementation team should understand the users' regular workflows (user journeys) and what is intuitive and natural with the way they work. This upfront design effort will help prioritize the features and design efforts for the new system implementation and ensure that users are understood and engaged from the outset of the project.

As we mentioned earlier when discussing product selection, integration with other systems is core to nearly every KM implementation project. There are some up-front activities that should be started as soon as possible on any KM implementation. First, it is important to have a system inventory that includes information about the system, its purpose, its security model, and the type of information that it stores. If it is a search or knowledge graph implementation, it helps the team understand where information is stored. If it is a content management system, this information helps us understand which information belongs in the new system and which information belongs elsewhere. The better this is understood, the better the new system can be integrated into the overall IT landscape. The second design activity is to produce a high-level logical and physical architecture for the new application. This activity allows the infrastructure team to prepare the servers for the installation of the application, and it also allows the KM implementation team to make sure that the new system meets all IT security standards. The implementation uses an Agile approach; as such, some of this will change as we learn more. These designs can remain high level since we know it will change over time. It is simply critical to start these activities right away so that the actual implementation is not delayed due to infrastructure or security issues.

Content modeling is another critical design activity that needs to be started early in the implementation process. Content modeling is the process of defining a consistent metadata structure for content across the enterprise. Over 80% of content in any organization is unstructured. Metadata adds structure and describes the content so that people and systems understand what is in the content. Content cannot easily be shared across the enterprise without additional structure. The content modeling process can identify the structures of the content in the system you are working with as well as the required structure of the content that your new system will interact with.

A taxonomy is a set of controlled vocabularies used to describe or characterize explicit concepts of information for purposes of capture, management, and presentation. Taxonomies allow organizations to categorize information in a consistent fashion across the enterprise. This allows users to share and view information across systems in a consistent fashion. Taxonomies typically are used to generate the facets in enterprise search implementations. They also populate much of the metadata defined in the content modeling design process described earlier. Every KM project we have ever worked on has required a taxonomy in order to capture, share, and manage information. It is truly a foundational element of KM system implementations.

Security is another important consideration in any KM system implementation. KM systems make it easier to share and view content created by others. Not all content should be viewable by all people. As a result, it is important to think about who can see content and how content will be properly secured. Most systems use a combination of groups, roles, and permissions. This approach allows for a lot of flexibility, but it can be complex, and it assumes that there is a user store in place that is accessible by the application. An experienced technical analyst will need to understand the security model that the business requires and figure out how that can be implemented within the application and the infrastructure systems in place at your organization. Implementation of your new application can begin before this analysis is complete, but this analysis needs to start immediately to make sure that your application will be able to provide a security model that is usable, maintainable, and aligns with the business needs.

Hit type analysis is a process specific to search implementations. The best search applications think of search results as unique assets with different information for each asset. For example, a project has one set of specific descriptive information including things like client, technology, team, or start date. A person or document would have very different information. A person would include title, organization, role, and contact information. A document might have the topic, type, and author. Hit type analysis is the process of identifying these unique asset types, their specific descriptive information, and then mapping the source of that information. Hit type analysis defines how search indexing works and what information is needed to create a great search experience.

An ontology is a defined model that organizes structured and unstructured information through entities, their properties, and the way they relate to one another. An example can be seen in Fig. 16.1. An ontology defines the way that a graph database is structured. Ontologies are typically organized around things like employees, products, projects, customers, and topics. When properly implemented, knowledge graphs are able to quickly produce relevant information from across multiple systems in a way that makes sense to the user. This design work is an important part of any knowledge graph project and typically begins once the data sources of the graph are known.

These unique design activities all play important roles in implementing KM solutions that integrate well in an organization and provide the right information to people at the right time.

16.4 Implementation and Testing

There are a number of significant challenges with implementing KM solutions. We talked about some of these challenges earlier in this chapter. Things such as complex integrations and enterprise-wide implementations are best handled by starting small with targeted groups and solutions and growing them over time. One challenge that is not addressed by these pilot rollouts is understanding how people will interact and use the new system. The way in which people look for and share information is not easily documented. There is no simple user journey describing what causes a person to look for information or decide to share information. As such, understanding the expected workflow and features for each new KM system is not reasonable. An Agile approach to implementation provides the opportunity to get a number of checkpoints with real users along the way. It also allows for a baseline system to be implemented quickly so that it can be adjusted as people begin to work with it and find out what they really need.

The first step of any implementation is to install the software and get it set up for use. While the development team is working on the vanilla installation, the rest of the team can focus on building a backlog of features that will need to be implemented over time. These features can be gathered as a team and agreed upon between the

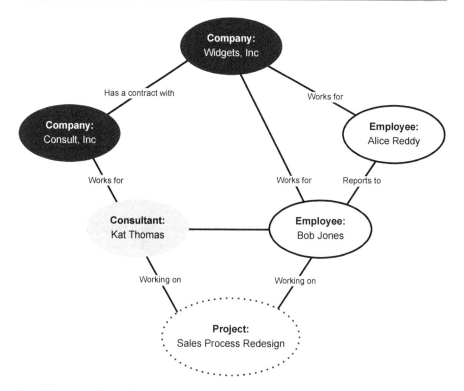

Fig. 16.1 A sample ontology showing how companies, consultants, employees, and projects can be modeled. © 2021, Wahl/Hilger, reused with permission

KM leaders and the group for which the pilot is being produced. Once the initial list is in place, these items need to be prioritized. A single individual should be appointed as the product owner responsible for prioritizing stories and answering open questions for the development team. It is important to note that you do not need a complete and prioritized backlog before beginning implementation. The project team can begin work once there is at least one complete sprint of prioritized backlog tasks. Once the software is installed and the prioritized backlog is ready, the development can begin.

There are a number of ways to run Agile sprints. The most common approach is scrum, which involves one-, two-, or three-week sprints where the project team has the following ceremonies or meetings each sprint:

- Backlog refinement
- Sprint planning
- Daily scrum
- Sprint review
- Sprint retrospective

Backlog refinement is a meeting where the project team and the product owner meet to gain greater understanding of backlog tasks and to prioritize what comes next in the upcoming sprint. Sprint planning is the kickoff meeting for each sprint. During sprint planning, the team commits to a series of tasks and prepares the business as to what it will see at the end of the sprint. The daily scrum is a quick (ideally 15 minute) meeting where each team member and the product owner update the team on what they are working on. The sprint review occurs at the end of the sprint. Typically, the work of the team is demoed during the sprint review to gather feedback from the business users. Finally, the sprint retrospective is the time when the team meets to talk about what went well and what could be improved. Agile approaches are based on a spirit of continuous improvement. These retrospectives allow the team members to learn from one another and to identify new and better ways to move the project forward.

In our experience, this Agile approach ensures the most interaction between the development team and the eventual users of the system. Business users are seeing new features every sprint and can comment on what they see and not some words written in a requirements document. Because there is no formal project plan based on a number of assumptions or prescribed requirements, the development team is able to adjust to the kinds of changes that naturally come up during a KM implementation project.

There are two other benefits to this type of approach. First, the software and new features are tested each sprint. This upfront testing allows for corrections to be made sooner, and it also allows the team to release working software to users sooner, since there is no planned testing phase at the end of the project. While this may feel uncomfortable to people not used to working in a true Agile environment, leading technical organizations around the world including IBM, Cisco, and Microsoft use this approach and have consistently found that software development is more consistent and reliable with this iterative approach.

The second benefit has to do with gaining buy-in to the new system. At the end of each sprint, users are seeing new features that they often get excited about. In addition, when there is something they do not like, it is corrected in a later sprint, and the business users see that they will get what they want and not have to put up with a system that meets only part of their needs. In most cases, development teams that follow this Agile approach find that the business is truly excited and anxious to start using the new system. They know what it is and how it will work and become evangelists as to what will be launched. An Agile implementation process is one of the best ways to ensure early and rapid adoption of your new KM system.

While an Agile approach is not the only way to implement new systems, we have found that it is one of the best and most reliable ways to implement these complex solutions in a way that gets users excited about what they are getting. The iterative process allows the business to get previews as to what is coming and allows the development team to adjust their plans when new requirements or needs come up. Harvard Business Review's article "Embracing Agile" asserts that Agile methods have been largely responsible for innovation and successes in software development over the last 30 years, transforming both management and IT processes

(Rigby et al. 2016). Now, Agile methodology is benefitting countless organizations across many different industries, and although the concept can be daunting, the simple and progressive steps laid out above will help to ensure success in any organization new to the iterative approach.

16.5 Rollout

Once the pilot is in use and it has met the original objectives spelled out during the strategy planning phase, it is time to begin to roll the product out to the rest of the enterprise. This can be a challenging endeavor, but it should be tackled in the same iterative fashion as the implementation of the first pilot, as shown in Fig. 16.2.

Identify the next group to expand the pilot with. This group should have shown interest in the solution, have content or processes that make it likely to be a successful project, and have people available to help with the implementation. As you are deciding which group to roll the software out to next, create a demo/roadshow to share with others. This will generate interest in the KM system and help spot good candidates for the next release. Once the candidate has been selected, the next phase can begin.

Each new group should receive a kickoff showing the product and agreeing on an initial scope for the project. Once this is complete, the iterative implementation process described in the prior section can be followed, with one exception. Since the software is already live with another group, it is important they are made aware of any upcoming changes and provided a chance to assist with the prioritization based on their current usage. Typically, the product owner from the initial implementation is added to the sprint reviews of the current implementation so that this person is aware of the changes that are occurring and can offer suggestions based on their

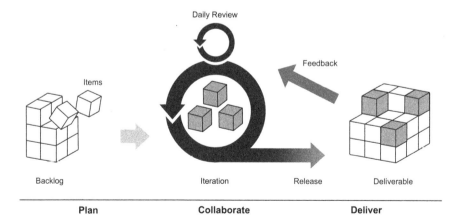

Fig. 16.2 Representation of an iterative Agile implementation process for pilots and product rollout. © 2021, Wahl/Hilger, reused with permission

current usage of the product. This process can be tricky with the first new group, but it gets easier as the product matures.

Once the second group has launched, a third group should be added. The project team should focus on making the addition of a new group to the process as repeatable as possible. Our most successful projects have used checklists of what it takes to be ready to join and who should be prioritized. They standardize the process and make sure that adding new groups is streamlined each time. After the first three or four groups, new groups should be added in weeks, and the process for adding new groups becomes less about new development and more about processes for onboarding new teams.

This phased rollout approach has a number of benefits when rolling out enterprise-wide KM solutions.

- The business gets to use software sooner and does not have to wait for a long, complex implementation.
- The development team gets to build competency with the tool in small increments and grow over time.
- The initial groups using the software become its champions and help create interest with other groups.
- A backlog of groups waiting to use the software naturally creates excitement that helps ensure visibility and adoption over time.

Enterprise software rollouts are difficult, but an iterative process of exposing the software to more and more users ensures a greater chance of success and a better product over time.

References

Agile Manifesto (n.d.) Manifesto for agile software development. https://agilemanifesto.org/. Accessed 11 June 2021
Rigby D, Sutherland J, Takeuchi H (2016) Embracing agile. Harvard Business Review. https://hbr. org. Accessed 06 Aug 2021

Common KMS Project Challenges and Mistakes

17

This book serves as a guide to ensure that your KM systems projects will run smoothly and successfully, from initial strategy and planning to design, implementation, operations, and long-term evolution. As we have asserted throughout, there are many risks and reasons as to why a project like this might be derailed or struggle, and this book endeavors to offer actionable guidance that will keep these risks and reasons from surfacing. Though the list is long, these are the most common project challenges and mistakes we have seen that have led to a major project issue or overall project failure. Ideally, you can see all of these as themes that we have addressed through the book and have already equipped you to address through each phase of your initiatives.

Missing the "Why?"

KM systems projects will fail when the organization cannot agree upon the answer to a simple question: why are we putting this system in place? Not only must the answer be clear, your leadership and stakeholders must concur. Without a defined answer to this question, organizations end up with internal competing priorities and different expectations as to what the end state should look like. It is notable that most organizations believe they possess a shared understanding, but once we start asking individual sponsors and stakeholders what their definition of success is, the answers can be dramatically different. Ensure you counteract this misalignment by putting a great deal of time into defining, socializing, and periodically revisiting the target state. Use personas, journey maps, and user stories to make the impact of the new KM system clear, and allow stakeholders to truly visualize the impact. Coming back to the target state over time to check in and ensure no major priorities have changed is also a key component to maintaining alignment.

Lack of Leadership Support

One of the most common reasons KM efforts fail is they do not possess the appropriate level of support from leadership. This does not just mean a lack of funding or prioritization, though those are certainly dire issues. In order for KM efforts to succeed, they need active support from leadership, with executives modeling and reinforcing the behavior changes that must occur for the KM effort to truly stick. Leadership support is also critical to remove project blockers and resistors in the organization. As we have discussed throughout this book, the most effective means of engaging leadership is to tie KM efforts to business value and, wherever possible, hard return on investment. KM systems plans must be put in terms of benefits to the business in order to generate and maintain leadership support.

Missing Design Foundations

Chapter 18 details the most important foundational design elements to make sure your KM system will make sense to your end users and will improve the usability and depth of content over time. Too frequently, however, we still see organizations making a major investment in the purchase of a new technology without putting the time and effort into designing and instantiating these foundational design elements within the tool. Foundational design elements like taxonomy, content types, and hit types all build on the system's information architecture so that end users will find it intuitive, and the right information may be found and discovered. In short, the foundational design elements are central to the activities discussed back in Chap. 1 regarding the KM Action Wheel. Organizations that fail to budget for the time, cost, and effort it takes to adequately understand their users, design those elements, and ensure they are put in place will often see an initial burst of activity for their new KM system, but they will then experience a steep drop off as users realize the new system does not reflect the way they think or want to do business.

Lack of End User Engagement

Keeping with the theme of the previous issue, many KM systems efforts have failed because they do not engage the very people who are supposed to get value out of them. Too frequently, KM efforts are designed without sufficient engagement from end users and business stakeholders. This commonly results from KM practitioners and project owners making too many assumptions about what the end users really want, what troubles they are having, and how they would like to see things change or as expressed above, focusing too much on the technology elements of the system and not enough on the foundational design elements. Even if the practitioners guess correctly, end users typically revolt against change to ensure their voices are heard if not all of their needs have been sufficiently met. In this book, we have detailed the many types of workshops, focus groups, and other user-centered design activities that help to engage users. If you cannot say what is in it for the end users associated with each aspect of the system you are putting in place, you should question whether you have spent enough time with your users or if you are making assumptions for them. Between strategy, design, implementation, and long-term iteration, a key success factor for KM systems is to ensure users are engaged and empowered to guide the effort.

Excessive Complexity

Yet another major reason for KM systems project failures is that they are designed in an overly complex manner. This is not only a reason why many efforts fail, but also the reason many never move past the planning phase. KM, as a field, has always suffered from struggles regarding complexity and clarity. When you consider the many definitions of KM itself and the vast array of topics, processes, and technologies that can fit within the KM bucket, it is not surprising that many organizations end up with a confused and overly intricate KM strategy and systems plan. To counteract this, focus on the iterative approaches and leverage Agile design and development as we detail in Chap. 16, identifying pilots and other foundational efforts that can show real value, measured in weeks and months instead of years. What this means, in practice, is that KM systems should not be deployed as a "big bang" major rollout. Leverage pilots and incremental extensions to test, deploy, extend, and repeat. This vastly decreases the overall complexity of KM systems efforts, spreads out the budget and risk, and ensures you have plenty of time to learn from your stakeholders in order to improve the overall system for your enterprise.

Missing "Celebratable Moments"

As we describe in Chap. 1, KM projects too often talk in terms of features and functions, instead of business outcomes. In addition, overly "big bang" sprawling KM projects wait too long to demonstrate value to their end users by showing them something real they can use. Projects that take too long to show value often struggle to get or maintain the necessary traction and buzz to keep going. To that end, ensure your KM systems projects have celebratable moments. These are seeded throughout an initiative to deliver periodic communications to stakeholders to ensure they see progress and have real elements to which they may react. Moreover, these moments become a key component of your change management plan, as they allow your team to show progress and demonstrate the practicality of the project approach and KM system in the context of actual work.

Lack of Integration

If we were to boil down one of the most important aspects of a KM system, it would be connectivity. That can be connectivity of people to people, people to content, or people to learning. Another important aspect of connectivity is connectivity to other systems and repositories of content. A successful KM system will be one that creates bridges and connections between various systems. However, a common mistake with KM systems implementations is that implementers fail to identify integration points for their new KM systems. At best, this means your organization is missing opportunities to build connections between systems. At worst, this lack of consideration will yield user frustration, confusion, and even potential redundancies between systems. Integration is not just cross-linking. True integration between systems, via shared taxonomies and ontologies, content types, APIs, and data, will result in seamless systems where the users focus on the content they need and not the system they are in or where the content is housed; rather, they will trust through the integrated experience that they are getting access to all of the right knowledge and information they need to do their jobs.

Overt Focus on the Technology Part of the System

Are you surprised to see this in a book regarding KM systems? You should not be. We are at an incredibly exciting time in KM technologies, where many of the promises from a decade ago are finally a reality. Auto-tagging tools are much more accurate than they used to be, ontologies and the semantic web are creating functional webs of structured and unstructured content, and enterprise search tools are making it easier to intuitively find and discover what you care about. However, KM initiatives frequently fail when the technology alone is regarded as the KM solution. The technology itself needs to be considered as the enabling tool that surfaces the overall KM solution. The way we talk about people, process, content, culture, and technology is very specific. Technology is listed last, and it is only one of five elements. Yes, technology is how KM programs become real and impactful to many of the people within your organization, but those programs will not work if you only talk about the technology and fail to consider the other elements of KM transformations and KM systems implementations.

According to Blackwell and Gamble, "people tend to use corporate knowledge bases where retrieval is also supported by local (internal) expertise and frames of reference. Thus, the creation of a knowledge base is really about creating an internal marketplace where people recognize what knowledge they need, the value of that knowledge, and its relevance to their current problem environment" (Gamble and Blackwell 2001). People, process, content, and culture all contribute to the capture, harnessing, and usage of intellectual capital in the organization. Similar to a giant library full of information, a KM initiative will be difficult for users to navigate and understand the value of without the right guidance and involvement from the business, which provides the context and input to ensure the system is intuitive and adds business value the end users will recognize.

Perhaps most specifically, your KM systems efforts will fail when organizations avoid what, for many, is their number one issue: old, incorrect, and outdated content. In fact, in many organizations, four out of five documents/pieces of content would fall into this category of disrepair. Ensuring the quality of your content is the most critical foundational element for KM success. We detail the specifics of content ahead in Chap. 19.

Lack of Sustainment

Even projects that experience initial buy-in and success still run the risk of failure if not properly sustained. The most successful KM systems are those that start out good and evolve to be great. Additionally, the most successful systems are those that will require the most maintenance, both because they will be business-critical to your end users and because the most used systems are those that have the greatest likelihood of falling out of sync with your enterprise. This may sound counterintuitive, but picture a great KM system like your favorite sweater. You wear it the most, it is your go-to article of clothing, and therefore to keep it from getting dirty or torn, it requires the most care. A well-used KM system is one that will have dynamic content loaded into it and will receive the most requests from end users to make changes and additions. All of this means it must be well managed and governed to ensure those changes and additions support the enterprise and not just the individuals or group making the requests. Organizations that do not make a long-term investment in the communications, iterative adjustments, updates to processes and technologies, and continued engagement efforts for their KM strategies will quickly see the interest and support for such initiatives wither.

One important piece of this sustainment is system governance. Efforts that have not put a long-term plan in place for KM strategy, system, and content governance may see initial successes, but they will turn into failures over time. Indeed, early KM successes that do not have the benefit of effective and comprehensive governance will quickly turn into failures, as systems and content trend toward chaos. Governance may not be the most exciting element of a KM system implementation, but in order to achieve sustainable evolution of your KM programs, it is absolutely critical. We define KM governance to include vision, roles and responsibilities, policies, procedures, communications, education, and analytics. Together, these elements will define a KM ecosystem that will yield continuous improvement instead of system entropy.

Reference

Gamble P, Blackwell J (2001) Knowledge management. Kogan Page, London

Foundational Design Elements

18

Throughout the book we have referenced the importance of getting the foundational design elements right. These foundational design elements are common threads of success in virtually any KM systems effort. Oftentimes, when we hear an organization complaining of lack of findability, poor content quality, and systems either running out of control or falling into disrepair, we find these foundational design elements to be lacking.

In addition, these foundational design elements often act as the binder between different KM systems. When these elements are put in place consistently across multiple different systems, those systems integrate more effectively, and the overall user experience across the enterprise is improved. Since these foundational elements translate so clearly to user interface and experience, consistency across systems means lower cognitive lift and higher user satisfaction.

As discussed already in Chap. 2, getting all of the following right requires a great understanding of your organization and a clear understanding of your user types (personas) and their goals (user stories). Each of these foundational elements will benefit from end user contact early and often during the design process, as well as substantial effort in user validation and testing.

Describing these elements as foundational in nature does not just mean they are a gateway to other designs or features; it also means they are critical to get right. Systems designed on poorly conceived foundational elements will suffer in usability and sustainability and will be difficult to get back on track no matter the effort. In short, put the time and effort it takes into getting each of these elements right to ensure your KM systems projects start off well and have the potential to succeed and grow.

J. Hilger, Z. Wahl, *Making Knowledge Management Clickable*,
https://doi.org/10.1007/978-3-030-92385-3_18

18.1   Content Governance

Content governance defines the roles and responsibilities, policies and procedures, communications, education, and marketing regarding the content that will go into the KM system. Put simply, it defines who is allowed to do what, provides consistent guidelines for decision-making and quality control, and ensures the right people are informed, aware, and educated regarding what to do and how to do it.

An effective content governance plan will include the following:

- Business Case—This will include a justification for why governance is required, including how it will help the users and the organization.
- Roles and Responsibilities—This section will detail, simply, who is allowed to do what regarding the creation, editing, and deletion/archiving of whatever information management components are being governed.
- Policies and Procedures—The policies and procedures you define should be linked to the aforementioned roles and responsibilities. In other words, your policies and procedures define how decisions are made, changes are actualized, and rules are enforced. Wherever possible, these policies and procedures should be built directly into the system.
- Communications, Education, and Marketing—Often overlooked, the communications, education, and marketing of governance and the components they cover are critical to the success of an information management initiative. Our experience is that individuals can seldom be cajoled into following governance rules, but if they are properly educated as to the value of what they are being asked to do, they will generally comply.

The most mature content governance plans will also cover governance over the taxonomy and ontology designs, guiding the creation, editing, or removal of synonyms, terms, and metadata fields. This level of control is essential to successfully iterating a design to ensure that it changes as your content and use cases change, yielding a long-term sustainable design that consistently serves the user's needs.

18.1.1 Why It Is Important

Content governance will ensure the content within your KM systems starts out high quality and then continues to improve over time. No KM system can be successful without high-quality content that users get value from and trust is correct. Content governance guides the content creation, publishing, and maintenance processes for your KM system to ensure the right content gets in, that it is reviewed for quality and clarity, and that it is well maintained over time (meaning the content improves, is updated when it should be, and removed when it is no longer timely or offering value).

Lack of governance is responsible for many KM systems failures. If the governance is not in place to ensure the quality and appropriateness of content, KM systems may fail quickly. Users may be willing to explore a new system after launch, but if they do not find valuable content therein, they are unlikely to return. Even if an organization begins with quality content within a KM system, without governance, the quality of the content is likely to deteriorate over time. We have found that 80% of poorly governed KM systems are made up of outdated, duplicate, near duplicate, or simply incorrect content. This occurs when users can publish anything they choose unchecked. Good governance, on the other hand, provides the necessary reviews, guidelines, and training needed to ensure content quality steadily improves.

18.1.2 Best Practices and Approach

Ensure Your Model Fits the Organization

One of the most important success factors for governance design is to ensure the model you choose fits your organization. The first part of this is to determine whether your organization needs a centralized or decentralized governance structure. An organization needs to determine if they want to leverage a select group at the administrative level to make content decisions or allow a larger selection of end users to own content governance.

Both models have their benefits and drawbacks, and these decisions are often contingent on the organization itself. Command and control type organizations tend to do well with a centralized model, whereas loosely managed organizations tend to gravitate more toward decentralized models. Organizations that are highly risk averse and require flawless delivery of content should leverage centralized models, whereas more consensus-driven organizations that are willing to accept some level of content risk are more likely to succeed with a decentralized model.

Beyond deciding which model to adhere to, organizations must also consider how tightly or loosely they want to govern the content. This entails asking how strictly end users will be expected to adhere to the governance plan. In a tight governance plan, there will be rigid controls and a clear chain of command through which authority has to be passed to make any changes. For organizations that are particularly risk averse or who have more sensitive content, this may be the better solution. However, a rigid hierarchy can make it difficult for an organization to adapt and capitalize on changing business and content needs.

A loose governance plan enables individuals or lower-level teams to have the autonomy and authority to experiment and make decisions about the content. While this approach allows for content to be more dynamic, having more end users make changes risks inconsistency within the system. The loose structure also heightens the possibility that a KM system becomes bloated with lower-quality content. If in doubt, we recommend that organizations start with a tight governance plan, recognizing that governance may shift to a looser structure as both the system and the role of end users change. In any scenario, having an ill-fitting governance model that does not mesh with the organization can prove detrimental to the sustainment of the system and the content within. An organization may choose between loose or tight governance, centralized or decentralized, any combination, or anything in between. The key is to be purposeful about what will be the right fit to accomplish your organization's goals for KM.

Design for the User

Too frequently, governance plans are designed to be overly formal and complex, using language, diagrams, and imagery that is more complex than it needs to be. When the topic of governance comes into play, people often formalize language and write in an almost "legal" type of format, rather than creating clear directions and guidelines that a non-technical user can clearly digest and act upon.

Regardless of whether the user of the governance plan is a seasoned IT or KM expert or someone who has never heard of KM before, a governance plan should always be designed for the non-technical user. In essence, the governance plan should be as easy to read and use to a brand-new employee as it would be to those who created it. There are many ways to augment the simplicity of a governance plan to make sure that anyone can use it to accomplish the tasks described within.

Most importantly, avoid overly technical jargon, and make sure that the document does not assume too much knowledge regarding key terminology or roles. Utilize graphics in order to convey essential points, such as governance procedures and roles. Doing so will cut down the amount of text needed to explain critical information.

Additionally, recognize that in most scenarios, a reader is not going to want (or have time) to read the entire document in order to figure out how to appropriately make changes to the content. Therefore, the governance plan should be designed as a "one-stop shop" reference guide, with sections linking to other parts of the document as necessary in order to guide readers through options and alternatives.

To further strengthen the usability of a governance plan, make sure that each section opens with the appropriate contextual information (definitions of what metadata, top-level, and lower-level values are, applicable roles, etc.). While this may result in a repetitive document, it alleviates the need for users to have to sift through other parts of the document to find the context they need so that they can move forward.

Build the Governance into the Tool

Content governance plans that do not fit into the chosen knowledge management system offer little to no value. What this means in practice is that content governance plans need to be signed with roles, permissions, and policies in line with what the tool can do. Roles and responsibilities should be aligned with the permissions in the tool, and processes and policies should be implemented as workflows and decision trees. Regardless of whether an organization has chosen a technology and subsequently written a governance plan or vice versa, the needs expressed in a governance plan need to align with the capabilities of the chosen tool.

If the rules and tools align, there will be opportunities to build the governance plan into the technology. Building governance directly into your tool(s) will ensure adherence to the plan and make it easier for the end user. Governance plans that are only hefty written volumes are easily ignored, but governance plans built into the technologies are easy to follow in ways that will be seamless for the users.

Be as Clear as Possible
A well-thought-out governance plan ensures that important decisions regarding the content never have to be based on limited information or instinct. Rather, a robust governance plan provides users with as many tools as possible to ensure the process for making changes is calculated and logical. These tools can take a variety of forms, such as a simple list of questions or a formalized decision tree. These can be as simple as requiring a specific naming convention for content (i.e., simple and clean language) or mandating that a piece of content follow a very specific format. Regardless, governance policies that leave little to no room for interpretation will help to improve consistency, but they will also provide the governance team with an important tool to help explain why particular requests were either approved or denied. When denying requests, having a clear policy to reference will help those making the requests from feeling that they are being treated unfairly, thereby improving the likelihood they will continue to use the system and even make future requests that are more in line with the written policies and procedures.

18.2 System Governance

Like content governance, system governance establishes the roles and responsibilities, policies, procedures, and communications, but it oversees the KM system itself rather than the content. Whereas content governance covers how content is created, edited, deleted, and archived, system governance covers the ownership and responsibilities of the KM system and the related decision-making regarding how the tool should change over time.

Few, if any, KM systems will be just right when deployed. Given their iterative nature, the use of Agile principles, and the ever-changing nature of organizations and their people, system governance is critical to ensuring the KM system starts out good and trends toward better. System governance should cover:

- Clear lines of authority, responsibility, and ownership for the system and its features.
- The prioritization (and reprioritization) of new features and functionality.
- Oversight for user privileges, ensuring the right people have access to make changes.
- Trends in the usage of the system, reacting to dropping usership and leveraging analytics to identify issues or gaps that need to be filled.
- Communications over how the system is being used, the value it offers, and changes that are being put in place.

18.2.1 Why It Is Important

System governance is what ensures your KM system improves over time, rather than falling into disrepair or spinning out of control. Ungoverned or poorly governed systems will either stagnate, as a lack of dynamism and support results in users losing interest or reverting to old habits, or run out of control, as users work in the system to the point of breaking it. In the latter case, a system may initially have been rolled out as a result of interest and support from users. Despite their good intentions, however, users have a way of breaking ungoverned systems. Through use, if they are given too much administrative control without the appropriate guidance or structure, they will begin to take a tool designed with best practices for the enterprise and turn it into a tool that only works for them or their specific business area. When this is happening across the system by multiple users, it will quickly fall into chaos, resulting in the same old issues of findability, reliability, and usability.

A well-governed system, on the other hand, will leverage human inputs and feedback along with analytics, combined with the strategic goals of the organization and direction from leadership in order to iterate the system toward constant improvement. This will result in a system that continues to serve its intended purpose, yielding the business value expected and resulting in the overall return on investment. Governance also plays a major role in surfacing and acting on user feedback, which means a well-governed system is also more likely to innovate based on the ideas of its users, ideally identifying new ways to support the organization and solve business challenges.

18.2.2 Best Practices and Approach

Define Clear Ownership

One of the biggest challenges with an enterprise-level KM system is that multiple stakeholders across the business and IT, different regions, and potentially different parts of an organization will all seek control. We often encounter "turf wars" between different executives or different business groups, all wishing to control the initiative to ensure their priorities are met. Though governance alone will not fully address that challenge, it does play an important role in documenting who has decision-making power over what. This reinforcement of roles and responsibilities is valuable both in the initial design phases as well as the ongoing maintenance and iteration of the system. Though several models can work, from single points of decision-making, to pyramid decision-making where bigger, more impactful, and more costly decisions are elevated, to models where committees vote when there is disagreement, clarity is critical. Regardless of your specific model, ensure there is clear documentation for who makes which decisions and ensure there are "tie-breaker" mechanisms in place to avoid deadlocks or confusion.

Leverage Analytics

After the system is deployed, analytics can play a major role in helping to prioritize new features, new content, or overall system changes. Analytics can inform the governance team, for instance, on where there are gaps in the KM system. Are a number of users consistently navigating to an area but then abandoning the effort without completing an action? That is a strong clue there are usability issues with that area or users are not finding what they are expecting there. Are users trending heavily toward searching over browsing or vice versa? That is a clue that one of your main findability methods may require attention. More specifically, are you seeing a great number of search actions but a low number of pieces of content being opened or accessed? That points to the fact that your search functionality needs work. These and other data points can be captured automatically through system analytics if thoughtfully configured and monitored, providing the system governance team with clear inputs that will allow them to focus their attention on what needs work.

Create Two-Way Communications

One of the most valuable change management approaches to build and sustain support and usage of a KM system is a healthy and active two-way communications plan. Having a well-defined, two-way communications plan as part of your system governance means you will have a channel (or better yet, channels) to receive feedback and requests from users. This feedback is likely to be more negative than positive, not as a reflection of a system, but simply because users are more likely to provide feedback when they are unhappy about something. Though many organizations are inclined to hide this negative feedback, if used correctly, it can be a great opportunity to increase buy-in and demonstrate the governance team and project stakeholders are invested in making the system better over time. Publicly responding to this feedback, with either an affirmation that you are taking action to address the issue or an explanation as to why you do not plan to do so, is a powerful means to demonstrate to your users you are listening to their feedback and taking thoughtful action when it is appropriate. To be clear, it is completely reasonable to say no to a user request, as long as you can explain why you are saying no.

Show Consistent Improvement

Many KM systems will see a burst of activity when they are first deployed, but some will see a steep drop off in usership within the weeks thereafter. Some of this is to be expected, as curious "first time" users will explore the system and then settle into routines, using the tool and getting consistent value from it. Another reason for drop off, however, maybe that some initial users encounter usability issues or, more broadly, do not find interest or value in the system when it is first released. Demonstrating consistent improvement in the forms of new features, new content, and richer interactions will all serve to maintain the interest of your existing users and also lure back some of the early disinterested users.

Consistent improvement in content and features is also an important tool to keep your content contributors adding to the system. Continued investment in the development of the KM system will spur user action, reminding them to actively contribute their own knowledge and content to the system, thereby making the overall system richer for all users.

Market the Value

Active participation in KM systems seldom just happens. The system governance plan must include a firm strategy for communications, education, and marketing, all key components of a change management plan to drive early adoption and ongoing participation. One of the most important types of communication is outcomes, or value based. How is the KM system resulting in value to the organization and the users themselves? Oftentimes, the best approach for communicating value is to leverage a series of different techniques, ranging from data based to a more anecdotal story based. On the data-based end, these communications should tie directly to return on investment and the KM value and business value discussed in Chap. 1. Ongoing and consistent reports noting key value metrics like number of searches completed, number of pieces of content found, number of discussions had, number of active users, number of new people connections made, and number of new pieces of content added or created are all-powerful metrics to track over time and share on a regular basis. Perhaps more impactful due to its specificity, however, are story-based communications. In these cases, specific outcomes and points of value are communicated in the form of news items or blog-type articles to demonstrate value. For instance, one month the story might be about how a cross-continental new relationship between two specialists was made via the tool, and these individuals are now fostering a new community of practice. Another week might speak to how a member of the organization's sales team was able to close a deal faster by using the content within the tool. Planning these ongoing communications will keep users engaged and may also help some users to better understand how they too may get value out of the system. Regardless, communications like this require time and attention to develop, and an effective governance plan should include the resources necessary for this, including an appropriate budget and identified resources.

18.3 KM Organization

The KM organization will be the specific organizational entity to own KM systems and associated activities. It is not to say that this group will be doing all the knowledge management work within the organization or owning all KM systems, in fact, that should not be the case. Instead, this is the group that drives KM, sets KM policies, and typically houses KM systems governance or content governance. Core responsibilities of a centralized KM organization typically include:

- Setting the overall strategy for KM transformations and KM initiatives.
- Engaging the organization in KM initiatives (big or small) and aligning different areas of the business to achieve enterprise goals.

- Serving as the nexus for governance, training, and communications related to KM.
- Cataloging feedback and analytics to consider and make shifts to KM systems and the transformation roadmap overall.

18.3.1 Why It Is Important

In organizations where ownership for KM is either unclear or nonexistent, programs seldom move past the discussion or planning phases. KM does not just happen, and a KM organization is critical to ensure the appropriate communications, leadership, and coordination are all in place to remove roadblocks, get the right people and groups aligned, and ensure a common understanding of KM goals, initiatives, boundaries, and overall value. In short, the successful KM transformations and dynamic KM systems exist in organizations where KM is a clearly defined role within the organization with set authorities, job descriptions, and reporting structures.

18.3.2 Best Practices and Approach

Don't Necessarily Replicate Your Organization's Model

The natural inclination for many organizations is to model their KM organization design, decision-making, and overall KM workings after the organization as a whole. Though this is likely the right starting point for many organizations, it should not be the foregone conclusion. Many organizations, especially those in heavily regulated industries or those that have a long history, have organizational models that are designed to obtain consensus on all decisions. This protects them from risk and can help to build consensus, but it also slows progress, limits innovation, and runs the risk of generating generic decisions based on the lowest common denominator. Some organizational models, similarly, are designed for stability and consistency but result in reinforcement of the status quo, rather than the new idea that might solve old problems. Traditional organizational models also run the risk of shutting down conversation, rather than engaging all constituents in ideation and identification of areas for improvement.

As you consider the design for your KM organization, including how decisions should be made, what the reporting structure should be, how communications are handled, and how others within the organization are engaged, consider the fact that a KM organization may be the place to pilot or test a different decision-making model for your organization. Moreover, to ensure the KM organization has the appropriate flexibility, speed, authority to make decisions, and positioning to drive innovation, consider stepping away from your standard organizational model.

Secure Time and Budget

Too many organizations regard KM roles and responsibilities as a part-time or even unofficial job responsibilities. For some organizations, those that are particularly small, simple, and heterogeneous in operations and their use of knowledge, this may well be acceptable. However, for most true enterprise organizations that are seeking to operate mature KM organizations and systems, KM cannot be regarded as a hobby.

To demonstrate the importance of KM and KM systems within your organization, ensure you are securing the appropriate budget to staff the organization. This also means defining KM as an official role or role within the organization with supporting job descriptions, competencies, and performance plans. Specifically, KM should not be an add-on responsibility, but rather it should be a specific role against which the employees are evaluated and compensated.

Hire, Train, or Outsource

If you are creating a KM organization for the first time, like many organizations, your KM initiatives will rise and fall based on the people you place within the effort and empower to own KM within the organization. The most successful KM people are those who bridge technology and business, possess strong communication and facilitation skills, can think and lead strategically, and have experience educating and, really, marketing their ideas and the overall value of KM to drive support and consensus within the organization. That, by any standard, is a tall order. As you are looking to staff your KM organization, make sure you have a plan for how that will be done. Do not assume that simply posting a job requisition will yield a slew of appropriate candidates. We are always looking for this skill set and seldom find individuals who match all of these criteria to our satisfaction. If you do plan to hire for these positions, ensure you have a great deal of lead time and are prepared with a Plan B if you are unable to fill the positions.

Two other options to build out your organization are to promote from within and train promising individuals up or to outsource through independent contractors or consulting firms. Promoting from within and upskilling existing employees is often the primary approach we recommend for organizations. This approach has several advantages. For one, these are people who already know how to be successful within your organization and have proven to be reliable and able to stretch, learn, and grow. Much of the KM systems experience we detail in this book can be learned, taught through classes, and developed through the right experience, so if you are starting with a strong internal candidate, you have the potential to build your own KM leaders in a way that will fit your organization. Another benefit of promoting from within is that you can choose how to develop these individuals with training and learning (internal and external) that match the goals of the organization. For instance, if a major component of your KM systems will include search, you will want to ensure this person develops search skills and exposure to the latest tools in the market. If, on the other hand, there is a records management focus for your KM initiatives, you will be able to direct learning in that space. Stated more broadly, by upskilling deliberately, you will have the opportunity to develop KM experts who perfectly match your environment and needs.

The limitation of upskilling is that these people will seldom have the deep experience in the field to be able to spot patterns and tell stories in the way a more seasoned KM professional would be able to do. In this case, leveraging consultants and contractors is another alternative for consideration. There are many consultants and contractors across the broad domain of KM. These include true practitioners and more academic thinkers, as well as KM consultants, focused on technology versus those focused on the softer side of KM. If you plan to go the route of outsourcing your KM organization, make sure you know exactly what you are looking for, so you do not end up with the wrong kind of person. Of course, the major downsides to outsourcing are the lack of internal understanding and the missed opportunity to build internal capability/capacity. The cost of outsourced experts may also be prohibitive, and some organizations have different views of contractors/consultants for you to be aware of, ranging from regarding them more highly for their expertise or considering them as untrusted since they are from outside the organization.

For most organizations, we recommend a collection of hiring, promoting/ upskilling, and outsourcing. Know specifically how you plan to use each type of resource, what your timeline is, and how you will encourage knowledge transfer and collaboration to best use the expertise of your resources over time.

Be Clear About Lines of Authority and Reporting

We often get the question of where a KM organization should fit within the overall organization. Specifically, to whom should the KM organization report and with which internal functions should the KM organization be collocated? There is no single right answer to this, but carefully considering the positives and negatives of the various options will help to ensure the early success and long-term sustainability of your KM organization and associated systems.

Taken as a whole, the most successful KM organizations, enterprise transformations, and substantial KM systems efforts tend to be housed in one of three areas. The first is reporting to the COO. At its core, this makes a great deal of sense for organizations that are seeking to invest heavily and see tremendous changes in the way the organization operates when it comes to KM. The high-profile location of the organization ensures appropriate leadership attention and funding and also sends a clear message regarding the organization's support for KM.

The second, and increasingly common location, is within or alongside the organization's learning and development group. Referencing back to the value of KM, so many KM outcomes are based on an employee's ability to learn and perform based on the knowledge of the organization. Tying KM to learning and development is, therefore, a natural fit, and it creates a very specific set of anticipated outcomes or "why statements" to connect KM to business value for the organization. Of course, placing KM with learning can also limit the potential perceived scope or impact of KM and KM systems to just those related to learning and development, so this consideration will be important, especially for organizations that are seeking wholesale change and broader impacts beyond employee knowledge and development.

The third placement for a KM organization that consistently yields good results is an organization's internal library staff. This is a more traditional placement of KM and tends to be most effective for KM initiatives and systems that are focused on harnessing an organization's content for use and reuse in all its forms. As many KM professionals have a traditional library background, housing or collocating KM with library services is a natural fit.

Investing in content and system governance will always require an investment in people who will maintain it. Gamble and Blackwell note that "84 percent of high-impact applications were associated with a continuing investment in content creation and maintenance. This requires two types of people--subject matter experts to decide what goes into the content and librarians to extract, organize, and manage the content" (Gamble and Blackwell 2001). Though we disagree with the very specific point that librarians are required, the gist of this statement is correct. The most successful systems will include provisions for the long-term involvement of subject matter experts to represent the organization and its knowledge, as well as a collection of KM, content, and system experts to ensure that knowledge is curated as high-value content. By establishing KM as a clearly defined and essential part of an organization, you will avoid people assigned to KM roles feeling as though their work is not important.

18.4 Taxonomy

Taxonomies, also known as controlled vocabularies, are words organized into lists or hierarchies that consistently describe an organization's content. The difference between a traditional taxonomy and a business taxonomy is shown in Table 18.1. Our standard taxonomy definition is:

Controlled vocabularies used to describe or characterize explicit concepts of information for purposes of capture, management, and presentation.

Table 18.1 Comparison of traditional taxonomy and business taxonomy for use in KM systems

	Traditional Taxonomy	Business Taxonomy
Purpose	Categorization	Findability
Designed By	Scientists/Librarians	The Business
Managed By	Scientists/Librarians	The Business
Used By	Scientists/Librarians	Everyone
Complexity	Deep, Wide, Detailed	Flat, Simple, Deconstructed
Key Characteristics	Mutually Exclusive, Collectively Exhaustive	Usable, Intuitive, Natural

Heather Hedden, author of *The Accidental Taxonomist*, describes a taxonomy as a tool to "aid users in locating desired content by topic-terms, which reflect both the terminology use of the users and of the content" (Hedden 2021). This is a great addition to our core definition of taxonomy, as we will address the importance of standardized language and simplified terms later on in this chapter.

Put simply, an organization's taxonomy design will provide a clear structure to organize and connect content and other knowledge entities. The components of a taxonomy design are:

- **Metadata fields**, to identify the ways that information should be classified, categorized, organized, or combined. For KM systems, examples of common metadata fields are topic/subject, document type, and intended audience. A simple way to consider metadata fields is as the question that can be used to learn about an organization's content. For instance, what is the content about, what type of content is it, or for whom is the content intended? The ways that you would naturally answer those questions translate into your taxonomy design.
- **Taxonomies**, to populate each of the metadata fields. For each metadata field (as in, each way you choose to describe/classify/categorize your content), a discrete taxonomy will control the terms that can be used to populate the field. The taxonomy will contain the words and phrases that will answer the question and should provide an exhaustive selection of terms to cover the organization's content. Taxonomies can be flat (as picklists) or hierarchical in nature, with hierarchical taxonomies delivering "parent" and "child" terms, creating relationships between larger and smaller groupings that can be used in a number of ways to build connectivity and findability of content. Though hierarchical taxonomies are traditionally much more common, as modern KM systems have allowed for more metadata fields and taxonomies to be managed discretely and as taxonomies are more commonly surfaced as front-end navigation and search features, flatter and simpler taxonomies are becoming more prevalent and should make up a meaningful part of your overall taxonomy design.

Figure 18.1 shows a simple representation of these terms in practice. On the left, the metadata fields are shown, with the representation of taxonomies (on the right) used to populate each of the metadata fields, translating to metadata values applied to each piece of content.

As the graphic shows, a taxonomy design will also designate whether a field can be populated with one or multiple values from the taxonomy. In more complex enterprise designs, a complete taxonomy design typically includes conditional metadata as well, meaning some of the fields and associated taxonomies will only be applicable to a subset of content, depending on the type or nature of the content. We typically describe this in terms of primary fields (those that should be applied to all content) and secondary fields (those that should only be applied to a subset of content). For instance, topic or subject is an example of a primary field in that any piece of content will possess one or many topics/subjects. On the other hand, length or time would be an example of a secondary field, given that asking, "how long

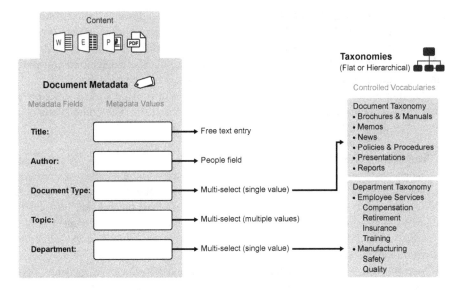

Fig. 18.1 How taxonomies are used to populate metadata. © 2021, Wahl/Hilger, reused with permission

is it?" or "what is the running time?" would not be legitimate questions to ask for all content but only a subset thereof.

Overall, taxonomy designs can run from very simple to highly complex, and they can serve a specific system or the entire enterprise. Most organizations struggle to design, implement, and maintain valuable taxonomies that truly represent their business and serve the needs of their end users. Those organizations that do invest in taxonomies consistently have greater success with their KM systems and are better poised to achieve advanced KM systems features.

18.4.1 Why It Is Important

As we already discussed in Chap. 10 on taxonomy management systems, taxonomies allow organizations to categorize information in a consistent fashion so that it is universally accessible, even across application silos or repositories. When we apply this to the value of taxonomies, it basically means that organizations with mature taxonomies, taxonomy management systems, and taxonomy and content governance are more likely to have content that is findable and discoverable in all the ways an organization is seeking. More specifically, some of the most important benefits of taxonomy are:

- **Organization of Content:** Taxonomies, when applied as tags on content, give structure to unstructured content. This is true not just for files and documents but also for people, products, data, systems, and virtually any other entity an organization manages. When organizations apply taxonomy to this content, they are connecting it all, making it easier to manage, and describing it consistently in ways that result in improved collaboration across the enterprise.

- **Findability and Discoverability:** Taxonomy can be surfaced as intuitive navigation, used to improve search weighting, and translated into visual filters or facets as part of a search solution. In short, taxonomy makes search better and overall improves the findability of content, improving the flexibility and usability of KM systems to make it easier for people to find the content they are seeking. Moreover, taxonomy can play a role in relating disparate content (i.e., content of different types, in different locations, in different formats, and for different audiences) and making it possible for users to discover more content than they were aware existed. This concept of discoverability basically means that users are finding content they did not go looking for but which will help answer their questions or complete their mission. Improving discoverability drastically reduces the time wasted in organizations when people spend time recreating knowledge or content that existed within the organization but of which they were unaware.

- **Improved Management of Content:** With taxonomy applied as tags, content will be better governed, resulting in improved management of content, less duplication of content, and improved direction of the right content to the right people. This means that organizations will experience less overall risk due to the wrong content being found and acted upon, potentially resulting in serious consequences. Overall, taxonomy is a content management tool that means your content is better and more reliable. Depending on the industry, this may even mean less regulatory risk, better litigation preparedness, and, certainly in some industries, lives saved.

18.4.2 Best Practices and Approach

Hybrid Approach

Similar to the overall approach to KM assessment we describe in Chap. 3, a taxonomy design effort is well suited to use a combination of human-driven inputs like workshops, focus groups, and interviews combined with more technology- and content-centric approaches. This combination of techniques for taxonomy design will produce a taxonomy centered around your end users' actual business needs and goals but will also work within the context of your current and planned content and systems.

Define and Document Your Purpose

Taxonomies, despite a lot of improved understanding over the last decade, can still be somewhat esoteric to the non-indoctrinated. As a result, many organizations still suffer from a lack of understanding regarding the reasons for taxonomy (as well as a profound lack of understanding of their complexity and the challenge in designing and maintaining them). Every taxonomy design effort should begin with a clearly documented and shared understanding of the who, what, and why of taxonomy. Who is our audience? What are we "taxonomizing" or tagging? Why are we doing it, and what is the business value that will be derived?

A taxonomy designed for a specific system and a small subset of content is a much simpler challenge than an enterprise taxonomy that will be used to maintain an organization's complete set of information (structured and unstructured), people, products, and processes. Before embarking on a design effort for taxonomy, ensure it is properly scoped and the use cases are clearly understood.

Leverage the Business and Subject Matter Experts

Taxonomies as we have defined them are specifically designed to help business users organize, manage, find, and discover content. It is critical to ensure these business users are involved in the actual design effort to ensure their goals are clearly understood and the taxonomy leverages organization and vocabulary that will be comfortable, intuitive, and familiar for them. Every design decision should come down to that which would best serve the end user. This is also why the development of personas is so important. An early stage in any taxonomy design effort should be the identification of your audience/users and a clear understanding of your "lowest common denominator" user. If you can design for that person, you will best serve the interests and needs of all your end users, whether they are customers, the public, your own employees, or a mix.

In a typical taxonomy design effort, we recommend that dozens if not hundreds of business users and subject matter experts be engaged in the process. For some, this means an upfront role in developing personas or brainstorming metadata fields; for others, it means helping to identify taxonomy terms. For many others, it may even mean participating in testing and validation exercises to surface where the taxonomy works and where it requires additional iteration.

> **Tip:**
> Taxonomy testing and validation commonly calls on more traditional usability testing techniques like A-B testing, card sorts, and "find-it" exercises. As you are planning a taxonomy design effort, ensure you are leveraging your organization's web design and usability resources to help test and validate the usability of the taxonomy.

Understand Your KM System's Limitations and Associated Workflows

A taxonomy can only be as complex as the system(s) into which it will be housed and surfaced. Not all KM technologies possess robust capabilities for managing taxonomies or applying tags. Before you start designing, understand the constraints of your technologies. If you already know the technology or technologies in which you'll be working, ensure you understand their capabilities and constraints related to taxonomy management and tagging. If you have not yet selected your technologies, ensure you consider requirements related to taxonomies. Of course, knowing whether or not your organization has or will have a taxonomy management system will also have a major impact on the potential complexity of your taxonomy design. Similarly, if you will have the technology to leverage auto-tagging, you will be able to design a more robust tagging scheme, whereas if you are relying solely on humans for tagging, you will need to consider fewer overall tags and simpler taxonomies (less granularity) in order to minimize the time your taggers are spending.

You should also consider governance requirements regarding stages of review before content is published and how many people you will be asking to publish content and use the taxonomy to apply tags. Depending on the type of system, type of organization, and purpose for the system, the content creation and publishing workflows can vary wildly. Some systems have content published only by a few, full-time content strategists. Others have a much broader content management approach where any user of the system also has the ability to publish into it. The number of tags you can expect to have consistently and correctly applied to your content is heavily dependent on who will be applying those tags. Systems with a broad base of content publishers must sacrifice some level of taxonomy and tagging granularity for overall usability.

Simplify Your Vocabulary and Separate Your Structure

When it comes to successful taxonomy designs for KM systems, choosing "simpler" is almost always the right choice. This is true for the language you choose for your taxonomies as well as for the structure of the overall taxonomy design.

For the language within your taxonomy, consider following typical web writing conventions of using vocabulary at no more than a seventh to ninth grade reading level, as the Literacy Project has determined to be the average reading level of US adults (Literacy Project 2017). Readability indexes, in particular, provide guidelines for business writing and ensure the users of your taxonomies will have no issue understanding the meaning and intent of the words within your taxonomies. Rudolph Flesch published his first readability formula in 1948, and the Flesch Reading Ease Formula has remained a reliable and efficient index used by Microsoft Word and US government agencies today (Flesch 1948). Using similar indexes and word processing software will enable you to quickly gauge the readability of your taxonomy. It will also be easier to internationalize the taxonomy, should the need arise, translating it more effectively and directly into other languages. When considering the words for your taxonomy, also strive to avoid your own organization's inside terms, marketing terms, and generic corporate speak, all of which typically has to be learned rather than being intuitive. Acronyms and abbreviations are also to be avoided at all costs for the same reason.

From a structural perspective, the thinking on taxonomies has changed. Taxonomies have historically been hierarchical structures with increasingly detailed and complex terminology at each level. Taxonomies from years past would also commonly mix together different types of terms (i.e., subject, type, and audience) in different branches of the same taxonomy. Some of this design complexity was based on a background overly dependent on library sciences, rather than considering the usability for business users, but much of it was also driven by the limitations of KM systems, forcing multiple disparate keywords into a single metadata field or limiting the number of taxonomies or terms that could be managed within the system or applied to content.

The thinking on taxonomy design has matured, and the systems capabilities have largely followed. Most systems now support a larger number of taxonomies and discrete metadata fields, meaning that each independent metadata field can be populated with its own taxonomy. This means each individual taxonomy can be simpler and likely flatter, resulting in greater usability and lower administrative burden. With the addition of a taxonomy management system, synonym terms and conditional taxonomies also become much easier to manage, further improving the usability and sustainability of the taxonomy while simultaneously resulting in less terms and hierarchy.

Leverage Existing Taxonomies and Other Resources

Most organizations already possess a plethora of starting points for taxonomies, even if they do not think of them as such. Consider the various folder/file structures, picklists, and glossaries existing in your organization all as potential starting points for a taxonomy design effort. In many cases, the right terminology already exists, and the key is to align it into the appropriate structure, removing conflicts between competing lists and vocabulary sets.

Leverage analytics to the greatest extent possible as well. Understanding what words people are searching with, what information they are accessing the most, and how they are navigating a site are all extremely valuable tools for taxonomy design. For instance, recognizing a particular term that has been searched more than any other can be an important key to recognizing that term should be included in a core taxonomy design. Equally, knowing what your most sought-after content plays a critical role. Analytics of this type can also help to prioritize content for a first implementable version of a taxonomy, focusing on high-value, sought-after content, and then iterating beyond it in future efforts.

The content your organization possesses can also play a major role in accelerating a taxonomy design effort. Analyzing existing content to see the terms and tags that have been applied to it in the past can provide great insights into the natural vocabulary of your content managers. Going deeper and reviewing common and prominent phrases in the content will also provide a key input into the taxonomy design. Though this can be accomplished manually by experts with time, taxonomy management systems can vastly accelerate the speed and accuracy of content reviews, especially when you are dealing with a large corpus of content (measured in the tens of thousands of pieces of content or more). Work that used to take months can now be accomplished in minutes with the right tool. Taxonomy management systems, as described in Chap. 10, have the ability to auto-tag content, recommend new terms, and validate the frequency of terms in the corpus of documents in the organization.

Plan for the Long Term and Ensure Governance Is in Place
Just like a KM system itself, no taxonomy will ever be truly complete. An organization's needs and strategies change, as do missions, services, products, and employees. As a result, content is constantly in flux, and a taxonomy design must be adaptive in order to address these changes. Moreover, on an average taxonomy design effort, the world of potential users will not be able to respond to it until after it is deployed. Even leveraging an array of interviews, workshops, analytics, and user testing and validation techniques will still be unlikely to engage a majority of your potential users in the design process. Ensuring analytics and feedback mechanisms are in place to "hear" from all of your users after the initial release will put you in a good place to improve the taxonomy iteratively.

As discussed in the preceding sections, having taxonomy and content governance in place to guide the iterative design and improvement of the taxonomy will ensure you're trending toward higher usability and value of the system overall.

18.5 Content Types

At its most basic level, a content type is a template that defines the structure and format of content. For instance, an organization may define a content type for meeting notes, resulting in greater consistency for each actual meeting's notes to come thereafter to have a similar organization and formatting. One of our colleagues, Tatiana Cakici, uses the metaphor of baking to describe content types. In her analogy, the content type is like the baking pan, and the actual content is the batter. In this analogy, anything baked with the pan will have the same shape (as in, format), but the taste and texture is dependent on the batter (content) itself (Cakici 2018). This metaphor paints the right picture for content types in that they have everything to do with structure and treatment of the specific type of content and less to do with the actual content itself.

Our more formal definition of a content type is:

> A reusable definition of format and metadata for a category of content, with its corresponding taxonomies that allow you to manage information in a centralized, reusable way.

More mature content types also include the following:

- Data Entry Form—A definition of how content creators or content editors will create or edit a content item for the given type of content.
- Front-End Wireframe—A wireframe that shows how content will be presented to end users after the content type has been used to create a new piece of content.
- Writing Guidelines—Direction regarding content length and format to guarantee that every new piece of content is created consistently according to standards and best practices, including tone, writing style, tense, and point of view.
- Metadata Fields—Definition regarding required and optional metadata fields.
- Workflow—Process steps that govern the roles and responsibilities regarding creation, approval/review, and maintenance for each content type.

18.5.1 Why It Is Important

Like taxonomy, content types are a core building block for KM systems. They provide structure that results in consistency for how information is captured and how it is shared or presented. They also guide the overall governance of content, meaning that content types do not just help better content to be created, they help ensure that the content stays up to date and pertinent. The most significant benefits of content types are:

- **Ease and Quality of Content Creation**—As with any well-designed form, a content entry template will help to speed up the content creation process. Less time formatting and thinking about content organization or placement means time saved, or more time spent on content quality. A well-designed content type will serve as a guide for what belongs within the piece of content, meaning both quality and overall consistency will increase.
- **Simplified Maintenance**—With well-organized content types, making changes to update content will also be easier and faster. Users can more easily find the content that needs to be changed through its metadata. In addition, properly structured content allows for publishing a single piece of content to multiple products so that writing only needs to be done once. Finally, large complex documents like technical documentation can be divided into smaller chunks. When one chunk is updated all of the documents that use that chunk of content are automatically updated as well. For instance, if a phone number or contact name changes, content types, and chunked content could allow for the change to be made in a single place and have it automatically proliferated to all applicable documents that use that information.
- **Improved Consistency and Findability of Content**—Of course, the corollary of content entered with improved quality and consistency is that the output of that content type entry, each content item visible to end users, would also be of higher quality and consistency. This is especially true of mature content types that include writing guides and publishing workflows. Findability of content generated using content types will also be improved when tags powered by taxonomies are applied as part of the content type process, and workflows ensure those tags and other metadata are applied consistently and completely.
- **Enterprise-Level Content**—Content types also improve enterprise-level consistency, meaning, regardless of the system that houses the content or the system where the content is displayed, any and all content can be consistent. This reduces cognitive lift, or the mental energy it takes people to comprehend a document. If all are familiarly structured, readers can consume the knowledge within more effectively. In more advanced scenarios, content types also help with content portability, where using a headless CMS solution allows for content to be displayed in different ways and in different places while leveraging the same root content. This means that a single piece of content can be published once and rendered in different formats to support different systems and user experiences depending on the use case and how the end user wishes to consume the content, across multiple systems, platforms, and devices.

18.5.2 Best Practices and Approach

Understand Your Content and How Your Users Want to Use It

Content types, like all foundational design elements of KM systems, require that your actual content and what your users want to do with that content is clearly understood. Do not just jump into the design of content types without having a clear understanding of what you are trying to accomplish for your end users. Content type design should be preceded by a content inventory or content audit to understand the makeup and distribution of your content, as well as a clear definition of your users, creation of personas, and detailed persona user stories that center around how they will find, discover, and act upon your content. See Table 18.2 for a standard content inventory template.

With that knowledge, you may then prioritize the design and implementation of content types that will accomplish your identified user goals. For example, if you identify your primary user goal for knowledge base articles to be for quick access and knowledge at the point of need, ensure the content type is designed with the short answer directly at the top and preceding levels of detail and follow-up beneath it. If, on the other hand, you find your primary user goal is learning and long-term development, design your content type to holistically explain the topic and then explain it in greater detail with required references and secondary opportunities for learning in the ensuing section. Knowing how your content will be used is a requirement for designing good content types.

When designing content types, also recognize that you need to consider both the content entry experience (the experience of the content publisher), as well as the content consumption experience (the experience of the content consumer, ranging from finding it to using it). These two experiences can be drastically different, with these discrete types of users possessing different motivations and levels of expertise.

Iterate Design and Implementation

Not all content types should be implemented in one mass. Many organizations fail in their content management initiatives because they create too many content types up front that confuse their users. Like many elements of KM design, highly iterative and methodical approaches to design and implementation are highly recommended. An iterative approach will allow you to deploy content types quicker and learn from their deployment regarding what is working and what is not, applying this learning to improve the design and deployment of forthcoming content types and improve the overall process. Moreover, iterative design and implementation will align with a gradual process of migrating existing content to leverage the new content types. Since this is often a manually intensive process, gradual deployment of content types aligns with the way the migration effort should actually be done.

Of course, with an iterative approach, deciding which content types to design and implement first becomes an important consideration. Understanding your actual content will play an important role in this decision. Generally speaking, you will want to prioritize high value, high access content for your first content type implementations. Based on your system analytics and understanding of your users,

Table 18.2 Standard content inventory and cleanup template

	Identify Content				
Document / Content	Current content location (H: Drive, OneNote)	Target Audience	Action (migrate, delete, archive)	Where to migrate?	Retention period for records management
1.					

	Identify Metadata						Track Migration			
Topic	Document type	Business area	Benefit	Audience	Vendor	Content owner	Target Migration Date	Status (complete/pending)	Notes
(cont. from line 1)									

identify the content types that are commonly accessed and relied upon heavily by your end users. Focusing on these content types for early implementation will ensure your users feel the positive impact of content types, helping them to support the content migration initiative and ensuring they get real value out of it. Balancing this high-value content prioritization, you may also wish to identify content types that are of a simpler format and represent a smaller percentage of your actual content. These two factors mean content may be migrated into the new content type faster and easier, lowering the time it will take to complete the particular migration and easing the burden on your content publishers.

Define Your Content Type Scope

Before you begin designing content types, ensure you are clear on what you want your content type to do. Content types at their most basic are templates or forms to chunk content into, but more mature content types can also include a data entry form, front-end wireframes, writing guidelines, metadata field definitions, and workflows. Ensure you have defined what your content types will include so you can begin the process consistently. Again, what you choose to include depends on the specific use cases you have identified and what your goals are as a result of implementing content. If you are just seeking more consistently formatted content, the bare minimum of a content type may well suffice, but if you are seeking to transform your content practices, enable content chunking and assembly, or introduce more automation into content delivery and sharing, the optional elements of a content type will be important to achieve your goals.

Consider the Content Lifecycle

As you are planning your content types, ensure you are considering the complete lifecycle of the content, from creation, to approvals, to publishing, to editing and updates, and finally to deletion, archiving, or disposition. Moreover, ensure you are considering the ways that content will be delivered and/or found. By considering these different stages, you will have the ability to predict how the content will be used and therefore what the content type should include to make these various use cases most successful for the end user and the organization.

In particular, considering content maintenance and the editing process will be helpful. Typically, static content is easy to maintain, but dynamic content, or content that has dynamic parts to it, becomes much more difficult to maintain. Content types can help with this challenge. If you can identify and isolate the most dynamic portions of a piece of content, both human and automated processes can help to ensure the content stays up to date and is easier to maintain. For instance, historically, phone numbers and e-mail addresses in some forms of content are highly dynamic. As people move within an organization or leave entirely, the content needs to be updated. With content types and by isolating, for instance, the phone number field, you are establishing an avenue to update the phone number once and have it proliferated to all the places in all of the content where that phone number is used.

This same concept holds true if some elements of a piece of content are more sensitive or will require additional reviews and approvals. By considering what, specifically, a manager or reviewer will need to approve, the content type can be designed to make that review and approval process focused on just that sensitive content. This can simplify review and approval cycles and allow content publishers to better manage the overall publication process.

Right-Size Content Types

Many organizations make the mistake of creating overly complex and granular content types, and they also make the mistake of creating many more content types than might be necessary. Content types do not need to be complex, and you may not need as many of them as you think.

Ensure each content type you create has a clearly unique purpose, whether that is distinct field requirements, different workflows, or different metadata requirements. Do not confuse a content type with a document type. Typically, many document types can be served by a single content type. For instance, a report, meeting minutes, and deliverable (three distinct document types) could all be served by a single content type. Typically, large and complex organizations may develop a set of 10 to 20 content types that will work for the vast majority (over 90%) of their content. Recognize there will always be outliers, but not every single piece of content requires a unique content type, and some truly outlier content might not need a content type at all.

Recognize, too, that content types do not need to be highly complex. Some basic content types may simply have a large field for body content entry along with a title and basic metadata. Yes, some content types may be much more complex, but recognize that the more complex a content type is, the more time it will take for the publisher to enter content into it. Ensure that time is being well used, and be willing to sacrifice some level of granularity for higher usability and overall adoption.

Test for Usability and Intuitive Use

We discuss usability throughout the book, and its importance in considering content types is of particular significance. Publishing content using content types, ideally, should not have to be taught. Content type entry and configuration should be incredibly intuitive. Content published via content types is more consistent, easier to find, and easier to manage, so ensure you are designing content types that are simple to use in order to encourage their active and complete use. When considering usability testing, as we talked about with the content lifecycle discussion in the previous section, ensure you are testing both the content input (publishing process) as well as the content output (end user consumption process). Ideally, you will also test the content editing process, as this is also one of the most common circumstances where content types will come into play.

18.6   Search Hit Types

The best search experiences treat search results as unique information assets that support the searcher's eventual goals. We call these types of search experiences action-oriented searches. An action-oriented search is a search that is made up of a collection of different types of search results, each of which supports a specific type

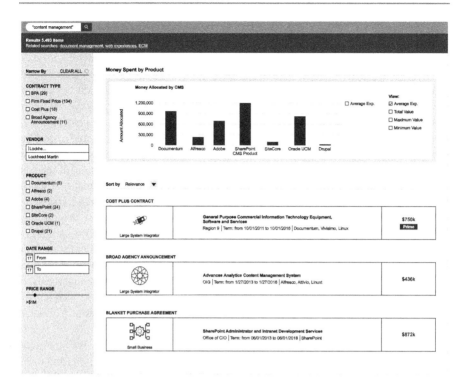

Fig. 18.2 Example of a search results page that includes facets, different result types, and aggregated information. © 2021, Wahl/Hilger, reused with permission

of information and the action people would like to take with the search. The most visible example of an action-oriented search can be seen on Google. Search for pasta on Google and you will see a result screen with many different types of search results. An example of this type of result screen is shown in Fig. 18.2.

Note that there are four very different types of search results on this single page view. The first result is a summary of where money is spent. This graph allows the searcher to see a quick overview of information found across the enterprise. It does not come from any single piece of information. The second, third, and fourth search results are similar, but they reference different types of contracts. Each of these hit types has its own look and own set of information that is specific to the type of information asset that is being displayed in search. Hit types are the building blocks of great search experiences, and a hit type analysis will ensure that each result type is well designed and documented in a way that ensures a successful search project.

18.6.1 Why It Is Important

Enterprise search is a critical part of any KM transformation, but because of its complex nature, it can be difficult to address effectively. According to the IDC, the average worker spends 25% of his or her day searching for and analyzing information

(Muldoon 2007). That is a large chunk of the working day, and this statistic reveals how important improving and streamlining the search process is to make an organization more competitive. Further studies conducted by The Search Network in 2020 reveal that only 22% of organizations report workers to be satisfied with their current search technology, proving that investment in search functionality is well worth it for many organizations (The Search Network 2020). Nearly every company we have ever worked with is frustrated with their existing internal search. Search is one of the most important tools in knowledge management, yet it rarely works well. People expect the Google search experience and too often, organizations fail to deliver on this promise. Hit types and hit type analysis ensures a search design that replicates many of the best features of Google and also ensures a user-centered search experience that focuses on what searchers are trying to accomplish and not just what they are trying to find.

Over time, we have learned that search works best when the search tool recognizes each search result as a thing and not a string. Early search experiences provided a set of results that were a list of links with brief descriptions. In those days, the search engine was finding documents or web pages that had text that matched the text in the search box. It would return a list of links to those documents, and the users were forced to research each document to see if the answer they were looking for existed within the document. This led to very poor search experiences and dissatisfaction with search as a whole.

Changing the focus of search from a list of documents or web pages to a unique set of "things" that people search for allows for better answers to questions and more successful searches. Frequently, the "thing" that a person is looking for is not in any single document or web page. For example, information about a person or a project is likely spread out across multiple systems. A focus on hit types allows the search team to identify the things people search for and how to best show them to searchers so that they get the answers they need.

18.6.2 Best Practices and Approach

Hit type analysis is the process by which we define the hit types or information assets that should be included in search and how the information within each hit type will be captured. The benefits of this approach are that it allows for the design of both the visual representation of search results along with the technical documentation as to how the search results are indexed and configured within the search engine.

The first step is to identify the common search problems and the difficulty in finding content within the organization. We typically do this with a workshop where users learn about the basics of search and then talk about the information they have trouble locating and why it is hard to find. For example, one client needed information about projects the other team members were working on. The challenge was that project information is not kept in a single place, and the search was more about which projects a person was working on rather than searching for a specific project. These search challenges help us understand the search features that are needed to deliver an overall search solution. Table 18.3 shows a common list of problems and the search features that best solve those problems.

Table 18.3 Common search problems and the search features that can solve them

Common Search Problems	Features to Solve the Problems
Too many irrelevant search results	Faceting
	Best bets / Promotions
	Boolean search
	Action-oriented result types
	Personalized relevance
Complicated terms	Synonyms
	Type ahead
	Suggested terms
Heterogeneous search results	Action-oriented result types
	Knowledge graphs
Content has no metadata	Auto-tagging
	Knowledge graphs
	Suggested terms
Content does not exist	Content management system
	Knowledge graphs
I can't find duplicates	Sort by date

(continued)

Table 18.3 (continued)

Versioned content	Action-oriented result types
	Date filters
	Related search results
Date-based content (news)	Sort by date
	Date filters
	Related search results
	Knowledge panels
Topics	Auto-tagging
	Suggested search terms

Fig. 18.3 Common information assets. © 2021, Wahl/Hilger, reused with permission

Employees	Products	Communities
Partners	Events	Clients
Offices	Meetings	Companies
Projects	Conferences	Industries
Tasks	Documents	Components
Plans	Processes	Countries
Class	Procedures	Regions

Once this workshop is complete, a search expert can prioritize the primary search features that need to be included in the search and develop a search framework that identifies the general look and feel of the search results page. This design work is typically done by someone with user interface experience.

The next step is to identify and prioritize the information assets that the search will need to support. The information assets are the unique types of assets that users search for within the organization. Figure 18.3 shows a sample list of common information assets that exist within an organization.

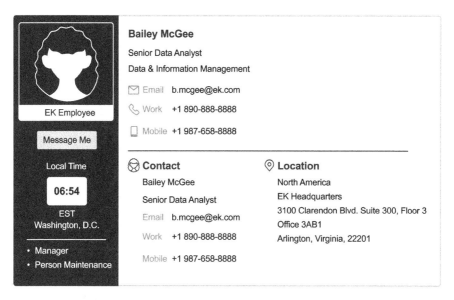

Fig. 18.4 Example of a person hit type with contact information. © 2021, Wahl/Hilger, reused with permission

1099 Tax Form

Used For: Reporting various types of income other than wages, salaries, and tips.

Used to Report Earnings On: Rents, Royalties, Prizes and Awards, Medical and Health Care Payments, Crop Insurance Proceeds, Payments to an Attorney, ...

Types of 1099:   ⬇ 1099-INT   ⬇ 1099-R   ⬇ 1099-MISC

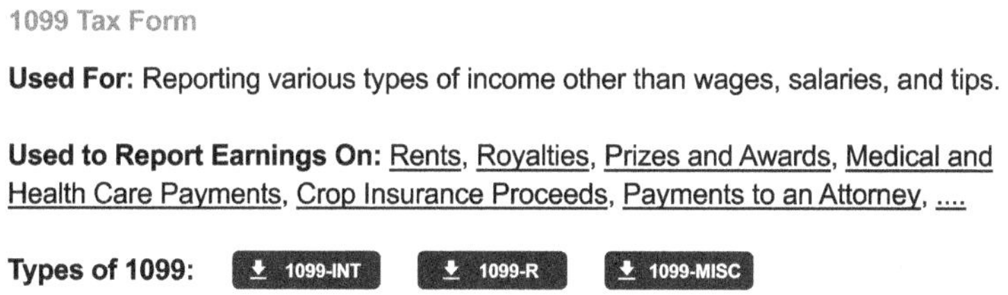

Fig. 18.5 Example of a document hit type. © 2021, Wahl/Hilger, reused with permission

Typically, we host a series of facilitated working sessions where we ask searchers to list the two or three most important search assets that they regularly search for and then prioritize the most important ones. Once these are prioritized, we take the top two or three in each working session and design the search result. This design effort is the key to action-oriented search. The design needs to meet two key purposes. First, the design should show all of the information that a user would want to know about the information asset before selecting it to see the details. Second, the design should support the actions the user might take with the asset. For example, a class hit type would have a button for registering in the class. Another example would be a person hit type which would have an e-mail address, phone number, and instant messaging link, as in Fig. 18.4. Figure 18.5 is an example of what a document hit type would look like, and Fig. 18.6 represents a general result.

Once the initial wireframing of the search results is complete, we have a good sense of the information that needs to be indexed and presented in the search

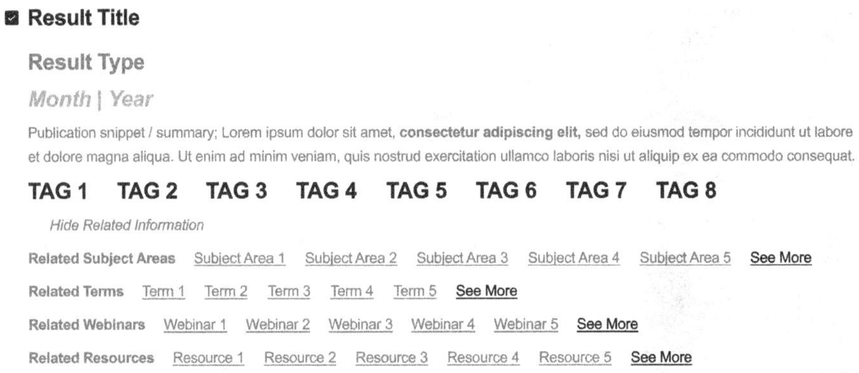

☑ **Result Title**

Result Type

Month | Year

Publication snippet / summary; Lorem ipsum dolor sit amet, **consectetur adipiscing elit,** sed do eiusmod tempor incididunt ut labore et dolore magna aliqua. Ut enim ad minim veniam, quis nostrud exercitation ullamco laboris nisi ut aliquip ex ea commodo consequat.

TAG 1   TAG 2   TAG 3   TAG 4   TAG 5   TAG 6   TAG 7   TAG 8

Hide Related Information

Related Subject Areas   Subject Area 1   Subject Area 2   Subject Area 3   Subject Area 4   Subject Area 5   **See More**

Related Terms   Term 1   Term 2   Term 3   Term 4   Term 5   **See More**

Related Webinars   Webinar 1   Webinar 2   Webinar 3   Webinar 4   Webinar 5   **See More**

Related Resources   Resource 1   Resource 2   Resource 3   Resource 4   Resource 5   **See More**

Fig. 18.6 General asset search result format. © 2021, Wahl/Hilger, reused with permission

application. The final step is to map the data elements required in the search to their source locations. This information is collected by the search analyst and the technical team that supports the various applications that are being indexed for search. As part of this process, the analyst lists each of the pieces of information that need to be included in search. They then answer the following questions to understand where the information exists, how it is collected, and how the search engine is configured.

1. What application or information repository stores this information element?
2. What is the name of the field where this information is captured?
3. Is this element used for faceting (i.e., does it show up in the facet list on the left-hand side of the search results)?
4. Should this element be searched? (In most cases, the search engine should not search information elements like dates or where the number of unique results is very small.)
5. Is this element used for sorting search results?

Once this information is collected for each unique hit type, the search can be developed pretty quickly. The front-end developers have wireframes showing how each search result should look, and the search developers know which information to collect in each index and how the search engine should be configured for each piece of information.

In our experience, a proper hit type analysis creates better search experiences, provides quick and simple documentation for the product, and makes the development of search much faster because the developers have the information they need to build the search quickly and efficiently.

18.7   Change Management

Change management is a term used widely not just in KM initiatives and IT initiatives, but throughout organizations to express the design and development of a specific plan to drive adoption, ease business challenges associated with change, and effect lasting change on the part of stakeholders. As Brent Hunter notes in *The Power of KM,* organizational change management is a critical part of the foundation of KM, as change management deals not only with ushering positive change into the organization, but also with the psychological effects of change on humans. Hunter states, "Without proper change management, KM initiatives are in danger of either never taking off or faltering after being launched" (Hunter 2016). Change management, unfortunately, is often treated as a nebulous concept, rather than a specific set of measurable steps and actions. Too often, especially in KM initiatives, we have seen change management invoked as a panacea to drive change and adoption without a clear action plan. This action plan must address the human and organizational dynamics that will come with change by providing support, assurance, and clear communication for people through transitional phases, including executives, stakeholders, and employees. This is the surest way to ensure buy-in and acceptance of the changes being introduced.

> **Tip:**
> Change is always a risk, for by their very nature, humans can be resistant to change and hesitant to adopt new habits. Remember that an important dynamic of change management is that things may get worse before they get better, for implementing lasting organizational change is a long and complex process.

18.7.1   Why It Is Important

The old adage of "if you build it, they will come" has never been accurate for any type of system implementation, and KM systems in particular do not follow this idea. Change is hard, and changing the way one does business is particularly hard. KM systems implementations, therefore, need a clear strategy and defined ownership and accountability for who, how, and why the change will be communicated. If you revisit the common KMS project challenges and mistakes we discuss in Chap. 17, you will note how many have to do with a lack of understanding, lack of communication, or failure to achieve and convey business value. An effective change management plan will help to mitigate many of these risks by providing:

- A clear communications plan, including the audience for the message, mediums for communications, and key points and elements for the communications.
- Approaches to measure efficacy and adoption of the system and to report up and out on those measurements in order to share successes.

- Focused and ongoing activities for coaching and end user support to initiate and sustain the desired change and adoption over time.
- Two-way communications plan to not just communicate to end users but engage them in conversation and solicit feedback in order to consistently improve the user experience, thereby guiding the iterative improvement of the system and further engaging your stakeholders and end users.

Collectively, a well-executed change management strategy with these elements will ensure the potentially large investment in a KM transformation and guarantee the associated KM systems pay off and realize the promised ROI. It is also noteworthy that when following an Agile approach, some KM systems will deploy a minimum viable product, which might not have all of the compelling features or interface in place yet to impress stakeholders. A good change management plan will also help to set expectations for each release, so all concerned parties know what to expect and will not be disappointed by specific releases. This will help to ensure the continued attention and support of sponsors, stakeholders, and end users together, giving the KM transformation a true opportunity to make progress and show meaningful value.

18.7.2 Best Practices and Approach

Be Clear About Your Goals

One of the most important ways to ensure that a change management plan is impactful and measurable is to clearly document what your goals are. Include what change you are looking to see, what level of change would be considered a success, and over what period of time you will be seeking to make this change. Being able to clearly articulate exactly what you are seeking to achieve will allow you to plan and scope your change management effort most effectively. It will also give you the ability to report more clearly on what success looks like, which is an important measure to share upward to leadership. We have also found that having a concretely articulated goal or set of goals keeps you or others from moving targets. If everyone agrees on the type and level of change you are seeking at the outset, you will know exactly what you are aiming for. As a result, the question of whether success was achieved will not be debated in a later conversation.

Map Your Stakeholders to Communications

Expanding on the guidance to be clear about your goals, it is critical to predefine whom you are asking to change and how you are asking them to change. A simple visual of how communications with stakeholders should move forward is in Fig. 18.7. Different types of stakeholders and end users will be asked to change in different ways. For instance, for an executive, you want him or her to consistently direct people to the new KM system and champion it to leadership. For a subject matter expert who regularly creates new content, on the other hand, you want him or her to use the new system, adopting new workflows and technologies within it and following the content governance guidelines regarding structuring and tagging

Fig. 18.7 Simple visual of constructive KM conversations in action. © 2021, Wahl/Hilger, reused with permission

Table 18.4 Simple chart to map motivations of different stakeholders

Stakeholder Type	Behavior Change	Motivations	Planned Activities	Success Measures

content. This is a much greater change that will require greater reinforcement and support. It is also valuable to understand the different motivations of these different types of end users and stakeholders. To plan this, we often use a simple chart like Table 18.4 to ensure we have a clear understanding of the different stakeholders and associated messages.

This allows us to be clear on who, specifically, we are asking to change and what we are asking them to do. It also allows us to map this with their motivations so we can be sure to articulate the benefits to them in messaging, planned activities to outline how we will drive their specific behavior change, and success measures to inform how we will measure whether the change activities are having the desired impact.

A key takeaway from this is to ensure you are fully customizing your change activities. The frequency of communications, medium by which communications are delivered, and the messages themselves should all be unique to the stakeholders with whom you are seeking to communicate.

Define Ownership and Accountability

Throughout the design and implementation stages of a KM strategy project, it is likely that dedicated staff and clear ownership of responsibilities is well in place. However, the post-implementation phase ends up less clearly staffed and defined, especially relating to change management and communications. To ensure the planned change and communication activities continue over the life of the KM system, especially in the first year after release, plan in advance for ownership of planned activities with associated accountability and measures to ensure the necessary activities take place.

A RACI chart is a great tool for ensuring the ownership and accountability is established at the outset as part of a change management plan. RACI essentially clarifies roles for each task that is part of a business project, and it is composed of simple language that makes it easy for an organization to define roles and responsibilities. The RACI chart dates all the way back to the 1950s, when it was first known as the "Decision Rights Matrix" or "Responsibility Charting" (RACI Solutions n.d.). Today, the RACI matrix is used by a large variety of companies, particularly large and complex ones that must constantly deal with the challenges of growth. RACI stands for:

- Responsible: Identifies who is responsible for completing a task.
- Accountable: Identifies who is responsible for reviewing the task and ensuring it is completed satisfactorily. This would also typically be the person collecting the analytics or other measures to ensure the task generated the anticipated outcome.
- Consulted: Identifies the person or people who can provide guidance and input to ensure the task is completed in the manner intended.
- Informed: Identifies the person or people who should be kept informed on activities and progress. These are also likely the people to whom milestones and successes would be reported.

A RACI chart is simple, but it also creates a collective view of responsibilities on a set of tasks. It is the only project management tool that deals solely with people and their roles in a process. When a complete KM system deployment with a change management initiative quickly becomes deeply complex, a RACI chart can ensure the right people are focused on and involved in the right activities at any time.

Leverage Analytics and Concrete Measures

The mistake that too many organizations make regarding change management initiatives is that they fail to provide concrete and measurable goals and outcomes as part of the initiative.

As we discuss in the preceding sections, setting clear goals and objectives is key to a change management plan, and ideally, the achievement of those goals and objectives will be measurable and observable in clear and quantifiable terms. In other words, setting a change management goal that says "people adopt the new KM system" demonstrates intent, but it is difficult to measure as it is open to interpretation. Instead, the change management goal might include several of the following:

- Ninety percent of users remain active in the system (at least one action performed per week) over the course of the six months following release.
- Total user actions remain steady or increase over the first year following release.
- Seventy-five percent of users contribute a new piece of content to the system within three months of release.

Equally, a goal that "people are happy with the new KM system" is too loose, and it does not offer a definition of what satisfaction means. Instead, the following is clear and measurable:

- Over 50 percent of users respond to the 3-month system satisfaction survey and provide an average satisfaction score of 7.5 or higher (10-point Likert scale).
- Sentiment analysis of user feedback shows positive feedback on 70 percent or more entries.

Alternatively, user actions can also be a strong indicator of "happy" users, so the following would also be applicable:

- Average number of user actions increase (per user) by over 20 percent over the first six months.
- More than 1000 users link to the new KM system (referral) from their e-mail or other system.

Each of the above provide a clear line of measurable success. Conversely, should any of the above not be attained, each is written in such a way to spur investigation or action in order to attain the desired behavior.

Plan for the Length of the Transformation

Change is not easy, and KM certainly is not easy, so it is imperative that change management initiatives plan for the length of the transformation. Change needs to be sustained in order to avoid people falling into old behaviors. Moreover, a typical KM system will evolve over time, introducing yet more change. This is even more accurate when dealing with true Agile deployments that may add significant additional features over the course of years.

As you seek your budget and plan your resources for a KM transformation and implementation of KM systems, ensure you are planning for the entire length of the engagement. Oftentimes, the cost of change management will actually increase over the first year after release, as you learn more about what is working and what is not and attempt to engage (or re-engage) your users and stakeholders.

A complete KM transformation is a costly endeavor, both in capital and the time of your stakeholders. Ensure the effort "sticks" by investing over the long term.

Do not Be Afraid to Market

Marketing is often considered something for customers, not employees, but it absolutely has a place in any KM change management initiative. Employees, just like customers, need to understand what is in it for them and get excited about the potential for new systems and what the change can do to benefit them. Marketing can take any number of forms, ranging from info sessions and promotional giveaways to multiple forms of media delivery to drive home messaging.

One of the high-value and low-cost forms of marketing we are seeing great traction in is the development of a short "commercial" to promote the KM system. KM systems can be difficult to grasp, but creating a strong visual of what the new system may look like and what users will be able to do with it can create a strong buzz around KM that gets users clamoring for the new system. The intent with a video like this is not to explain every feature or function and not to spell out every use case; instead, it should help the user visualize the value that may come from the new system. The following is the beginning of a strong narrative for a video like this:

> Imagine running a simple search and seeing highly pertinent results assembled from throughout <organization>, providing everything from short and simple answers that will help you perform a task to detailed how-to's, innovative discussions, and opportunities to connect with <organization's> leading experts.
>
> The <new KM system> will enable you to ask questions in plain language and get a wide selection of results from which to choose.
>
> Imagine being able to leverage the learnings and materials from all past and current projects, saving you time, helping you to perform your work better, and leveraging the wealth of past and current work done throughout <organization>.
>
> The <new KM system> will include a project navigator, placing all of <organization's> project resources at the ready, assembling and recommending that which will best suit your changing needs.

Though simple in language, this type of audio/visual marketing presents compelling ideas and outcomes that can get users excited, while showing them key features of the new system. Videos like this make excellent change management tools, and they can even help early in a KM transformation to secure leadership support and budget.

References

Cakici T (2018) What is a content type? Enterprise knowledge. https://enterprise-knowledge.com. Accessed 16 Sept 2021

Flesch R (1948) A new readability yardstick. In: DuBay W (ed) The classic readability studies. ERIC Clearinghouse, pp 96–99

Gamble P, Blackwell J (2001) Knowledge management. Kogan Page, London

Hedden H (2021) Taxonomies and sitemaps. The Accidental Taxonomist. http://accidental-taxonomist.blogspot.com. Accessed 17 Sept 2021

Hunter B (2016) The power of KM. Spirit Rising Productions, San Francisco

Literacy Project (2017) Illiteracy by the numbers. https://literacyproj.org. Accessed 17 Jun 2021

Muldoon M (2007) Why search initiatives often fail. KM World. https://www.kmworld.com. Accessed 29 Jul 2021

RACI Solutions (n.d.) What is RACI? An introduction. https://www.racisolutions.com. Accessed 28 Aug 2021

The Search Network (2020) Search insights 2020. OpenSource Connections. https://opensourceconnections.com. Accessed 28 Jun 2021

Content

19

Content is the fuel of any knowledge management system. The most compelling features and user interfaces do not matter at all if the systems do not contain (or provide access to) valuable content that will help to complete a user's missions. Having already mentioned content more than one thousand times by this point in the book, this chapter is not meant as an introduction to content. Instead, this chapter will ensure you understand the different ways to think about content, ensuring you are considering the appropriate scope and scale of content when planning, designing, and implementing your KM systems.

19.1 Types of Content

We use the word content in a very broad way to express an organization's explicit knowledge and information assets. We typically restrict this scope to those that are in a digital format, rather than wading into the quagmire of old boxes of paper files, but of course, there can be exceptions to even that. Overall, however, the following subsections will help to constrain how you scope the types of content you wish to address as part of your knowledge management program and KM systems overall.

Knowledge Versus Information
Every organization should expect content that is knowledge, as well as content that is information. The simple difference between the two is that knowledge contains expertise and experience, whereas information, though still critical to an organization, is simply consists of facts, without the context of the aforementioned expertise or benefit of any expert analysis upon it. To use a metaphor, if you are looking for a good restaurant, information would be someone listing the highly rated restaurants in your area, whereas knowledge would be someone recommending a place he or she had been and explaining why you might enjoy it.

Too many hours have been spent on overly academic arguments trying to draw a clear line between knowledge management and information management, or more

J. Hilger, Z. Wahl, *Making Knowledge Management Clickable*,
https://doi.org/10.1007/978-3-030-92385-3_19

precisely, between the definitions of knowledge versus information. An article by Knowledge Management Tools even observes, "you will often find KM solutions even today which are essentially nothing more than information or document management systems, which handle data, information, or perhaps even explicit knowledge, but which do not touch the most essential part of KM: tacit knowledge" (Knowledge Management Tools 2014). Information can help create and refine knowledge, but the critical difference between the two disciplines is lost in many organizations. The focus on differentiating between the two misses the key point that mature organizations will need both, and the tools, processes, and approaches to capturing, managing, and sharing both knowledge and information heavily overlap. It is important to understand the broad difference between the two in order to explain it and plan for both, but in reality, most mature KM systems will hold both knowledge content and information content, and in most cases, any given piece of content will contain elements of both knowledge and information.

Though the two terms should not be used interchangeably, it is important to note that they often are. Instead, consider that all knowledge is a type of information, but information itself is not knowledge. Both knowledge and information fall under the definition of content.

Tacit Versus Explicit
Tacit knowledge, also known as implicit knowledge, is that which is held in one's own head. Tacit knowledge is based on one's own learning and experience, making it extremely valuable but also difficult to translate into a digital and repeatable format. Explicit knowledge is more concrete, and in our parlance, it typically takes the form of digital content. Both types of knowledge are represented in Fig. 19.1. To use the same metaphor as before, if I am looking for a good restaurant, an example of tacit knowledge would be asking individuals knowledgeable about the city and the restaurant scene for recommendations, whereas explicit knowledge examples would include checking local food blogs online, going to a restaurant review site, and flipping through a local restaurant guidebook. Both of these types of knowledge are valuable, of course, and your situation and circumstances will determine if one or both suits your goals and needs.

Both tacit and explicit knowledge are necessary within an organization, but as this section will later describe, they must be synthesized for an organization to effectively keep up with the times. A 2017 article by Olivier Serrat describes how tacit and explicit knowledge are "mutually complementary forms of meaning." He includes a diagram of an iceberg to illustrate his point, which shows the surface 20% of an organization's knowledge to be explicit, or media based, while the other 80% dwells underwater as tacit knowledge. Serrat goes on to discuss patterns of interactions that affect the relationship between tacit and explicit knowledge. Externalization is the most critical to reach effective KM: it is "the process of articulating tacit knowledge into explicit knowledge by means of metaphors, analogies, or sketches" (Serrat 2017). We hope that the diagrams, illustrations, charts, and graphs interspersed throughout this book will serve as simple yet effective examples of externalization, as the creation of explicit knowledge becomes increasingly necessary.

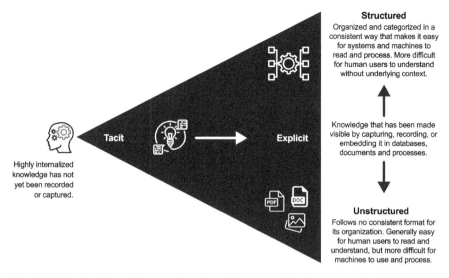

Structured
Organized and categorized in a consistent way that makes it easy for systems and machines to read and process. More difficult for human users to understand without underlying context.

Knowledge that has been made visible by capturing, recording, or embedding it in databases, documents and processes.

Unstructured
Follows no consistent format for its organization. Generally easy for human users to read and understand, but more difficult for machines to use and process.

Tacit

Highly internalized knowledge has not yet been recorded or captured.

Explicit

Fig. 19.1 Visual of knowledge as tacit and explicit, structured and unstructured. © 2021, Wahl/ Hilger, reused with permission

The importance of explicit knowledge over tacit knowledge is a critical element of KM strategy and KM systems. Many organizations are dealing with the loss of tacit knowledge as employees retire or leave the organization for a different opportunity. This is known as brain drain or human capital flight, and it constitutes a huge loss of productivity and cost to organizations, as their knowledge is literally walking out the door. The term "brain drain" was coined in post-war Europe, as skilled scientists and other technical workers emigrated to North America in search of better opportunities, higher pay, and an overall increased standard of living. Those fundamental causes of brain drain have remained fairly constant as this phenomenon has impacted the modern business world, and the primary solution seems to be offering highly skilled, intelligent workers chances for advancement and innovation (JEC Republicans 2019). As we detail in Chap. 1 on KM business value, counteracting this brain drain is a major source of ROI in KM initiatives. By identifying processes and systems that help to capture tacit knowledge and translate it to content that can be captured, managed, and shared in KM systems, the organization is not just stopping the brain drain, it is also creating a version of that knowledge which other users can access, learn from, and act upon. Even without the brain drain, in situations where an individual is still with the organization, tacit knowledge capture and knowledge transfer are hugely valuable in order to save the right people the time of repeating the sharing of their tacit knowledge over and over, instead having it placed as content in a way that others may access it when needed. As a result, organizations that effectively create efficient and innovative KM systems will not just better retain the knowledge, they will likely retain more highly knowledgeable workers who recognize their organization as future oriented and a place where their knowledge is leveraged and appreciated.

Put simply, using KM systems as an avenue to translate tacit knowledge into explicit knowledge in the form of content is a key element of KM and a core use case of KM systems. When done correctly and consistently, it represents a major source of value and ROI and can translate to a major source of competitive advantage and productivity improvement for most industries.

Structured Versus Unstructured

The monikers of structured and unstructured refer to how well the content is organized, both internal to the piece of content but also within the system in which it is housed. Structured content, like that you would find in a database or application like a CRM or financial management system, is organized and categorized in a consistent way that makes it easy for systems and machines to read and process, but it is more difficult for (most) humans to understand and act upon independent of a user interface or data visualization tools. Unstructured content is the opposite. It is typically designed for human consumption, so it is much easier for a typical end user to understand, as it includes the context for it to make sense independently. However, KM systems and machines struggle to understand it in a way that makes it relatable or findable.

To put this in terms of our restaurants' metaphor, you may identify a local food blog written as a loose narrative, which would be considered an example of unstructured content. Alternatively, you could go to a restaurant booking or review app, filter in "top rated," and then limit your results based on location range and price range. This would be an example of structured content.

KM, of course, can help to add structure to unstructured content. Many of the techniques and systems discussed in this book are designed to do just that. Specifically, using content types and applying consistent metadata tags from taxonomies are key approaches that add structure to unstructured content. Likewise, applying ontologies is an advanced means of adding structure that enables automated relationship building and vastly improves the findability and discoverability of content.

It is important to note that structured and unstructured content is not a black and white distinction but rather a spectrum. Not all content should ever be fully structured, but in many cases, a successful KM transformation will include a marked increase in the structure of key content types and sources. Again, there are many ways to gradually increase the structure of content, not just through taxonomies, content types, and ontologies. Some simple means of increasing structure include improving detail and consistency of file naming conventions, improved granularity of the placement of content in systems and folder structures, and consolidation of content from multiple disparate sources and file drives to a more cohesive and purposeful set of locations.

Content Items Versus Assembled Content

As we move into more advanced content strategy and content management systems, content can also be differentiated based on whether it is a complete piece of content (assembled content) or an element of the whole (content item or content particle). These concepts come into play in systems that are dealing with content chunking and

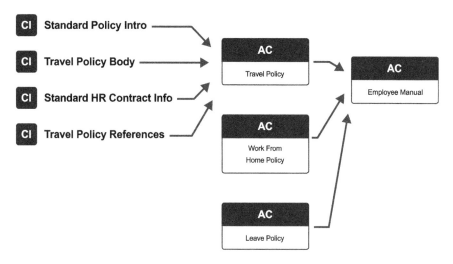

Fig. 19.2 The relationship of content items to assembled content. © 2021, Wahl/Hilger, reused with permission

content assembly as we detailed in Chap. 14. The naming, as well as the somewhat esoteric concept, can make the difference between content items and assembled content confusing, especially when you consider that in some cases, content items that will be combined to form a piece of assembled content are themselves made up of smaller content items. Figure 19.2 shows an example of this in practice, demonstrating that content items assembled into a piece of content can then in turn be used to assemble an even larger piece of content.

These complexities are important to recognize when you consider architecting your system, especially recognizing that though all of this is content, content items and different "levels" of assembled content may each have their own content types, metadata requirements, and governance and workflow requirements. Moreover, the placement of content items within KM systems will likely be different than that of assembled content. In short, this is not something that should be made up in an ad hoc fashion. A clear understanding of your content items and assembled content plans and needs should be in place before selecting your systems or beginning the content design process.

Tip:
Bringing together the concepts of content items, structured content, and Enterprise AI, it is noteworthy that the more granular your content items and the more structure you have applied to them, the more they can be leveraged by knowledge graphs and other AI mechanisms to automate content assembly, power chatbots, and drive recommendations engines. As you are planning your content strategy, consider the content you will want to leverage in AI solutions and prioritize the structuring and granular chunking of that content.

Content Unbound

As a final consideration of the types of content, you should consider as part of a comprehensive KM systems strategy, recognize that the boundaries of what has historically been considered content are quickly expanding, and they can be unique to your organization as long as you understand the business justification. Content traditionally was considered to be files like Word, PowerPoint, and PDF documents. Over the years, it has expanded to include all digital assets within an organization, including images, videos, drawings, and more. As we have detailed throughout this book, it has further expanded to include data sets and structured data housed within applications. That is a fine and broad boundary for content in some organizations, but for most, especially moving forward and following the guidance in this book, it is incomplete.

As you plan your KM transformation, ensure you are considering content as anything that should be created, captured, managed, enhanced, shared, and/or connected within the organization. Put more simply, your complete definition of content should include anything you want to be found or want to relate to other content. In most organizations, this means employees will be considered a type of content or, rather, their metadata will be (i.e., employees' skills, job experience, position, and responsibilities). As you progress the way you think about content, your products and services, components/materials, and physical office locations may also be considered.

Considering content in this broader way will allow your organization to connect and discover all traditional and non-traditional types of content collectively. Users may go searching for the short answer to a question, ideally finding it quickly but also discovering a host of other types of content that can help them act, learn, and perform. Imagine, for instance, an enterprise search that does not just return the short answer but also reveals experts from whom to learn more, a community of practice where the topic is being discussed, a learning opportunity to sign up for, a video to watch, and an office location where a discussion on the topic will be facilitated.

19.2   Content Cleanup

We have found that large organizations are typically managing 80% more content than they actually should be. These four out of five documents are made up of duplicate, old, obsolete, and incorrect content. This happens naturally over time, especially for organizations with poor content and system governance or governance which is not being enforced or followed. How often have you heard the story of someone finding an incorrect or outdated policy or procedure, or finding multiple versions of the same document and not knowing which is the right one, or worse yet, finding and acting on a piece of old information that resulted in them performing an action or advising a client incorrectly? In even more dire circumstances, incorrect information can be shared externally or placed incorrectly, resulting in accidents and regulatory fines. Poor content maintenance has a major cost to it. Each of these cases is a problem related to the content within systems more than the systems themselves.

The basic problem is that in too many systems, it is easier for users to recreate a document or upload a near duplicate version of the original than to edit the original. Part of this is a lack of governance, part of this is poor system design, and part of this is simply a lack of education. At the same time, organizations are maintaining these systems from an IT and functional perspective, ensuring up-time and software updates, but many miss the equally critical importance of content maintenance, where content is regularly reviewed to ensure it is still pertinent and accurate.

These issues result in whole enterprises that are overwhelmed with content they do not actually need or want indexed in their core systems. Of course, for records management and compliance purposes, there may well be a requirement to keep it, but that does not mean it should be placed prominently in a location where it keeps users from finding and acting on the information they actually need and can trust.

Overall, content cleanup efforts are often problematic areas of avoidance in an organization as they are considered incredibly complex, terribly labor intensive, and difficult to measure meaningful progress. Given the abundance of content and content stores within an organization, many have simply tried to start over with new repositories rather than cleanup or migrate content. This, of course, compounds the issue over time, as some content ends up not just duplicated within a system, but duplicated across multiple systems, as key content is copied from old to new systems without any thought or methodology guiding the process.

In order to ensure your content is ready for a new or updated suite of KM systems, a content cleanup effort may well be required. This typically begins with a content inventory to understand the current state of your content. This may have already been accomplished as part of a current state analysis of KM, but if not, conducting a content inventory will help to answer where your content is, what types of content you are dealing with, the dynamism of your content, and the general state of your content regarding how current it is. A content analysis, ideally, will also leverage metrics to inform how frequently the content is being accessed and edited, which are important inputs to help simplify and speed the content cleanup process.

To ensure content cleanup efforts proceed at your organization and can demonstrate meaningful progress, consider the following three steps to focus work:

1. **Prioritize systems, departments, and/or content types**—Rather than looking across an enterprise and wondering where to begin, consider focusing content cleanup activities on specific systems, departments, and/or content types. In these cases, it is often valuable to start with smaller systems/departments/content types to demonstrate that the content cleanup challenge is surmountable and also to learn how to improve the cleanup process through a smaller or simpler starting initiative before wading into those that may be more complex. You may also want to prioritize high-impact systems, departments, and/or content types that will have a visible positive impact on a wide set of users. This result will help to gain support and buy-in for further content cleanup activities as you progress through the organization. In short, find a small but impactful set of content that can be cleaned up, prioritize this, and use it as an exercise to hone your cleanup methodology and market the value and outcome to the organization.

2. **Use analytics**—When large and complex organizations consider the time and effort of cleaning up potentially millions of pieces of content, the sheer time it would take often becomes a deterrent to moving forward. Analytics can quickly help to eliminate a major percentage of content that would require a human review. Setting some simple rules and assumptions regarding the usage of content can help to narrow content cleanup activities down by several factors of size and complexity. Specifically, if content has not been accessed/opened by anyone or if content has not been modified/updated by anyone for a given period of time, it can be considered archivable. There are of course exceptions to this that will need specific consideration, but generally speaking, if no one has opened or edited a document in over a year, it is likely of minimal business value. Some organizations may wish to get more granular than this and make exceptions for high-value content to be held in perpetuity, such as final deliverables or corporate policies, but the broad guidance nonetheless holds true and can quickly eliminate a major amount of content.

3. **Leverage technology**—In more advanced cases, your KM suite of technologies can also help to identify duplicate and near duplicate pieces of content. Many legacy systems are full of iterated versions of documents that have since been finalized. For example, in one organization planning to migrate its document management system, we discovered it had been holding over one hundred different versions of a single marketing plan. This commonly occurs when an individual saves a document locally and then uploads it as a fresh document instead of leveraging version control capabilities. In organizations with multiple content repositories, this is even more of an issue, with multiple duplicates or near duplicates present in each system. Semantic analysis capabilities included in some enterprise search or auto-tagging tools can automatically identify these duplicate or near duplicate pieces of content, largely automating the process of eliminating them.

Say your content inventory initially identified an unwieldy collection of 5,000,000 pieces of content across your enterprise. If we were to assume it would take a human three minutes per piece of content to perform a cursory review and determine whether it should be kept, updated, or archived/deleted, you would be looking at 250,000 hours of work! No organization would ever make that investment. However, if you focus on a specific, high-value set of content within a prominent (but smallish) department, you are likely looking at no more than 50,000 pieces of content. When you then leverage analytics and a semantic analysis to eliminate old, outdated, duplicate, or near duplicate content, you are left with only 10,000 pieces of content for a human review. That represents a much more achievable 500 hours of work, something a few interns with guidance from some of your SMEs and your KM and content teams could accomplish in less than a month.

Another approach to thinking about content cleanup, standard in the knowledge and information management space, is called a ROT analysis. ROT stands for **R**edundant, **O**utdated/**O**bsolete, and **T**rivial. You can find definitions of ROT using either the term outdated or obsolete dating back to the early 2000s, and it has since become a widely accepted approach in most organizations and government entities across the USA. A ROT analysis provides a basic set of questions or guides to help eliminate content that no longer belongs as part of your core indexes. This helps speed decision-making as part of a content cleanup, improves the consistency of that decision-making so that multiple people will be making more standard decisions, and helps to remove judgment calls or guesswork as part of the cleanup process. Examples of simple (and measurable) questions that can be used to assess your content are as follows:

- Is the item redundant?
  - Are there duplicates or near duplicates of the same item?
  - In the case of near duplicates, is there a requirement to keep both versions?
  - In the case of near duplicates, do the differences make a meaningful impact on the meaning or usage of the content?
  - Can the information be found in an alternative location and/or format that is more effective or valuable?
- Is this item outdated or obsolete?
  - Has it been more than <time period> since it was last updated?
  - Has it been more than <time period> since it was last accessed?
  - Is the information within the item still relevant?
  - Is the information within the item accurate?
  - Is there a newer version?
  - Is the item subject to a retention schedule?
  - If the item is subject to a workflow or review and update process, is it compliant with these reviews and timeframes (i.e., has it gone through the workflow reviews and been approved)?
- Is this item trivial?
  - Is this a business-related item that offers value?
  - Does it reference current business processes, people, products, etc.?

Each of the above questions would require additional guidance and definition by your organization, but they nonetheless represent a potential starting point to add a consistent and logical decision-making process to a content cleanup effort. There also exists ROT analysis software that a company can invest in, which can be used to automatically locate duplicate files, manage junk files, and optimize storage. It was originally meant for improving SEO on public sites, but these same tools can be used to crawl many internal sites to find duplicate or near duplicate content.

As another way of thinking about content cleanup, we have created our own acronym of NERDy content. This acronym represents descriptions of content that should remain following a cleanup, and it can be used to prioritize the content on which to focus cleanup activities. It is closely aligned with content ROT, as well as the aforementioned prioritization and focusing techniques for content cleanup. NERD stands for:

- **New**—Simple sorting will reveal the newest version of documents and the latest thoughts from your experts. The newest content within an enterprise is often pertinent and of high value, meaning it is good content to prioritize.
- **Essential**—Company policies and legal restraints will guide that which is necessary for regulatory compliance, and your business users can help to identify business-critical information. Essential content is non-negotiable. It must be kept within the enterprise.
- **Reliable**—Content must be trusted. Reliable content means that you have eliminated the old, outdated, and obsolete content that often gums up a system and are maintaining the "right" versions, leaving the rest to the archives or to be deleted.
- **Dynamic**—With the recognition that many types of content are fleeting, including news, memos, and meeting minutes, the dynamism of content is a strong indicator that it should be maintained. In other words, if content is being updated, business users have deemed it valuable or necessary.

Focusing on NERDy content can help bring attention to where it can offer the strongest results. NERDy content prioritization can also help as a prioritization strategy when going beyond just removing or archiving content as part of a cleanup. More complex content cleanup efforts are not a matter of simply keeping the "right" stuff and removing the "wrong" stuff; they also require expertise in order to improve the readability, accuracy, and consistency of content through rewriting, reformatting, and revoicing. The same logic and approach hold true for these efforts, where the first step will be to clean out any content that can simply be deleted or archived, with the remainder being prioritized and assessed for reformatting, rewriting, or revoicing.

In cases of content that needs this additional effort, your organization should plan for the human cost of these activities and consider outsourcing simple but time-consuming activities like reformatting, leaving any time from your own experts focused on rewriting high-value content and reviewing the work of others. Though important, these intensive content cleanup efforts can be laborious, and we have consistently seen internal stakeholders push back on the time and effort it will take. It is often thankless work and will require significant leadership support and planning regarding change management and communications to conduct at the enterprise level. Small and focused content cleanup efforts that leverage iterative and Agile processes are much more likely to succeed in these cases as well.

19.3   Content Migration

Beyond cleanup, and still more advanced, some KM transformations may require content migrations. In these cases, the content is not just being cleaned up, it is being moved or reentered as chunked content or content items.

Content may be migrated from one system to another when old systems are being retired or replaced or when several systems are being replaced and consolidated into a single enterprise solution. These content migration efforts can be time consuming and complex, but they can yield enhanced content if conducted correctly. The most important factor in a content migration is to ensure your business is aligned on the purpose and value of the content migration. Too frequently, these complex content migration efforts are begun without fully understanding the level of effort required, the desired outcomes, or the best practices to get the most out of the effort. A content migration should be treated more like a project, with clear scope, timelines, and success criteria. The following steps will help to ensure successful content migration efforts for your organization:

1. Agree on content migration scope, including:
   - Target Content—Clearly document what content is being moved and why. As discussed in the preceding section, do not be afraid to focus only on a particular section or type of content in order to identify a scope that is reasonable over a nominal amount of time.
   - Migration Activities—A content migration is infrequently just the act of moving a piece of content from point a to point b. Will your migration include content chunking, rewriting, revoicing, or tagging of content? Ensure you know exactly what the definition of done is for each content type.
   - Migration Roles and Workflows—Define who will be responsible for the content migration. Oftentimes, especially in large and complex organizations, several roles will be defined for a content migration, with one group performing the work and at least one other reviewing and approving it. In some organizations, the work will be distributed across a large number of people, while in others the work will be centralized.
2. Cleanup—Conduct cleanup activities prior to migration so as not to waste effort migrating content that will not be kept.
3. Document and Educate—Clearly document your content migration approach, required activities, roles and responsibilities, and overall timeline for the work. Make sure to include any guidance on the required activities. For instance, do not just instruct a migrator to tag content; ensure you have clearly spelled out how and why to tag the content. Once your documentation is clear and your migrators have been identified, conduct training and coaching to ensure they understand the "how" and "why" of the migration, and plan for ongoing coaching activities to guide them along the process and support them in this challenging and often monotonous task.
4. Test Approach—Before moving forward, select a semi-random sampling of content for your migrators to migrate. This testing stage will prove your planned migration approach works and your migrators will be able to carry out the effort with the given guidance and to the level of consistency expected.
5. Conduct Migration and Report—Once validated, move forward with the content migration itself, ensuring your migrators are supported with ready guidance and coaching. On a regular basis, report on progress and assess if the projected speed and accuracy of the effort are on track with the plan. Adjust this as necessary,

potentially pulling in other migrators or downscoping the amount of content to be migrated.
6. Conduct a Retrospective—Once completed, conduct a retrospective with your content migrators to learn how to improve the process for the next tranche of content.

Tip:
In some cases, technology can help a content migration process along, speeding the tagging or placement of content. The same technologies that can auto-tag content may be used to help automate a content migration process. As with tagging, however, do not be overly reliant on these tools, as even in the best circumstances, human oversight and review will be necessary. Auto-tagging works best when it is first tuned and validated as part of the process.

Though oftentimes complex, content migrations are excellent opportunities to improve your content as it is being migrated. With the right planning, a content migration effort will also be a content enhancement effort, resulting in content that is easier to read, find, and maintain.

References

JEC Republicans (2019) Losing our minds: brain drain across the United States. United States Congress Joint Economic Committee. https://www.jec.senate.gov. Accessed 24 Jun 2021
Knowledge Management Tools (2014) Information management vs knowledge management. KM From A to Z. https://www.knowledge-management-tools.net. Accessed 17 Jul 2021
Serrat O (2017) Notions of knowledge management. Knowledge solutions. Springer, Cham. https://doi.org/10.1007/978-981-10-0983-9_30

Operations and Iterative Improvements

20

Like many complex enterprise applications, implementation is never complete. The information being captured by the organization and the processes that knowledge workers follow will continue to change over time. It is important that the operational support for these KM solutions is designed to grow and adapt over time. This chapter describes the basic operating principle for all KM systems with some more specific practices for some of the different types of solutions.

20.1 General KM Operations and Support

The support for KM systems should mirror the way these systems were developed. KM solutions need to adapt to the way people work, and it is very hard to truly understand and plan for the way that different people work across the enterprise. Agile approaches are best suited for solutions that need to plan for change like KM systems. Each application should have an Agile team that is designated as the support team. Ideally, this team is the same team as the one that implemented the solution initially, but that is not a requirement as long as proper turnover and training has been carried out. The application support team will be smaller than the original development team, but it should have a similar make up. The team should have a product owner that understands the true vision of the application and can help make decisions with regards to the prioritization of the enhancements that are typical for any newly developed application. The team should have analysts and user experience professionals who can understand how changes should be designed and communicate these changes to the users when they are launched. Finally, the team will need developers and at least access to an architect who can ensure that new features do not negatively impact system performance.

If the application was implemented using an Agile methodology, there will be an existing backlog of features that should be implemented over time. This backlog should be carried forward to the support team as the initial list of features to be added to the KM solution. When planning sprints, the support team should set aside

© The Author(s), under exclusive license to Springer Nature Switzerland AG 2022
J. Hilger, Z. Wahl, *Making Knowledge Management Clickable*,
https://doi.org/10.1007/978-3-030-92385-3_20

30 percent of their work for unexpected issues or bugs that need to be addressed right away. The rest of the time can be spent adding the new features from the backlog. This backlog will be revisited by the product owner each sprint as new features are requested. Often, these new features take priority over the original backlog of features that were never prioritized during initial development. The ability to respond to new feature requests and changes is critical to ensuring the long-term success of any KM solution.

The team should plan on releases every 1–2 months initially. This is critical to long-term adoption, as the business users will see that their KM solution team is responsive to their needs and that the solution better aligns with the way they work. Over time, as the applications stabilize, releases can be moved to a quarterly schedule with emergency bug fixes implemented on an as-needed basis.

In addition to the original and newly requested features, it is important to plan for application upgrades. On premise, applications frequently have upgrades that are required for implementation. These upgrades are rarely simple and require the application team to develop a plan to roll out the new version of software and test that it does not break existing features. If the application has automated unit testing built in, this is a slightly easier task. Either way, it is typically a significant undertaking. Ideally, the new release comes with new features, but sometimes the new features are of little value to the organization and the upgrade is required for support purposes. In either case, at least once a year, the development team and product owner should plan for an upgrade release. During the upgrade release, all other new feature development should be put on hold.

Given the schedule described above, it is common that mature KM solutions offer three functional releases and one upgrade release per year. People expect KM applications to adapt to the way people work and the information that they work with. Managed correctly, this approach should offer plenty of opportunities for these systems to grow and adapt over time.

20.2 Solution-Specific Support Needs

In addition to the support described above, there are specific support requirements for each of the different types of applications we have discussed in this book.

Content management systems need to adapt to align with changes in the content being managed. This is typically in the form of new content types. As new types of content are introduced to the organization, an expert in content engineering needs to determine if the content requires a new content type and what the implications of that new content type are. For example, a Web Content Management System (WCMS) may require new front-end pages to properly present the content on the website. New content types in a Document Management System (DMS) may have new metadata fields that could cause the organization to need to revisit the organization's taxonomy. We typically recommend that CMS support teams include or have access to an experienced content engineer who can determine what new content looks like and its implications across the enterprise.

Learning management systems need to continually align courses with skills, capabilities, and job roles across the organization. As organizations reorganize or new positions arise, it is important that the LMS continues to map to these important roles. As such, we recommend that organizations have a learning expert on staff who can map these new roles and requirements and determine what that means to the LMS implementation. Reorganizations create new roles that need to be mapped out. These changes affect the way courses are mapped to skills, skills are mapped to capabilities, and how capabilities are mapped to job roles. The learning management specialist can plan for these changes.

Collaboration suites are typically designed with a great deal of flexibility, so content types and managing change are not as critical. When supporting a collaboration suite, the most important role we have found is that of evangelist. The evangelist is regularly learning about new features and ways in which people work. Evangelists are always looking for new processes that can be automated or integrated into the collaboration platform. Collaboration platforms are only as good as their adoption, and the evangelist can make sure that more and more groups take advantage of the platform over time.

The data catalog needs a data architect involved in the project so that this person can ensure new data sources and data sets are included in the data catalog so that it remains a reliable source for all data across the enterprise. When a data catalog stops managing metadata about data, it ceases to add real value.

Taxonomy management systems teams need to be well aligned with the enterprise architecture group. As new systems are implemented, many of them need to be integrated with the taxonomy management system. The support team will need to be available to work with each new product implementation team to support the integration of the new software with the taxonomy management system.

The search-related solutions have a different set of needs. Both enterprise search tools and graph databases need an information architect involved who can identify new information assets. These information assets need to be modeled and added to the graph or the search tool so that these important tools regularly add new information asset types as information grows and changes. In addition, both of these tools need a search architect who can plan new indexing logic as new information repositories are identified and added into the enterprise search.

The combination of the general recommendations for operational support along with the system-specific recommendations shared above should help ensure that your KM implementation continues to meet the needs of today's knowledge workers and that it adapts to new and unplanned requirements that naturally arise.

Envisioning Success: Putting KM Solutions and Outcomes Together

21

Many of the KM systems described throughout this book can stand on their own. Having said that, there are a number of powerful KM solutions that can be developed using a combination of these different technologies. The solutions described in this chapter are built using one or more of the technologies we have already covered, and they solve more complex KM problems.

21.1 Integrated Knowledge Management Platform

What Is It?

There is no single software platform that can serve as an enterprise-wide knowledge management solution. A true enterprise knowledge management platform integrates information from multiple systems and exposes it in a single location that provides context and structure around the information in these separate systems and makes it searchable from within a single search interface. The ultimate goal of these platforms is to blur the lines between systems to make information available no matter where it is stored or managed.

When done properly, the KM platform gives knowledge workers easy access to the information they need along with content that provides context to what they are seeing. Knowledge workers can navigate through the site or use search to find answers to questions when they need them. Organizations with a complex set of IT applications that need to provide better access to information for their employees should prioritize the creation of an integrated enterprise knowledge management platform.

How Is It Built?

The integrated knowledge management platform is built on many of the tools and products discussed in this book. At a minimum, it will need the following tools, as shown in Fig. 21.1.

© The Author(s), under exclusive license to Springer Nature Switzerland AG 2022   299
J. Hilger, Z. Wahl, *Making Knowledge Management Clickable*,
https://doi.org/10.1007/978-3-030-92385-3_21

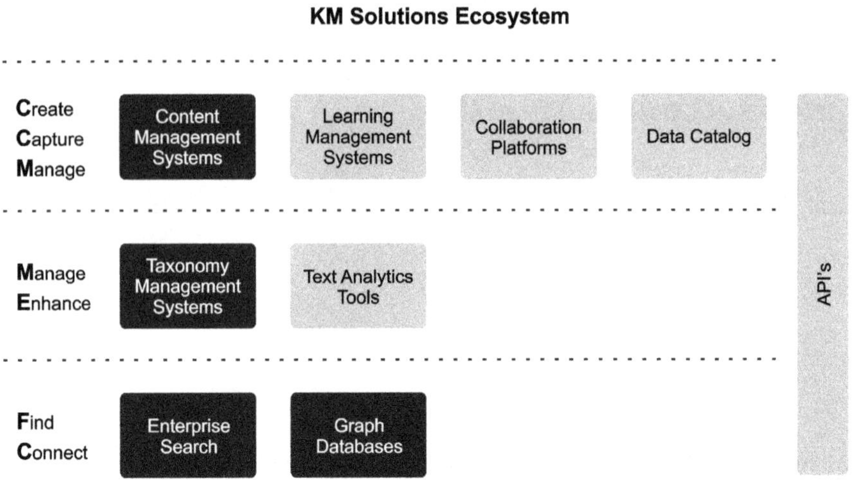

KM Solutions Ecosystem

Fig. 21.1 The shaded tools are the minimum required for an integrated knowledge management platform. © 2021, Wahl/Hilger, reused with permission

- A web content management system
- An enterprise search engine
- A taxonomy management system
- A graph database

The web content management system is used to develop the website that is the entry point for the knowledge management platform. In addition, authors from around the business can create content that provides context for the content found in other systems or fill gaps in content that is not available elsewhere.

The enterprise search engine will index content from the different information repositories in the organization and make all content accessible to the people who have permission to see it from the search screen in the integrated knowledge management platform. The search engine is critical to making access to content across systems easy and seamless. It can also serve as a way to expose content on the website that comes from other systems.

The taxonomy management system provides a single place to store and manage the enterprise taxonomy that fuels faceted search as well as guided navigation to content on the knowledge management platform. It also provides a way to auto-tag content so that users are not required to enter all of the metadata in all of their platforms.

Finally, the graph database serves two purposes. It serves as an aggregation tool to pull information from one or more data sources that can then be summarized as a single search result. For example, the graph database may pull together everything it can find about a person from multiple locations and then send it to the search engine as a person search result. The second purpose is to store metadata for content in repositories that do not support metadata. In this case, the graph stores metadata about content and a pointer to the content in its original location. This content can then be accessed on the knowledge portal with metadata even though the original source system did not allow for the capture of metadata.

Once these tools are properly integrated, organizations have a knowledge portal through which they can find all of the information of the organization in one simple and highly organized site.

Business Benefits

An integrated knowledge management platform pulls together information from across the enterprise in a way that makes it easily accessible and understandable to everyone in the enterprise. This type of platform is the basis of any large, enterprise-wide KM initiative. As such, the benefits of a KM platform are the same as you would see in any KM strategy project with one very specific addition. KM platforms make knowledge management real. KM initiatives are internal and often struggle to show ROI. Historically, many of these initiatives were people and process based, and executives struggled to see the value of the effort. An integrated KM platform is something that executives can see and touch and quickly benefit from. Many of our clients did not get excited about their KM transformation until the KM platform was in place, and they could quickly find information that historically was lost or required rework. The title of this book, "Making Knowledge Management Clickable," is based on our experience seeing organizations truly get excited about KM when they see a well-designed and highly functional KM platform.

In addition to justifying the KM investment, KM platforms help organizations in several other important ways.

- Improve employee engagement and retention
- Streamline common processes
- Improve the customer experience
- Increase efficiency across the entire organization
- Ensure compliance with laws and industry regulations
- Increase creativity and entrepreneurship across the organization

We are increasingly moving to a digital world with people working remotely. The ability to find information when there is no one sitting next to you is no longer a convenience. It is a necessity for organizations that want to be competitive leaders in their industry.

21.2 Expert Finder

What Is It?

A key for any successful KM initiative is to make it easy to find the person or persons that have the knowledge or experience to answer specific questions. An Expert Finder is a tool that allows knowledge workers within an organization to search for people based on specific skills or questions that arise. For example, a knowledge worker might search on a topic such as network architecture. The expert search would return a list of people who have shown some form of knowledge about the topic based on their training, degrees, or work experience both before and after they began working with the organization. The key to a successful expert finder is to find a way to automatically derive this information. The original expert finders asked employees to state their experience. This failed because users did not fill out this information, they did not keep it up to date, or they did not offer the right level of detail as to what they know. Modern expert systems use a knowledge graph to pull information about employee experience from multiple applications. This includes:

- The recruiting database with employee resumes.
- The HR systems with reviews and organizational information.
- A time tracking system with project information.
- Project collaboration tools with project material.
- Published documents/reports from both internal and external sources.

An expert finder that aggregates this information to gain a full understanding of an employee can provide information about their expertise without asking them to manually fill out information and keep it up to date. The result is up to date and detailed information about what each employee in your organization knows.

This new type of expert finder is also being called Employee 360. The idea is that organizations now have the tools to see a more complete picture of their employees including what they do, what they know, and where they work. The vision of Employee 360 goes beyond a tool for finding experts. Employee 360 allows organizations to better manage their employees' careers and provide information that allows organizations to better utilize their skills by placing them in the projects and roles that can best use their unique skills. For instance, a services organization could leverage an Employee 360 capability powered by a knowledge graph and combined with predictive analytics to identify trends in bids and sales and combine it with an analysis of employee demographics and skill sets in order to flag potential gaps in staffing before they even occurred. This could allow an organization to proactively train their people or make new hires to fill gaps in expertise before they exist.

How Is It Built?

The expert finder should be available both within the enterprise search application and also as a standalone service that can be exposed in whatever applications are best suited to allow people to search for experts. A modern expert finder system is made of the following solutions, as shown in Fig. 21.2:

- An enterprise search engine to enable the search.
- A graph database to aggregate personal information.
- A taxonomy management system to tag skills.

KM Solutions Ecosystem

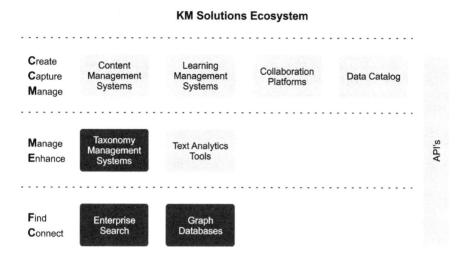

Fig. 21.2 The shaded tools are the minimum required for an expert finder system. © 2021, Wahl/Hilger, reused with permission

The enterprise search engine makes people searchable. The key to the implementation is that content created by people and their related project information is stored in the search engine along with the attributes about each employee. The search can then be exposed as part of the enterprise search, or the people index can be searched independently if you need an independent expert finder application.

The graph database is used to aggregate the information about each person from all of the applications and systems that store relevant information. This has a node for each person and then captures key information from each system about each person. This information is then sent to the search engine so that it is searchable. The graph database will also be used to show all of the information about the person when a person search result is selected.

Lastly, a taxonomy management system can be used to manage the skills that are important for your organization. The skills are either manually tagged in the source systems or auto-tagged by the taxonomy management system. These tags are stored in the graph database with each person so that the expert finder is automatically populated with individual skills about that person.

Together, these three tools make expert search a more dynamic and automated solution that evaluates expertise quickly and accurately.

Business Benefits

An expert search is a foundational tool for any KM initiative. KM is about making knowledge available at the point of need. We cannot expect everyone to document or share everything they know. As a result, it is important that any KM initiative has a way to find the people who have the answers. A well-done expert finder makes it easy for people to find others in their organization that can answer difficult questions.

Organizations that are able to implement an expert finder solution can expect the following benefits:

- Improved customer service because knowledge workers are able to get the right answers at the right time.
- Greater collaboration across organizational units.
- Improved employee productivity because employees spend less time looking for answers and are aware of the work of others.
- Increased job satisfaction and company loyalty because employees see the combined power of the knowledge workers of the organization.
- Insight into knowledge loss from people who leave an organization because the expert finder has information as to what they know and who else knows it.

The right expert finder enables a much more cohesive organization that makes tacit knowledge more accessible and allows people across the organization to better understand what they need to best serve the organization's interests.

If the expert finder is expanded so that the information about employees is more immersive and accessible outside of an expert search, it can be rolled out as an Employee 360 solution. The Employee 360 solutions enable a number of other capabilities, including:

- Project staffing and resource allocation
- Connecting remote workers
- Managing employee growth
- Managing employee competencies
- Workforce planning and recruitment

Greater insight into what an employee knows and does can be a real differentiator for organizations looking to increase their overall effectiveness and retain their best knowledge workers.

21.3 Data Mesh

What Is It?
Zhamak Dehghani coined the term data mesh. His definition is "a type of data platform architecture that embraces the ubiquity of data in the enterprise by leveraging a domain-oriented, self-serve design" (Moses 2020). To put it simply, a data mesh is a layer that sits on top of an organization's data and maps that data to a more business-centric model so that people across the business can find the data they need to make intelligent decisions.

We have worked with clients to model their business through an ontology and then mapped the ontology to the data in their internal and external data repositories. The result is a tool that allows business users to use natural language queries to find answers within their data. These solutions can be integrated with reporting products like Tableau so that any business user can mine information from the organization's data stores. Prior to data mesh solutions, business leaders would request a report, and a data expert would write SQL and build a report that the leaders could read. This often took days or weeks and distracted IT personnel from other initiatives while delaying management's access to information. Data mesh democratizes data so that it is more widely accessible across the enterprise.

How Is It Built?

A data mesh is a map that sits on top of all of your data stores. This mesh takes data elements from many different data sources and aligns them to a more business-centric model. Two of the tools that we have analyzed in this book are critical to a data mesh solution, shown in the shaded boxes in Fig. 21.3.

A data catalog stores information about the data elements, including things like field names, descriptions, and purposes of these fields. A data mesh solution requires this field and data set level information in order to support the mapping process. In addition, these tools support the data governance process, which is critical to ensuring that the data mesh mapping stays current as new data sources are added to the enterprise.

A graph database is used to map the business model (as part of an ontology) to the data elements that make up each of these entities/relationships. For this to work, an ontology needs to be created that aligns with the way the business thinks. This ontology identifies common business entities that are stored in the graph and mapped to data fields or data calculations from one or more data sources. Most graph databases offer this feature; it is typically called a virtual graph. Each node in the

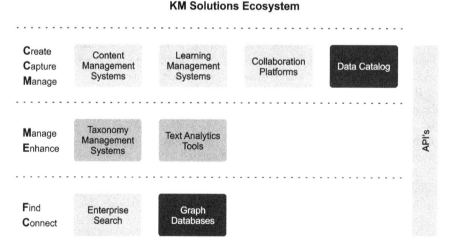

Fig. 21.3 Graph databases and a data catalog are critical elements for a data mesh, while taxonomy management systems and text analytics tools can also be used. © 2021, Wahl/Hilger, reused with permission

graph can have SQL associated with it that represents the node in the graph. When users ask questions of the graph which models the way people think, the question is turned into SPARQL to query the graph, and then the graph automatically executes SQL statements (in some cases, this information is already cached for performance) to query the information in the original data sets. This approach allows the graph to mirror the business and retrieve information from the data sets without the user having to understand the underlying relationships.

More and more businesses are querying unstructured information as well. In cases where the data mesh is expected to include unstructured data/content, there are two additional products that are frequently used.

A text analytics engine can be used to pull people, places, and things out of textual reports and then store them in the graph database. The business users can then query for structured and unstructured information from the graph at the same time.

Similar to the text analytics engine, taxonomy management tools can serve a similar purpose. Their auto-tagging capabilities can be used to extract/map information from text documents to a predetermined list of elements (the taxonomy), which can be queried in the graph in the same way that the text analytics tool allows for unstructured information to be queried. The difference between the two approaches is that taxonomy management systems assume a controlled list of terms while text analytics tools pull whichever terms they identify in the documents.

Data mesh and graph databases are changing the way organizations manage and query their data repositories by offering a business-centric view into data that has historically been organized based on the transactional system that was the source of the information.

Business Benefits

Data mesh solutions are very popular right now. They solve a problem that business intelligence groups have been wrestling with for years. Data is rarely stored in a format business executives find useful. Earlier solutions to this problem included long, complicated ETL processes that often had bugs and took time to run. Data mesh makes content available to a wider range of business users and lessens the load on IT to deliver answers to complicated business issues.

Business users have quick access to data that allows them to make better informed decisions. They are able to answer questions when they arise so that the decisions are not only better decisions but also timelier. These decisions improve strategic planning, enable better customer experiences, and help organizations save money on problems that are understandable much sooner.

In addition, data mesh solutions lower the demands on IT. Rather than having to build long, complex ETL processes or reporting tools, IT can define the relationships in the graph and allow for much greater self-service. IT is then able to focus on larger, more strategic initiatives that allow them to bring new technical solutions to the business much faster.

21.4   Semantic Hub, Data Fabric, and Knowledge Graph Solutions

What Is It?

A knowledge graph is an organized, central store of information linked to content across the enterprise. While it stands on its own as a solution it is also the foundation of Semantic Hubs and data fabrics that support structured and unstructured solutions. Similar to a data mesh, a knowledge graph organizes information in a way that models the business. These models align information across the organization based on things like customers, services, products, employees, and important topics. While data mesh solutions break down silos of data within data sets, knowledge graphs break down silos of information within documents. They link to documents and pull relevant information out of them to create a semantic information store that can support a wide range of information uses.

The most powerful part of knowledge graphs is the number of problems that they solve. A knowledge graph can be used to do the following.

- Provide recommendations
- Enhance search
- Optimize machine learning and analytics
- Power AI solutions like chatbots
- Monitor activity on social media or within the office

We have developed knowledge graphs that offer automated recommendations for related content, products, or courses an individual might use. Knowledge graphs provide a number of ways to fine-tune recommendations through things like personalization (characteristics of the person receiving the recommendation), subjects (recommendations for other contents with similar subjects), and reasoning/inference (relationships of these subjects based on similar characteristics). These tools can be implemented as a single recommendation application or as a series of widgets that can be placed on websites across the enterprise.

Google pioneered many of the ways in which knowledge graphs can be integrated into search. Features like knowledge panels and aggregated search results turn search results from a list of documents into an answer-first search experience. In addition, the way that information is stored allows for things like natural language search results and more related links to search results.

AI solutions that require two-way interaction like chatbots are built on knowledge graphs because the graph stores information in the way that people think. If people are asking questions about people, places, things, or topics of importance, the graph has captured information in that format and can more easily respond with an intelligent answer as opposed to a document that uses a term from the question. Nearly every major interactive AI tool that you work with today is built upon a knowledge graph. In-house solutions should follow the same proven approach to building these tools.

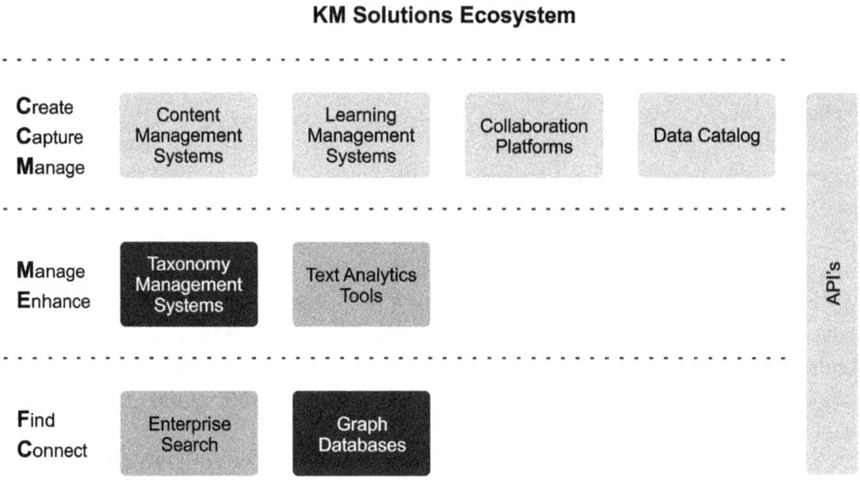

KM Solutions Ecosystem

Fig. 21.4 Tools used to support knowledge graphs, semantic hubs, and data fabric include graph databases, taxonomy management systems, as well as text analytics tools and/or enterprise search engines depending on the use case for the system. © 2021, Wahl/Hilger, reused with permission

Finally, knowledge graphs are also used to monitor and analyze information from one or more data sources. We have worked with organizations that mine information about key topics, customers, or services from both internal and external sources. This information can be shared with the employees or partners that need to be aware of these activities, or it can be analyzed to spot trends that need to be acted upon.

Knowledge graphs offer a single hub of information that serves as the backbone for a large number of cutting-edge KM services which improve the flow of information across the enterprise.

How Is It Built?

There is no single knowledge graph tool that supports all of the features of a knowledge graph, data mesh, or semantic hub. When we have built these tools for clients the end solution typically requires at least three of the products described in this book, as shown in Fig. 21.4.

A graph database is the data store for all of the information that is kept in the graph. It stores information based on relationships and allows for many of the features that enable people to query and find data across the enterprise.

A taxonomy management system that supports the design and management of ontologies, as well as auto-tagging capabilities, is a critical tool in the development of a knowledge graph. The taxonomy management system can be used to define and manage taxonomies that are used as properties for nodes in the graph. It can also be used to define the ontology (including entities and properties of each entity) and manage that structure. Finally, it can be used to auto-tag documents that are referred to in the graph.

In many implementations, the entities of the graph are not known in advance. In these cases, a text analytics solution that can identify people, places, and things and send them to the graph is very helpful. Text analytics libraries or platforms offer a powerful way to pull out information from documents, social networks, and text libraries and capture it in the graph.

Finally, some knowledge graph solutions require an enterprise search engine or a data reporting dashboard to support rapid querying of information from within the graph. When these queries are less complicated and of a high volume, it makes sense to put a search engine in front of the knowledge graph.

Business Benefits

A knowledge graph provides a central knowledge store that can make knowledge available through a number of different avenues. As a result, there are a wide range of business cases that these tools can support.

The recommendations component can be used in a number of ways. Organizations sharing information with customers and partners can use the recommendations capabilities to show their customers and partners the latest and most relevant information about the products or services that they care about. Organizations that use the recommendations for their employees can proactively send the employees information that helps them do their jobs more efficiently or to provide better customer service. Recommendations can also be used to automate product recommendations to increase product discovery and sales.

Search enhanced with knowledge graphs makes employees more efficient by showing them all information about a topic in a single location. They can also be used to improve customer or partner satisfaction by making it easy to see all of the information about products or services in a single aggregated location.

AI tools streamline processes and improve both customer and employee satisfaction by making it easy to find the information the searchers are looking for.

Finally, organizations can use knowledge graphs to monitor social media sites for information about their products or services. They can also use these tools to identify patterns in documents, reports, or social media that represent trends which the organization can use to improve products or services.

21.5   Enterprise Search

What Is It?

Most organizations are looking for their enterprise search solution to work like an internal Google. It takes more than a simple search engine to deliver a search solution that works across a wide range of information repositories. A true enterprise search solution will do the following:

- Include content from most major systems.
- Offer a consistent set of facets on all content.
- Replicate the security of the source systems.
- Aggregate information into people, places, and things.

Fixing enterprise search is the most common request we have received when helping clients solve their KM solutions. Making content findable quickly and easily is critical to supporting KM across the enterprise. When implemented properly, search becomes the first thing people go to when they are looking for information. It feels natural and makes it easy for knowledge workers to find the information they need to be more effective in their jobs.

How Is It Built?

A truly modern enterprise search implementation requires at least three major tools, shown in Fig. 21.5, and some work developing ontologies and taxonomies in order to be implemented successfully.

The enterprise search engine (or insight engine as they are called today) is the tool that enables the rapid search of information. It is the primary component in any enterprise search implementation. Content and the security settings are indexed in the search engine, and then search requests are sent to the search engine which responds with the search result.

Faceting is a key part of making search work for end users. A taxonomy management system is needed to ensure a consistent set of facets for information stored across multiple systems. The taxonomy management system is the place where the taxonomy is stored and managed. It feeds the taxonomies to the source systems so that every system uses the same facets for all of their contents. The search engine will then index the content and taxonomy information from the source systems to provide the faceted search. An example of the flow of information can be seen in Fig. 21.6.

Graph databases can be used to aggregate information from multiple data sources and send that information to the search engine so that it can be displayed as a search

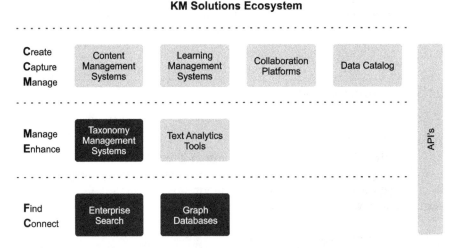

Fig. 21.5 The shaded tools are the minimum required for enterprise search implementation. © 2021, Wahl/Hilger, reused with permission

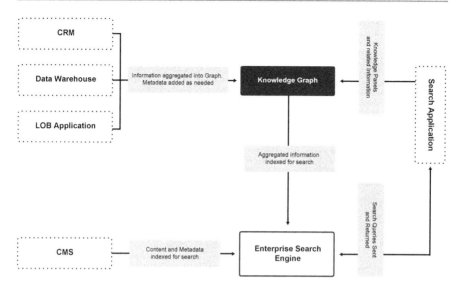

Fig. 21.6 The flow of information in an enterprise search system. © 2021, Wahl/Hilger, reused with permission

result of a knowledge panel. The knowledge panel is a concept pioneered by Google and one that can be replicated in any company search.

When combined together, these three tools can create the Google-like search experience that modern knowledge workers expect.

Business Benefits

An effective enterprise search gives knowledge workers access to the information they need to do their jobs in a timely and efficient manner. Knowledge workers will make better decisions that are more aligned with company and industry policies. They will also feel more fulfilled and happier in their jobs because they are confident in their decisions and feel supported in their work. All of this leads to greater employee retention, improved efficiency, and better customer service.

Organizations continue to try to do more with less. Organizations that equip their knowledge workers with quick and easy access to information have an incredible competitive advantage as the collective knowledge of the organization continues to grow.

Reference

Moses B (2020) What is a data mesh—and how not to mess it up. Towards Data Science. https://towardsdatascience.com. Accessed 12 Sept 2021

Closing

This book is the culmination of our collective (and shared) careers, over 60 years of combined experience written over the course of more than a year. We hope you have found it valuable and that it will serve as your definitive guidebook to how to make meaningful and lasting KM stick within your organization.

The field is changing quickly, and we imagine new technologies and techniques will quickly be added to those we currently list within this book. We hope you will tell us how you are doing with your KM efforts and what else would have helped you. Until then, best of luck moving forward!

Index

A
Access control, 136
Access Control Libraries (ACLs), 140, 168, 224
Adobe Experience Manager (AEM), 122, 123, 168
Agile, 71, 88, 89, 97, 125, 149, 228, 230, 232, 235, 236, 238, 243, 251, 278, 281, 292
Agiloft, 124
Alation, 188
Alignment, 7, 8, 35, 90, 128, 241
Analytics, 10, 11, 24, 26–30, 129, 130, 133–136, 166, 245, 290
APIs, 149, 182–184, 194, 217, 219, 221, 231, 243
Aprimo, 123
Artificial Intelligence (AI), 31, 209, 212
Asana, 149
Assembled content, 286, 287
Auto-categorization, 138
Auto-tagging, 29, 31, 95, 97, 136, 137, 169, 181–184, 193, 219, 244, 263

B
Backlog, 89, 233, 236, 238
Badging, 160
Basecamp, 149
Batch uploading, 127
Benchmark, 20, 32–57, 89
Benefits of KM, 210
Best bets, 171
Boosting, 174, 175
Box, 121
Business case, 59, 64, 248
Business content solutions, 120, 123

Business value, 1, 8, 25, 30, 73, 75, 81, 85, 89, 91, 93, 95, 96, 105, 107, 209, 211, 215, 252, 254, 257, 262, 277, 285, 290
Bynder, 123

C
Canto, 123
Change management, 59, 91, 253, 277, 280, 292
Chatbots, 200, 209, 212, 213
Collaboration platform, 150, 152
Collaboration suites, 150, 155
Collaborative editing, 125, 126
Collaborative workspaces, 125, 126
Collibra, 188
Componentized content, 125, 126
Connected search, 165
Content, 1–3, 5–11, 21–34, 45, 60, 73, 78–80, 82, 83, 91, 93, 96, 98, 104, 105, 119–139, 149, 151, 155, 157, 158, 165, 167–169, 171–175, 177, 181–184, 187, 193, 194, 200, 202, 204, 205, 208, 210, 217–219, 221, 222, 224, 230–232, 235, 239, 242–245, 248–251, 253, 258, 259, 261, 262, 264, 266, 267, 269, 272, 283–286, 293, 294, 296, 299, 300, 306, 307, 310
Content analysis, 25–26, 32
Content audit, 267
Content chunking, 212, 269, 286, 293
Content cleanup, 27, 28, 73, 211, 230
Contentful, 124
Content governance, 23, 28, 73, 83, 96, 98, 134, 210, 248–251, 254, 260, 265, 278

CPSIA information can be obtained
at www.ICGtesting.com
Printed in the USA
LVHW082113150422
716322LV00001B/1